THE BRITISH ISLES

ROBERT CROFT
SARAH DIXON
SIMON BURTON
BECKY BURTON
MARK PENROSE
DAVID PENROSE
JENNY LEINERT
KIM DIXON

Learning English

Green Line new 2

Unterrichtswerk für Gymnasien

von
Stephanie Ashford, Rosemary Hellyer-Jones,
Marion Horner, Peter Lampater, Harriette Lanzer,
Peter Pasch, Rolf W. Roth, Helmut Slogsnat,
Klaus Stenzel, Gunther Volk,
Margaret Winck, Harold S. Wonham
sowie
Claudia Finkbeiner

Ernst Klett Verlag
Stuttgart Düsseldorf Leipzig

Learning English

Green Line New 2

für Klasse 6 an Gymnasien

von

Stephanie Ashford B.A., Villingen-Schwenningen; Rosemary Hellyer-Jones M.A., Ehingen (Donau); Marion Horner M.A., Cambridge; Peter Lampater, Ehingen (Donau); Harriette Lanzer B.A., London; Prof. Dr. Peter Pasch, Tübingen; Rolf W. Roth M.A., Idar-Oberstein; Dr. Helmut Slogsnat, Neckargemünd; Klaus Stenzel, Bopfingen; Gunther Volk, Villingen-Schwenningen; Margaret Winck B.A., Tübingen; Harold S. Wonham M.Litt., Stone

sowie

Prof. Dr. Claudia Finkbeiner, Heilbronn

Beratende Mitarbeit

Dr. Rainer Berthelmann, Halle; Gisela Bullan, Cottbus; Jürgen Meyer, Itzehoe; Ilsabé Seils, Neubrandenburg; Günter Schubert, Kiel; Dorit Stribel, Nürtingen; Dr. Uwe Vogel, Leipzig

sowie

Jörg W. Mollenkopf, Giengen

Visuelle Gestaltung

Elsie Lennox, London (Zeichnungen);
Dieter Gebhardt, Graphic- und Foto-Design BFF, Asperg (Grundlayout, Graphiken);
Kirsten Walther, Bochum (Zeichnungen Vokabular, z. T. Grammatik)

Kassetten und CDs zu diesem Band

SB *Begleitkassette zum Schülerbuch* für zu Hause und für den Unterricht mit Unittexten, Liedern, Ausspracheübungen (Klettnummer 546228).
Die *Begleit-CD zum Schülerbuch* mit demselben Inhalt hat die Klettnummer 546283.

HV *Kassette zum Hörverstehen* für den Unterricht mit den Hörverstehenstexten aller Werkteile (Klettnummer 546229).
Die *CD zum Hörverstehen* für den Unterricht hat die Klettnummer 546284.
Lieferung direkt an Lehrerinnen und Lehrer, Schulstempel erforderlich.

Lernsoftware: Passend zu diesem Band gibt es ein Vokabel- und ein Grammatiktrainingsprogramm. Die Programme bieten abwechslungsreiche Übungsformen, zahlreiche Abfragevarianten, Leistungs- und Lernzielkontrolle und ein Lexikon mit dem Wortschatz der gesamten Lehrbuchreihe.
Lehrersoftware: Schulbuchtexte für den PC für die Bände 1 und 2 (Klettnummer 990213) Zusatztexte für den PC für Band 2 (Klettnummer 990263, Schulstempel erforderlich)

2. Auflage A 2 25 24 23 22 | 2009 2008 2007 2006

Alle Drucke dieser Auflage können im Unterricht nebeneinander benutzt werden, sie sind untereinander unverändert.

Die letzte Zahl bezeichnet das Jahr des Druckes.

Internetadresse: http://www.klett-verlag.de

Redaktion: Peter Cole M.A., Alison Imrie M.A.

Herstellung: Eveline Wiest, Stuttgart
Umschlaggestaltung: Christian Dekelver, Weinstadt
Satz: DTP-Verlag und Lihs, Satz und Repro, Ludwigsburg;
Bebop Sounds, Freiberg/Neckar (Noten)
Reproduktion: Repro Maurer GmbH + Co, Tübingen
Druck: Druckhaus Götz GmbH, Ludwigsburg
ISBN: 3-12-546220-7

9 783125 462205

Inhaltsverzeichnis

Hallo,
ich begleite dich auch durch dieses Buch und gebe dir ab und zu ein paar Tipps.
Damit du dich leicht zurechtfindest, erkläre ich noch einmal kurz, wie dieses Buch aufgebaut ist.

Jede der zehn **Units** (Kapitel) hat ein anderes Thema. Am Ende jeder *Unit* kannst du auf einer *Let's check*-Seite überprüfen, was du dazugelernt hast.

Auf Seite 98 beginnt die **Extra line** mit weiteren interessanten Geschichten, einem Theaterstück und ab Seite 106 mit Übersetzungsübungen.

Auf Seite 109 beginnt der **Grammatikanhang.**

Das **Vokabular** beginnt auf Seite 129. Hier findest du alle neuen Wörter aus den *Units*.

Wenn du einmal ein Wort aus einer früheren *Unit* nicht mehr weißt, kannst du in der **alphabetischen Wortliste** am Ende des Buches nachschlagen.

Und alle **unregelmäßigen Verben** stehen in einer Liste auf den Seiten 182 und 183.

Du solltest aber auch noch wissen, was die **Zeichen** vor den einzelnen Texten und den Übungen bedeuten:

- SB: Begleitkassette bzw. CD zum Schülerbuch
- HV: Kassette bzw. CD zum Hörverstehen
- Your turn: Hier kannst du über dich, deine Familie oder Freunde sprechen.
- Partnerarbeit
- Gruppenarbeit
- WORD POWER: Wortschatzübungen
- Wiederholungsübungen
- ⟨ ⟩ wahlfreie Aufgaben
- schwierigere Aufgaben, die wahlfrei sind
- für fächerübergreifenden Unterricht besonders geeignet

Alles klar?
Na, dann – viel Spaß!

Units/Steps | *Kommunikative Schwerpunkte Arbeitstechniken (AT)* | *Strukturen (R=Revision/Wiederholung)* | *Seite*

Unit 6 Food, food, food

Unit 7 A week in Scotland

Unit 8 Help

Welcome back

Step A

A new school year

It is the 4th of September and the boys and girls are coming back to Haywood School after their summer holidays.

1 Can you remember them?

Talk about the friends.

Example: David plays the guitar. His birthday is on the 11th of May.
His little brother's name is Mark.

guitar/ birthday: 11th May/ brother: Mark

two dogs/ parents: bike shop/ pond in garden

football/ from London/ ...

German/ David's cousin/ birthday: 7th Feb./ ...

sister: Kim/ cat: Tabby/ ...

Go on. Can you say more about the friends?

2 A game: I spy

Look at the picture and play with a partner.

You: I spy with my little eye
something beginning with 'S'.
Partner: A school bag?
You: No.
Partner: A sweatshirt?
You: That's right. It's your turn now.
Go on.
You can spy things in the classroom, too.

Step A

The wrong lesson

Robert: What's the next lesson?
Becky: Technology. Come on, we're late.
Sarah: Hey, where are you going? Haven't we got Drama now?
Robert: I don't know. Let's look at the timetable.
Becky: OK, er … second lesson. Yes, you see. Technology.
Sarah: But it's Tuesday today, Becky, not Monday.
Becky: Oh, of course.
Robert: So which subject is it now?
Sarah: Drama! Come on!

8 MD	Monday	Tuesday	Wednesday	Thursday	Friday
9:05	Science	Art	PE	Assembly/RE	Maths
10:05	Technology	Drama	German	German	PE
11:00	BREAK				
11:15	Technology	Humanities	Humanities	Science	Humanities
12:10	LUNCH				
1:25	Maths	English	Maths	Music	English
2:20	BREAK				
2:35	English	German	English	Technology	Science

3 The new timetable

RE: Religious Education
PE: Physical Education
Humanities: History/Geography

a) *Answer the questions.*

1. Which lesson finishes at half past three on Thursdays?
2. Which lessons are after lunch on Fridays?
3. Is there a Science lesson on Monday mornings?
4. What time is Humanities on Tuesdays?
5. What is the second lesson on Wednesdays?
6. How many PE lessons are there every week?

b) *Ask and answer more questions about the timetable.*

4 Listening practice: Lessons and days

Look at the timetable and listen to the dialogues. Which day is it?

5 Different timetables

Your turn

a) *Look at the timetable. Do you do the same subjects? Make two lists.*

b) *Talk about your lists.*
Example:
"We both do Maths.
They do Technology.
We do …
They don't do …"

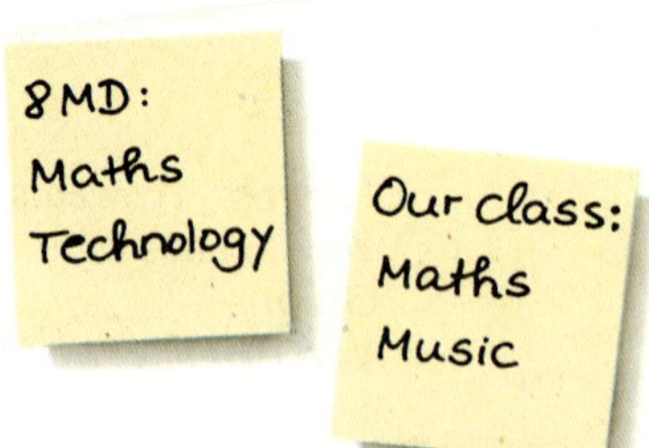

6 My English folder

Write your timetable in your English folder.

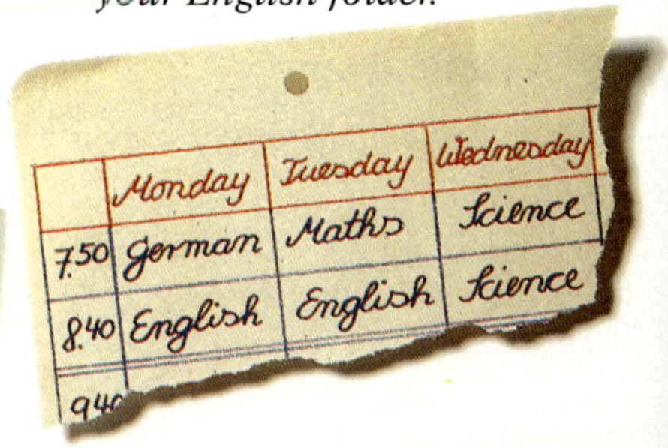

Step B

The junior play

It is morning break. Robert and his friends are looking at the notice board.

Robert: Hey, look! There's a meeting about the junior play.
Jenny: Oh yes? Which notice is that?
Robert: The one at the bottom. The meeting is today. Do you want to come, too, Jenny?
Jenny: Well, is it a nice play? I only like funny ones. What about you, David?
David: No thanks. I don't like plays.
Robert: But this one is really good. And they need a lot of people.
David: How do you know? Do you know what play it is?
Robert: Er ..., no. But the junior play is always good.

1 What do they do?

Ask and answer questions with a partner.

Do Does	Robert Becky and Simon David Jenny Jenny's parents ...	want to like live in know speak ...	German? what play it is? go to the meeting? plays? Nottingham? ...	–	Yes, ... do/does. No, ... don't/doesn't. I don't know.

2 Becky's room

Look at the picture and make sentences.

Example:
Becky has got two posters in her room, a big one and a small one.

3 Your class

Make sentences about people in your class and about you, too.

Example:
I'm wearing a red sweatshirt and Anna is wearing a blue one.

Step B

The new pupil

There is a new pupil in 8MD. His name is John and he comes from Chicago in America. Everything is new for him, but Becky is helping him.

John: Oh, just one more question, Becky.
Becky: Yes, what is it?
John: Well, I've got two Humanities books here. Which one do I need today?
Becky: Let me see. Er ..., we have History on Tuesdays, so you need the blue one. Come on, let's go to lunch now.
John: OK. What's for lunch today?
Becky: Well, there's sausages and chips or a salad. Which do you want?
John: Er ... I don't know.
Becky I'm going to have a salad.
John: OK.
Becky: There's a cheese salad or a ham salad. Which one are you going to have?
John: Cheese, I think.

4 Role play: What does John ask?

Of course John has got a lot of questions. Can you ask his questions and give the answers?

Example: John: When do we have lunch break?
Becky: At 10 past 12.

When		we	have lunch break?	go home?
What	do	you	have Art?	have for Maths?
Where	does	our tutor	play cricket?	get to school?
Who		I	eat lunch?	do after school? ...
How				

5 Which one do I need?

Becky is helping John. He is looking for the right things for his lessons. Make dialogues.

Example: I've got two Maths books. Which one do I need now? – You need the blue one.

Maths English Humanities PE Science

6 *Watch out:* 'Which' or 'what'?

1. ... time is our next lesson?
2. ... teacher do you have for English? Mr Stevenson or Mrs Dane?
3. ... subject have we got now? Drama or Technology? – Drama.
4. ... is in your lunch box? – Biscuits.
5. ... bus goes to Haywood School? The 43 or the 31?
6. I've got a new pullover. – ... colour is it?
7. There's ham salad and cheese salad. ... do you want?

Step C

Activities

1 Join a club

Find a club or activity for these people.
Example: Becky likes animals. She's going to join the bird club.

1. Simon is a computer fan.
2. John likes climbing.
3. David likes music.
4. Jenny likes badminton.
5. Robert likes drama.
6. Sarah is a sports fan.

2 Your plans

What are you going to do this year? Talk about it.

Example: I'm going to join the football club.

join … do … buy …
meet new people …

3 ⟨A poem: Back to school⟩

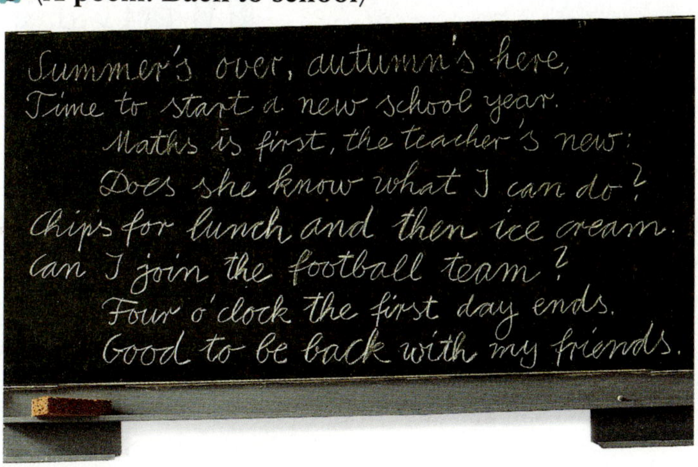

4 WORD POWER

These words look the same in English and German.

computer club
badminton
anorak
drama
jeans
club
hand

How many more can you find?

Step D

Simon's new friend

"Becky, is that Simon over there?" asks Sarah.

It is break time on Thursday morning and the children are in the playground.

"Oh, yes. He must be with a new friend," says Becky.

"That doesn't look like a friend," says Robert. "That's Barry Jenkins's brother Mike."

"But Barry Jenkins is a terrible bully," says Becky. "What's Simon doing with his brother?"

"I don't know," says Sarah. "But come on, we're late for Science!"

After lunch Becky looks for Simon in the playground, but she can't find him there.

"Robert, I'm worried about Simon," she says. "I can't find him."

"Oh, don't worry," Robert answers. "He's probably at a club or something."

"He can't be," Becky says. "He's only in the computer club and they have it on Tuesdays and Fridays."

At half past three Becky and Robert go to Simon's classroom. But the lesson is already over and Simon is at the end of the corridor. They run after him.

"Becky Burton! Robert Croft! Come here at once!"

They turn round. Their new Maths teacher, Mr Stevenson, is standing there.

"Don't run in school," he says. "Now off you go, and walk!"

Becky and Robert turn round. But the corridor is full of people now. They can't see Simon.

They leave school and walk home.

"Hey, Becky," says Robert suddenly. "There's Simon outside that shop."

"Which shop?" Becky asks.

"The one over there – the newsagent's."

"Oh yes," Becky says. "And he's with that Mike Jenkins. Quick. Let's hide!"

They hide behind a car and watch the two boys.

"What are they doing?" asks Robert.

Simon gets his purse out of his pocket.

He opens it and gives Mike some money.

"Come on, Robert," says Becky. "Let's go!"

And they run towards the two boys.

Step D

"You bully! Give my brother his money back!" shouts Becky.

"Go away, Jenkins!" shouts Robert.

"Hey! Stop it!" says Simon. "Mike's not a bully. He's my friend."

Becky and Robert look at Mike. That *is* a surprise.

"We're both computer fans," says Mike. "We want to buy a computer magazine together. They cost so much."

"Oh!" says Becky. "Er … I'm really sorry, Mike. It's just … well, your brother …"

"I know," Mike says. "My brother is terrible, but I'm not!"

1 Talk about the story

1. Who is Simon with in the playground?
2. What does Becky think of Barry Jenkins?
3. Where does Becky look for Simon?
4. When does she look for him?
5. Why is Mr Stevenson angry?
6. Where does Robert see Simon?
7. Where do Becky and Robert hide?
8. What does Simon get out of his pocket?
9. Why does Simon give the money to Mike?
10. Why is Becky wrong about Mike?

2 Tell the story again

Tell the story again. First look at your answers to exercise 1.

At morning break …
In the lunch break …
After the last lesson …
On the way home …
Then …

3 Listening practice: Simon's new school

Right or wrong?

1. Simon likes his new school.
2. Simon's teachers are terrible.
3. Simon's favourite lesson is German.
4. Simon gets homework every day.
5. Simon and Mike want to go to the climbing club together.
6. The school computers are terrible.
7. Simon has lunch in the canteen.
8. Year 7 has lunch first.

4 Sound practice: [θ] – [ð]

a) *Make two lists with these words. You can look at the word list on page 165 for help.*

nothing them together fifteenth brother month healthy father thanks another mouth this those thing

[θ]	[ð]
nothing	them

b) *Say these sentences again and again.*

[ð] – [z]
These clothes are his clothes and those clothes are their clothes.

[θ] – [s]
Three packets of sweets for thirty-three pence – thanks!

Step E

Let's check

1 Favourite subjects

What are their favourite subjects? Can you find out?

Example: 1. David likes music.

1. DIDVA – CISMU
2. NENJY – SHLENIG
3. KYBEC – NAGREM
4. BOTRER – AMDRA
5. ASHRA – SHMAT
6. MOSIN – CEESINC

2 WORD POWER

Find two more school words for every group.

1. Lessons: Maths – PE –
2. Places: classroom – hall –
3. People: pupil – teacher –
4. Activities: bird club – badminton –
5. Things: pens – books –

3 A game

Sarah and Becky are playing a game in the classroom.

Sarah: Look at my desk for a minute.
Becky: OK.
Sarah: Now turn round. Can you remember everything on it?
Becky: Well, you've got two pencils on your desk – a red one and a blue one.
Sarah: That's right.
Becky: And there are some books.
Sarah: How many?
Becky: Two yellow ones and a green one.

Go on. Then play the game with a partner.

4 ⟨Just for fun: A school joke⟩

Ken comes downstairs for breakfast. He sits at the table and eats his cornflakes but he isn't very happy.
"I don't want to go to school today, Mum," he says. "The teachers don't like me and everyone bullies me."
"But you must go," says his mum. "You're 38 years old and you're the headteacher!"

Adventures in Nottingham

Step A

The adventure centre

SB

Sarah, David and Mark are at Jenny's new house.

Mr Leinert: I'm going to take Jenny to 'The Tales of Robin Hood' next weekend. Who wants to come with us?
Mark: I do!
David: Can we all come, Uncle Mike?
Mr Leinert: Of course you can.
Jenny: 'The Tales of Robin Hood' – what's that? Is it a film?
Mr Leinert: No, it's an adventure centre. Look, here's a leaflet about it.
Jenny: 'Nottingham's Great Adventure'. Hey, everything is just like in Robin Hood's time! You meet Robin Hood and the outlaws in Sherwood Forest. And look – you can shoot with bows and arrows, too!
Sarah: And you meet the Sheriff of Nottingham. You know, Jenny – Robin Hood's enemy.

David: Oh, and look at this! The Sheriff's men catch you and take you prisoner.
Mark: I don't want to come!
Mr Leinert: It's OK, Mark. It's all in the adventure. Robin Hood's men hear the news and save you!

1 Telling Mrs Penrose

Now Mark is sure – he wants to come to 'The Tales of Robin Hood'.
That evening he tells Mrs Penrose all about it.

hear catch shoot
meet take go save

It's great, Mum!

1. You **go** to Sherwood Forest.
2. You … Robin Hood and his outlaws.
3. You … with bows and arrows.
4. The Sheriff … you in the forest.
5. His men … you prisoner.
6. But Robin Hood … the news.
7. Then the outlaws … you.

2 Role play

Make dialogues with a partner.

What can we do *at the weekend?*

on Saturday?
on Sunday / … ?

Let's *go to the cinema.*

go to an adventure playground.
go out on our bikes.
stay at home / … .

Oh yes! *Let's do that!*
Oh no! That's *boring.*

Great idea!
That's a good plan!

not very exciting.
silly!

Step B

Robin Hood

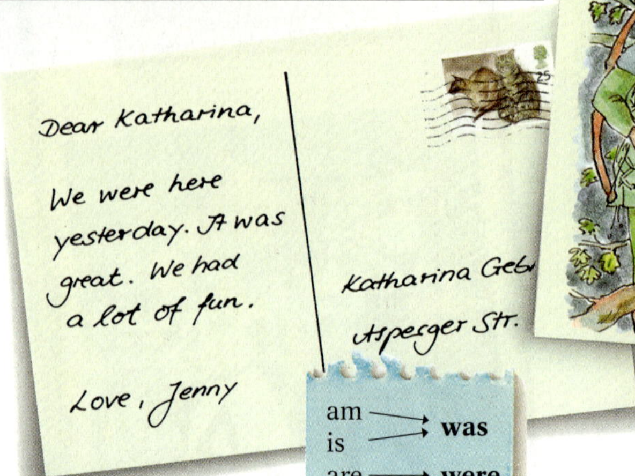

Robin Hood lived in Sherwood Forest near Nottingham. He and his men helped the poor people of Nottingham. The Sheriff only wanted their money. He often tried to catch Robin Hood, but Robin stopped the Sheriff's plans and often played tricks on him!

am → **was**
is → **was**
are → **were**
have → **had**
has → **had**

help → help**ed**
live → live**d**
play → play**ed**
try → tr**ied** [d]
stop → stop**ped** [t]
want → want**ed** [ɪd]

1 Yesterday

It is Sunday. Jenny *is* at home today. But yesterday she **was** at 'The Tales of Robin Hood'.

1. The weather *is* bad today. But (yesterday – nice)
2. It *is* really cold today. But (yesterday – warm)
3. David and Mark *are* with their parents today. But (yesterday – with Jenny and her father)
4. The Leinerts usually *have* lunch at one o'clock. But (yesterday – lunch early)
5. Mark usually *has* tea at home. But (yesterday – tea at the 'Hungry Outlaw' snack bar)

2 Can you remember?

arrive in Nottingham ✔

work in a shop on Saturdays

stay at Springfield Farm

live in Berlin

start the pond in their garden

Example: 1. Last autumn Robert **arrived in Nottingham**.

2. Last spring he and his mother …
3. Last year Kim …
4. Last autumn Becky and Simon …
5. Last winter the Leinerts …

3 Robin and his outlaws

Put in the verbs in the right forms.

1. Robin Hood … (be) an outlaw. He and his men … (live) in Sherwood Forest.
2. At that time Sherwood Forest … (be) very big. Nottingham … (be) a small town. But it … (have) a big castle, and it … (have) a Sheriff.
3. There … (be) a lot of poor people in England then. They … (need) things for their families, but they often … (have) no money. Robin … (like) them and often … (help) them.
4. He and his men sometimes … (stop) people on the Nottingham road. "Give us your money!" they … (shout). "We are collecting for the poor people of Nottingham!"
5. Nobody … (want) to give money to Robin. But there … (be) no way out! They … (open) their purses, and the outlaws … (collect) all the money together.

The weekend

Becky: Hi, Jenny! What was your weekend like? Did you have a good time?
Jenny: Great! Sarah and I were at 'The Tales of Robin Hood'. David and Mark were there, too.
Becky: Did Mark like it?
Jenny: Yes, he did. But he didn't like the Sheriff! He was scared of him at first!
Becky: Why? What did the Sheriff do?
Jenny: Nothing terrible really. But he shouted a lot. So all the small children were scared.
Becky: Oh dear! Well, I'm sure Mark liked Robin Hood.
Jenny: Yes, he did. Now he wants to be an outlaw when he's big.

4 Questions about the weekend

Example: 1. Did Jenny have a nice weekend? – Yes, she did.
2. Was Becky at 'The Tales of Robin Hood' on Saturday?
3. Were Mr and Mrs Penrose there, too?
4. Did Mark like 'The Tales of Robin Hood'?
5. Did he like the Sheriff?
6. Was he scared of him at first?
7. Did the Sheriff do terrible things?
8. Were the other small children scared?
9. Was Mark scared of Robin Hood?

Yes,	he she it they	was. were. did.
No,		wasn't. weren't. didn't.

5 You and your activities

a) *Ask your partner.*

Example: Do you often listen to pop music?

Do you	often usually sometimes always …	listen to pop music stay with your grandma/at a hotel/… play computer games/… help at home/in the kitchen watch TV/…	?

b) *Now ask your partner. Did he or she do these things yesterday/…?*

Example: Did you listen to pop music last night?

last night/yesterday
yesterday afternoon
last year/last weekend/…

6 Not a lucky day

Yesterday wasn't a lucky day for Mark. *Write about his day.*

Example: 1. breakfast time / ask David a question – David / not answer
At breakfast time he asked David a question. But David didn't answer.

2. after nursery school / wait for his father – Mr Penrose / not collect him
3. Grandma Penrose / collect him – she / not stay for lunch
4. after tea / show David a funny trick – David / not laugh
5. then / want to play with his mother – she / not have time
6. so / play a game with David – David / not like the game

A strange dream

The pupils in 8MD must write about a 'strange dream' in English this week.
Jenny reads her story to the class.

One night I had a very strange dream. I was at the Burtons' house, and Becky and Simon were with me. Simon said, "Let's play football," so we went into their garden. Simon got his football, and we started the game. Simon kicked the ball to Becky, but Becky couldn't get the ball. It went into the pond. "Don't worry, I can get it out!" I said to the others. I ran into the water. But suddenly the pond was a big lake. And the ball was at the bottom! I looked for Becky and Simon, but they weren't there.

*Then I heard a noise near me. "Croak! Croak!" I turned round and saw a big frog. "Get my ball," said the frog. "But it isn't your ball," I answered. "It's Simon's ball." "But I **am** Simon!" said the frog. Then suddenly Becky was there again. She had her swimming things on. She went into the water. Then she came up with the ball in her hands. She gave it to the frog and sat down on a big stone. But now her arms and legs were all green. She was a frog, too! Then I looked at **my** arms and legs, and **they** were all green. So I was a frog, too! What a shock! I woke up at once – it was so terrible.*

say → **said**
go → **went**
get → **got**
...

These are irregular forms. There's a list on page 182.

7 Irregular forms

Look at Jenny's story and find the irregular forms of these verbs.

come, hear, give, run, sit, see, wake

8 The Penroses and the Leinerts

Example: 1. Mr Penrose often *goes* to the new supermarket in Mansfield Road. Last Tuesday he **went** there with Mark.

2. (come) The Leinerts often ... to the Penroses' house. They ... for tea yesterday.
3. (sit) Jenny usually ... with Sarah in Maths. But last Wednesday she ... with Becky.
4. (give) Mr Penrose often ... Mark a banana for nursery school. Yesterday morning he ... him an apple.
5. (get) Jenny often ... letters from her friend Katharina. Last Saturday she ... a postcard from her.
6. (go) Grandma Penrose usually ... to the Twinning Office by bus. But yesterday morning she ... by car.

9 My English folder

Write about a 'crazy dream' in your folder.

Suddenly ... Then ... At once ...	I saw ... I went ... I heard ... ... said. I wanted to ... A ... came towards me.

Looking at the UK: In and around Nottingham

Every year there is a big fair in Nottingham – Goose Fair. It goes on for three days and is always in the first week of October. In Robin Hood's time, the fair was in the market square and they sold geese there. But now there are no geese and it is outside the city centre, near Mansfield Road. ▶

▲ This big old tree in Sherwood Forest is called the Major Oak. Robin Hood and his men sat under it and talked about their plans. Well, that is what people say. Some of the oaks in Sherwood Forest are over 800 years old.

There are a lot of exciting old tunnels and caves in the rock under Nottingham Castle. You mustn't get lost there! ▼

1 In and around your town

Talk about your town now.

- Is there a fair sometimes? When is it?
- Is there a forest near your town? Do you sometimes go there? What can you do there? Can you watch birds or animals?
- Are there caves? Can you go inside?
- Is there an old castle in or near your town? Or an adventure centre?

Step C

In the History lesson

Today 8MD are talking about the Middle Ages – around 1200.

Becky: What did people eat in those days?
Robert: Fish and chips?
Mr Lee: Well, they caught fish. But when Robin Hood lived, there were no potatoes in England.
Sarah: No potatoes? How terrible! Did they eat meat or cheese?
Mr Lee: Yes, they ate both. But usually only rich people had meat. People lived a very different life then. That was before they had bathrooms or hot water …
Jenny: So what did they do when they wanted to wash?
Mr Lee: They got water from the river in buckets.
Robert: Ugh! And what about school?
Mr Lee: Most children didn't go to school.
Sarah: No school? Why didn't we live then?
Mr Lee: Well, life wasn't easy for children. They started work as soon as they were old enough, usually before they were eight. And a lot of children died at a very early age.

1 What was it like in those days?

Ask a partner questions about life in Robin Hood's time.
Start with questions about these things.

have	~~bathrooms~~	candles	~~bikes~~
play	~~basketball~~	~~tennis~~	ball games
eat	bread	~~potatoes~~	meat

– Did people play … in those days?
– Yes, they did.
No, they didn't. But they played …
Maybe they did. I'm not sure.
I don't know.

And now – what about these things?

cars music bananas beds cheese bows and arrows …

2 When …

a) *How old were they?*

Example: Robert came to Nottingham when he was twelve. *Go on.*

Robert	come to Nottingham	12
Mark	start nursery school	3
Jenny	arrive in England	11
David	have his first guitar lesson	10
Becky	get Maxi for her birthday	8
Kim	start her Saturday job	16

b) *When did you …?*

Example: I got my first bike when I was six. *Go on.*

get your first bike / …
join the … club
have your first … lesson
get your cat / dog / bird /…
start school

3 Listening practice: Robin Hood's time

1. When did Robin Hood live?
2. Why did outlaws live in the forests?
3. Why didn't people know their age?
4. What were families like?
5. Were there a lot of old people?
6. What were towns like in those days?

Step D

Robin Hood and the Sheriff

One day, when the Sheriff's men were in Sherwood Forest, they caught Will Scarlet, one of the outlaws, and took him to Nottingham. "Ah! One of Robin Hood's men!" said the Sheriff when he saw Will. "Take him to the gallows in the market square tomorrow. Then everyone can see what happens to outlaws!"

That evening Robin and his men heard the news. "We must go to Nottingham at once and save Will!" said one of the outlaws.
"Wait," said Robin. "Will is a prisoner in Nottingham Castle. We can't get to him there. But we must save him! What can we do?"
"I know the hangman!" said Friar Tuck.
"Good! Now I've got an idea," said Robin. "Go to Nottingham right away ..."
"Can't we all go?" asked another outlaw.
"Wait, it's our turn tomorrow!" said Robin.

Early the next morning, Robin was on the way to Nottingham with twelve of his men. They wore coats over their green clothes, and under their coats they had their bows and arrows.

When they were on the road to Nottingham, they met a poor old man in a long black coat with a hood.
"Good morning, friend," said Robin. "That coat has a nice hood. Can I buy it from you?"
"This dirty old thing? You can have it for a pound!"
"Thanks," said Robin. He took the coat and gave the old man five pounds. "For you and your family. Take it! Goodbye!"
"Five pounds? But that's –" The old man wanted to say thank you, but Robin and his men were already on their way.

At twelve o'clock there were a lot of people in the market square. A man with a rope round his hands stood under the gallows. It was Will Scarlet. The Sheriff was there with twenty men.
"Well, where's the hangman?" the Sheriff asked his men. But they didn't know. They couldn't find him.
"He drank too much wine last night!" said one man, and a lot of people laughed. The Sheriff was angry now.
"We need a hangman!" he shouted to the people in the square. "Well? Does nobody want to do the job? For five pounds? For ten?"
But the people didn't want to help the Sheriff. So at first nobody answered.
Then an old man in a black coat with a hood came up to the gallows.
"I can do the job for you!" he said.
The people in the square were angry when they heard this. A boy threw an apple at the old man. A woman threw an egg.

"Come on! Do the job!" said the Sheriff, and he gave the old man the money. The old man went behind the prisoner. "What are you doing with that rope?" shouted the Sheriff. "Come on, you idiot! Do your job!" But suddenly the old man threw off his black coat and stood there – in green clothes now, and with a bow in his hands. "It's Robin Hood!" a woman shouted. At the same time, Robin's men took off their coats and ran through the crowd with their bows and arrows, ready to help Robin.

"Stop them!" shouted the Sheriff to his men. But the outlaws were ready for them. As soon as the Sheriff's men came near them, Robin shot an arrow from his bow. It went over people's heads – and straight into the Sheriff's hat. "Be careful, Sheriff!" shouted Robin.

This was enough for the Sheriff. He felt scared. In a minute or two he and all his men were gone. Now Will Scarlet was with his friends again. Before they all went back to the forest, Robin threw the ten pounds from his purse into the crowd.
"A present from the Sheriff!" he called.

1 Questions about the story

1. Who was Will Scarlet?
2. What did the Sheriff's men do when they caught him?
3. What did the outlaws want to do when they heard the news?
4. Why was the Sheriff angry?
5. What happened when the 'old man' went up to the gallows?
6. Why did the Sheriff and his men run away?
7. How did Robin help the people in the crowd?

2 Did you like it?

Talk about the story now. Did you like it?

I liked / I didn't like	the beginning.		That was	clever.
	the ending.			good.
	Robin's plan.			great.
	the bit where	Robin gave the man the money for his coat.		silly.
	…	the Sheriff didn't find the hangman.		boring.
		Robin shot an arrow through the Sheriff's hat.		funny.
		Robin threw money into the crowd.		exciting.
		…		…

3 Looking at English

Yesterday the weather **was** nice. "Yesterday" is a signal word for the simple past.

What others can you find? Write a list in your exercise book. Then make sentences with five of them.

4 Will Scarlet's story

Put in the verbs – in the simple past.

want ask
get happen

As soon as they … back to Sherwood Forest, the outlaws all … to hear Will's story. "What …?" they … .

throw take
hear catch
come say

"When the Sheriff's men … me, they … me to Nottingham Castle," … Will. "They … me into a small room with two other prisoners. Then the Sheriff …, and I … the terrible news – the gallows!"

see feel
come give
happen be
take see

"The next morning they … me bread and water for breakfast. Then they … me to the market square. I … terrible when I … the gallows! But when the 'old man' … up to me, I … at once – it … Robin! Well, you all know what … after that!"

5 The old man's coat

When the old man came home without his coat, his children said, "What happened, Father? Where's your coat?" "Well," he said, "when I was on the Nottingham road …" *Go on.*

6 Act the story

First have a look at the Robin Hood story and see how many parts there are. Then work in groups and write the dialogues. You can act the story in the classroom.

7 Listening practice: Friar Tuck's wine

Listen to the dialogue between the hangman and his friend. Can you answer these questions?

1. Where did the hangman meet Friar Tuck?
2. What did Friar Tuck have with him?
3. How did the two men spend the evening together?
4. What time was it when the hangman woke up?
5. Where was he?
6. Is the hangman's name *Jack* or *John*?

8 Sound practice

a) *Say these words.*

[t] work**ed** [d] liv**ed**, listen**ed** [ɪd] want**ed**, need**ed**

b) *Now read these sentences and then put the verbs in the right groups.*

We wait**ed** for ten minutes. Then the train arriv**ed**.
As soon as it stop**ped**, we all climb**ed** in and look**ed** for seats. Then the train start**ed**.

9 A game: Everyone's story

Tell a story together in class. But each person can only say one word.
Look at the example and go on.

Let's check

1 What can you say?

a) *Make six sentences. Example:* Last night I **helped at home**.

Yesterday On Sunday Last week Last …	I we	help at home ✓ watch a good film on TV have a late breakfast listen to the radio phone my best friend …

b) *Now ask a partner six questions. Example:* Did you help at home last night? – Yes, I did.

2 Dialogues

Example: 1. *Becky:* Let's *go* to 'The Tales of Robin Hood'!
Jenny: (no / there last weekend) Oh no, I **went** there last weekend.

2. *Mrs Leinert:* Let's *take* a photo of the new house!
   Mr Leinert: (no / two yesterday)
3. *Robert:* 'Robin Hood' is on at the cinema. I want to *see* it. Let's go together.
   David: (no / with Jenny last week)
4. *Becky:* What can we *give* Mum for her birthday? A new CD maybe?
   Simon: (no / one last year)
5. *Mrs Burton:* Can you go to the shops and *get* a new packet of dog biscuits?
   Becky: It's OK, Mum. (Simon / two packets yesterday)

3 Back in Robin Hood's time

Put in the verbs – in the simple past.

1. Only one in ten people … (live) in towns. There … (be) shops in the towns, of course, but they … (not have) shop windows.
2. The streets … (be) very dirty. People … (throw) their dirty water from upstairs windows. Pigs often … (run) from house to house. They … (eat) the rubbish in the streets.
3. Houses … (not have) water. People … (get) water from the river. Or sometimes a man … (take) water round the streets in big buckets.
4. Men and women often … (wear) hats, outside and in the house. Children … (have) clothes like their parents – but usually they … (not wear) shoes.

4 WORD POWER

a) *Do you know the words? They are all in this unit.*

1. Not a friend! 2. Saturday and Sunday. 3. There are a lot of trees in it. 4. You have it when you are sleeping. 5. You make chips from them. 6. It starts in the hills and finishes in the sea. 7. A lot of people all together. 8. A big bird on a farm – usually white.

ESOGO STREFO VIRER DROWC TEATOPSO YEMEN NEKEWED AMERD

b) *Make a sentence with each word.*

Nottingham Goose Fair

Step A

It's here again!

It is the first week of October – an important time of the year for people in Nottingham. The famous Goose Fair is here again! The fair is very popular. Everyone – young and old – visits Goose Fair … .

1 Listening practice: Goose Fair last year

a) *Listen to the cassette. John, the American boy, is asking about Goose Fair last year. What did everyone do at the fair?*

Please take notes for:

Becky David Robert

Becky – went with Sarah
– dodgems

b) *Talk about what they did.*
Example: Becky went to the fair with … . They … .

2 WORD POWER

a) *Find the opposites of these adjectives.*

cheap old little boring good right ↔ left / wrong

b) *Sometimes you can make opposites with 'un-'.*
You know: tidy ↔ untidy

So you can understand: unlucky unhappy unpopular unhealthy unimportant

Can you make sentences with these new words?

Step B

Thanks, Dad!

It is Friday evening, and Kim is at Goose Fair.
Sarah isn't so happy because she must stay at home.

Sarah: Why can't I go to the fair in the evening like Kim?
Mrs Dixon: Kim is older than you, Sarah, and –
Sarah: Yes, and she's luckier than I am.
Mrs Dixon: Oh, Sarah! Anyway, you're going to go with your friends tomorrow afternoon.
Sarah: Yes, but the afternoon isn't as good as the evening. Everything always looks bigger and better in the evening.
Mr Dixon: Goose Fair is fun in the afternoon, too, Sarah. But it isn't the cheapest place in the world. Here – you can have some extra pocket money this week.
Sarah: Oh thanks, Dad! You're the best!

old – old**er** – **(the)** old**est**
big – bi**gger** – **(the)** bi**ggest**
lucky – luck**ier** – **(the)** luck**iest**

good – **better** – **(the) best**
bad – **worse** – **(the) worst**

1 Sarah, Becky, Jenny, Robert, David

a) *What do you know about them? Make questions and answers with a partner. Look at the pictures in this book.*

WHO is the smallest/biggest of the friends / has got the oldest sister/youngest brother / speaks the best German/has got the biggest pet/ … **?**

Example: Who is the smallest of the friends? – David is the smallest.

b) *What do you think about them? Does your partner think the same? Work with these ideas:*

say (funny) things – be (clever/crazy) – look (happy) – have (good) ideas – wear (nice) clothes

I think Sarah looks the happiest.

Oh no, I think Robert looks the happiest.

2 Family pairs

Compare the people (and dogs).
Example:
1. Kim is older than Sarah. She is not as crazy as Sarah. Sarah is … . *Please go on.*

	younger bigger smaller older crazier funnier quieter	than …
not as	big old funny quiet crazy …	as …

1

2

3

4

In the park

It is Saturday afternoon. Robert and David are in the park. They see Simon with Maxi and Mini.

Robert: Hi, Simon. Where's Becky?
Simon: Oh, she's at the fair with Sarah and Jenny.
David: What? Goose Fair is more important than her dogs? Poor Maxi, poor Mini!
Simon: Oh, the dogs have fun with me, too, you know. We go for the most exciting walks together. I play more interesting games with them than Becky does.
Robert: Really? Then why are they running away?
Simon: Oh no! It's always so difficult when they run away. Maxi! Mini! Come back! You're the worst dogs in Nottingham!

exciting
– **more** exciting
– **(the) most** exciting

3 The most exciting game

Make dialogues with these ideas:

important school subject · expensive place for a holiday · boring activity · difficult game · famous pop group · exciting book · interesting film

Example:

I think English is the most important school subject.

I think Maths is more important than English.

I don't. I think Maths is the most important school subject.

4 A group activity

Make a poster about the people in your class.

WHO
– is the youngest/the oldest?
– is the biggest/the smallest?
– has got the most exciting video?
– tells the funniest jokes?
– has got the most interesting pet?
– …?

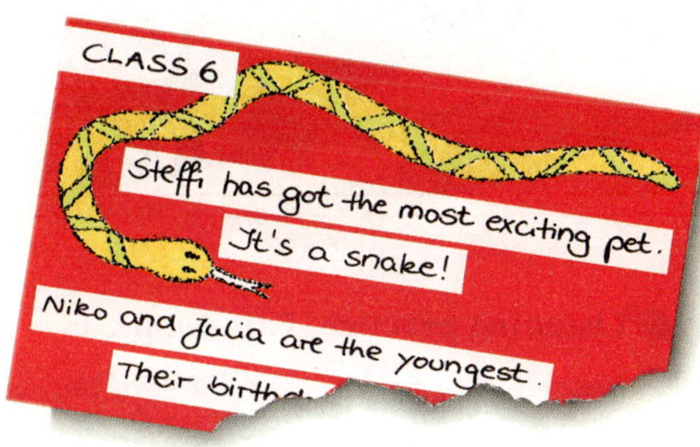

5 *Watch out:* more/most or -er/-est

Nottingham isn't the **biggest** (*big*) city in the UK. It's (*small*) … than London, of course. And maybe it isn't as important as London. But Nottingham is one of the (*interesting*) … cities, and it has a (*long*) … history than many others.
Everyone knows Robin Hood, the (*famous*) … outlaw in British history. People in Robin's time had a (*difficult*) … life than today. So Robin helped the (*poor*) … and the (*hungry*) … of them. The Sheriff of Nottingham wasn't as clever as Robin!
One of the (*old*) … fairs in the UK is in Nottingham, too. At first Goose Fair was a market – with the (*good*) … cheese in England – and people came from far away. Today it is (*easy*) … to visit Nottingham than in those days. The city is in the centre of England, so it is never a long way by car.

Unit 3

Step C

All the fun of the fair

1 Role play: Let's have a go!

What do you want to do at the fair?
Look at the pictures and act the dialogues.

2 Listening practice: Fair people

a) *Listen to the people. Can you find the right pictures? (Only 3 are right.)*
Start like this: The right picture for number one is picture ... .

b) *There is nothing on the cassette for two of the pictures in a). What can these people say? Write a little text, and act it in class.*

3 Sound practice

a) *One word has got a different sound. Can you find it?*

[dʒ] joke strange child dodgem Jenny   [tʃ] catch cheap picture church German

b) *Please say these sentences and then find more words with* [dʒ] *and* [tʃ] *sounds.*
Do**dg**ems aren't **ch**eap. – They're **G**erman **ch**ildren. – Let's cat**ch** **J**enny!

4 Looking at English

Look at the list of irregular verbs on page 182 and find the simple past forms of these verbs. Write them in your exercise book. Then make sentences with them. Example: buy – bought
Yesterday I bought a new CD.

buy ✔ write find drive
make put spend feel leave

5 When I was little

When I was little, I went to the fair with my parents. And I was scared of white knuckle rides. I only liked children's roundabouts. But now it's different. I go to the fair with my friends. And I love exciting rides!

turn

Talk about what you were like when you were little. What are you like now? Think about:

games bed time free time activities TV food clothes …

eat read wear go drink watch play …

6 WORD POWER

When you describe things, you can often compare them with other things. Find the right words, and finish the sentences.

1. (old) Ha ha. That joke is as old as **the hills**.
2. (white) Look at your dirty T-shirt! This morning it was as … .
3. (free) Come to the mountains and feel … .
4. (cold) Poor you! Your hands are … .
5. (black) Black cats are lucky. But they must be … .
6. (easy) Of course you can make a nice cake. It's … .

ice ABC night the hills ✔ snow a bird

SB

7 ⟨A song: I've got a lovely bunch of coconuts⟩

Down at Barney's Fair, one evening I was there,
when I heard a showman shouting underneath
a flare:
"I've got a lovely bunch of coconuts,
There they are all standing in a row,
Big ones, small ones, some as big as your head,
Give 'em a twist, a flick of the wrist,"
That's what the showman said.
"I've got a lovely bunch of coconuts,
Every ball you throw will make me rich;
Here stands my wife, the idol of my life,
Singing roll or bowl a ball a penny a pitch."

Step D

Two and one make three

Becky was really excited when she arrived at Goose Fair with Sarah and Jenny. But things started to go wrong right away.
"Hey, look! The dodgems!" Sarah shouted.
She and Jenny jumped into one car together, so there was no seat for Becky. She drove a different car. – Crash! Sarah and Jenny hit Becky's car from behind. "Ha ha! We must learn to drive!" Sarah shouted.
"Isn't this great?" Jenny laughed.
But Becky wasn't sure. She didn't think it was much fun without a partner.

After the dodgems Jenny wanted to have a go on the coconut shy. She didn't win a prize, but Sarah won a little teddy.
"Well done!" Jenny said. "Come on, Becky. It's your turn now. Maybe you can win a bigger teddy than Sarah's. What about that white one?"
But when Becky threw a ball, she couldn't hit the coconuts.
She hit the man behind the stall.
"Hey! Try to be more careful! That was the worst throw today," the man laughed. Jenny and Sarah laughed, too. But not Becky.
She felt angry. She didn't like it when people laughed at her.

Near the coconut shy they could see a white knuckle ride.
"Ooh, that's the most exciting ride at the fair," Jenny said. "Let's have a go on it."
But Becky felt nervous about rides like that.
"Look, there's a nice children's roundabout," Sarah said. "That's better for you.
You can wait for us there."
She and Jenny ran off for their ride. Becky walked away. She felt miserable now.
She remembered the fair last year, and the fun with Sarah.
Of course Jenny wasn't with them last year. Two was better than three … .

"Becky, wait! Where are you going?" It was the other two behind her.
"What do you want?" Becky asked. "Leave me alone!" She didn't feel very friendly.
"Becky, I'm really sorry about my roundabout joke," Sarah said. "It wasn't very nice of me. I know you don't like white knuckle rides."
"We didn't want to go for a ride without you," Jenny said. "We came to the fair together. So let's stay together. What do you say, Becky?"

1 Questions

a) 1. How did Becky feel when she arrived at Goose Fair?
2. Why didn't she have fun on the dodgems?
3. What did Sarah win on the coconut shy?
4. What happened when Becky had a go?
5. What did they see near the coconut shy?
6. How did Becky feel about rides like that?
7. Why didn't she wait for the others?
8. Who ran after her, and why?

b) *How can the story finish?*
What did Becky say to Jenny and Sarah? What do you think?

2 The story

Make a summary of the story in the simple present.
- *How many parts are there?*
- *Write down in one or two sentences the most important things about every part.*
  (First look at your answers to exercise 1.)
- *Say how Becky feels at different times in the story. That is important, too.*

You can start like this:
When Becky arrives at … she feels … . But she doesn't have fun on the dodgems because … .

3 Becky

I think she's silly at the dodgems. You can't always sit with a friend.

Yes, but I can understand how she feels. Everything is more fun with a partner.

a) *Is Becky silly? What do you think?*
Talk about what she thinks or how she feels –
at the dodgems/at the coconut shy/at the white knuckle ride.

b) *What can you say about the other people in the story?*
Are they nice/not so nice/silly/friendly? *Say why.*

4 Poor Simon

Simple or progressive?
Put in the right forms of the present.

play run go laugh

1. Simon often … football on Saturday afternoons. But this afternoon he … with the dogs in the park.
2. That's because Becky … to Goose Fair today. She usually … for walks with Maxi and Mini, of course.
3. Maxi and Mini never … away from Becky. But they aren't so good with Simon, and now he … after them!
4. "Ha ha!" Now Robert and David … at poor Simon. He doesn't like it when the bigger boys … at him.

Step E

Let's check

1 WORD POWER

Unit 3

Sometimes you don't know a word – so you find other words.
Say these sentences again, with the 'right' words. (They're all new in this unit.)

1. I think English is – well, you often need it. – It is **important**.
2. Robin Hood is very – er – everyone knows his name.
3. I like those shoes, but they're – well, they cost a lot of money.
4. We're lucky because our neighbours are – they're always nice and say hello.
5. This song on the radio is very – er – a lot of people like it.
6. Why does that man look so – well, he looks the opposite of happy.
7. This puzzle is – it isn't easy.

2 Let's compare

What can you say about these pairs of things?
Example: 1. Bikes are **cheaper** than cars. And they aren't **as dirty as** cars.

cheap ✔ nice exciting clever
friendly good expensive
easy dirty ✔ important
…

3 What they think

What do these people say? Make sentences.
Example:
1. *Sarah:* Tabby is the silliest cat in the neighbourhood.
2. *Becky*: Maxi and Mini are … .
3. *Simon:* Burtons' Bikes is … .
4. *Mrs Croft:* Robert! Your room is … .
5. *Jenny:* The Tales of Robin Hood is … .
6. *Mr Stevenson:* The pupils are … .

– untidy place/England
– silly cat/the neighbourhood ✔
– important people/the school
– exciting adventure/Nottingham
– nice dogs/the world
– good bike shop/Sherwood

4 What can you say?

Find the right answers.

1. "Look at that poster. There's going to be a fair next week."
2. "Let's go swimming today."
3. "Here, you can have my last sweet."
4. "Where were you yesterday evening? I thought you wanted to come to my house."
5. "I'm sorry I wasn't very nice yesterday."
6. "I had 20 throws but I didn't win a prize."

"Sorry. I haven't got time."
"Sorry. I had too much homework."
"Great! Let's go there."
"That's OK. We're still friends."
"Never mind. The prizes were terrible."
"Thanks. That's very nice of you."

The junior play

Step A

Costumes for the play

This Christmas the junior play is a ghost story. Jenny hasn't got a part in the play, but she is the prompter. Now she and Shabina Ismaili, from 9GN, are looking for costumes for the play. There are a lot of different clothes in the drama group cupboard.

Jenny: Look, Shabina. This long skirt is pretty! Maybe you can wear it for your part. A hundred years ago women wore really long skirts and dresses.

Shabina: Oh yes, it's lovely! – This short jacket is good, too.

Jenny: Yes, one of the boys can wear that. What have we got for the ghost? Let's look in this box.

Shabina: There are some useful things in here! These white tights look good.

Jenny: And here's a long white shirt. Oh dear, it isn't very clean. Well, we can wash it. Hey, look, there's a white beard, too. Great!

Shabina: Yes, that's important for the ghost. Let me try it on. – Aaah! Do I look frightening?

Jenny: No, you look silly! Come on, try the skirt on now.

1 My English folder

What clothes do you know in English?
Write a list in your folder.
What do you think are the nicest clothes?
Draw pictures of them, and write about them.
(You can write about your friends' clothes, too.)

2 WORD POWER

What other 'drama words' do you know? Start a list in your exercise book.
Later in this unit there are more 'drama words'. When you find them, write them down, too.
At the end of the unit you can put them in alphabetical order.

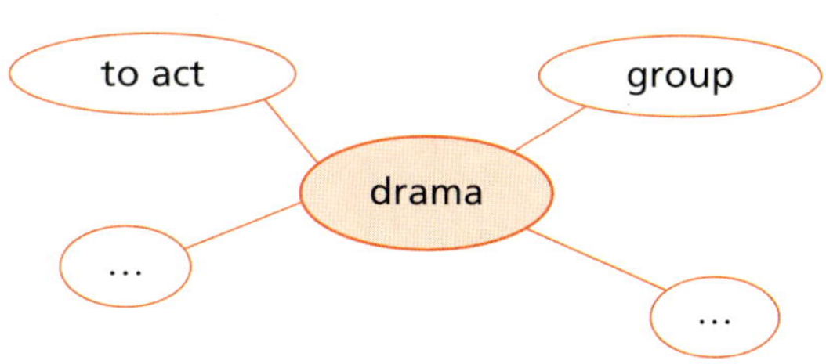

Step B

Robert the ghost

Robert has got a good part in the play – he is the ghost! He is very happy about this. But he is a bit nervous, too. A lot of people will be there … .

Robert: Hey, Mum! Next week at this time I'll be on the stage! I hope everything will be OK!
Mrs Croft: Of course it will, Robert.
Robert: But I'm so nervous. I'm sure I'll forget my words.
Mrs Croft: No, you won't. You know your part! Everyone will feel a bit nervous at first. But after a minute or two you'll be fine. It's the same with people on the radio.
Robert: But my part is so difficult, Mum. I'm sure people will laugh when they see me as the ghost.
Mrs Croft: They won't laugh, Robert. They'll all be scared! – Say something in your ghost voice again.
Robert (with a terrible laugh): I will be back on Friday the thirteenth … Ha – ha – ha.

Unit 4

1 The play

Put in 'will' or 'won't'.

I'll laugh	=	I will laugh
he'll laugh	=	he will laugh
they'll laugh	=	they will laugh
they won't laugh	=	they will not laugh

1. The drama group … act their play next week.
2. A lot of people … be there.
3. All Robert's and Jenny's friends … come, of course.
4. The Penroses … bring Mark with them, too.
5. David hopes Mark … be scared of the ghost!
6. Jenny is sure everyone … like the play.
7. But Robert thinks people … laugh at the wrong time.
8. Mrs Mason, the drama teacher, hopes Robert and his friends … feel too nervous!

2 Don't worry!

Say the opposite.

Example: 1. Oh dear, I'll be so nervous. – No, you won't! I'm sure you won't be nervous.
2. People won't like the play. – Yes, they will! Of course they'll like the play.

3. I'll forget my words.
4. I won't look good in my costume.
5. People will laugh when I come on the stage.
6. They won't understand the play.
7. People won't like the music.
8. The play will be terrible.

3 Kim

Kim often thinks,
"When I have children, things will be different …"

Say what Kim thinks.

When I have children, | I'll … / I won't … |

ask questions about school every day
try to understand their problems
be nice to them
give them enough pocket money
buy nice things for them
get angry about little things
listen to their music

Who knows?

Robert feels much better now …

4 What will happen?

What are these people thinking?

Example:

1. *Sarah:* If there's a table tennis club next year, **I'll join it.**
2. *Becky:* If I have time after school, …
3. *Robert:* If Mum has a lot of work, …
4. *Jenny:* If we have drama practice after school, …
5. *David:* If I don't have time today, …
6. *Simon:* If Mike lends me his new computer game, …
7. *Grandma Penrose:* If the weather is good at the weekend, …
8. *Mark:* If David takes my crayons to school, …

join it ✓
do my guitar practice tomorrow ✓
make tea for her ✓
go for a walk with Maxi and Mini ✓
play it at the weekend ✓
take the children to the seaside ✓
not go to Becky's house ✓
not lend them to him again

5 What will you do?

Think of next weekend.

If the weather is nice/…,			go to the cinema/the park/the mountains/…
If it's wet and cold/…,	I	'll	stay at home.
If I/we have time,	we	won't	watch TV/read …
If I/we have enough money,			play …/visit …
If my mum/dad says yes,			…

6 Sound and listening practice

a) [w]

I **w**on't be **w**ith you on **W**ednesday next **w**eek. **W**ill you be a**w**ay?

[v]

I'**v**e got se**v**en **v**ideos. The **v**et arri**v**ed **v**ery late in the e**v**ening.

[w] - [v]

We **w**alked to Lar**w**ood Gro**v**e **w**ith Da**v**id. Mr Ste**v**enson **w**on't **w**ait!

b) *Listen to these words.*

Make two lists and put the words in the list.

The Canterville Ghost

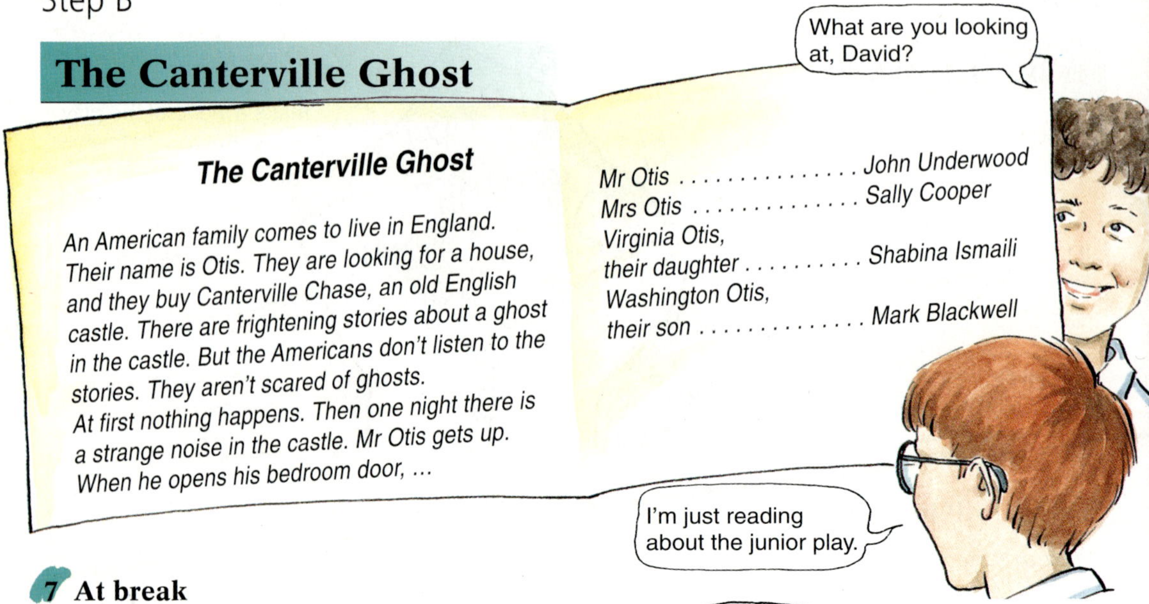

7 At break

look talk wait listen look think

a) What are they doing?
Example: 1. David is **looking at** the poster for the play.

at about to for

b) *Now ask a partner questions with 'who' or 'what'. He or she must tell you the answers.*
Example: 1. **What** is David **looking at**? – He's looking at a poster for the play.

8 Simon and the dogs

Put in the right prepositions.

Last Saturday Simon wanted to go … a walk with Maxi and Mini. "Are you sure they're OK with you?" asked Becky before they went … the house.
"Of course they're OK. You needn't worry … them!" said Simon. "We're only going to go … the park."
There is a big fish pond in Arnot Hill Park. Suddenly Mini saw a strange animal near the water. A frog! First she just looked … it. "What is this?" she thought. Then she barked … it – she made a terrible noise! Now the frog felt scared, and at once it jumped … the pond.
But Mini wanted to catch that frog. So she ran … it – and in a moment she was in the pond, too! "Is this a new game?" thought Maxi. "Wait … me, Mini, I'm coming in, too!"
On the way home, Simon met Robert and David again! They looked … the two wet dogs, and of course they laughed. "Don't laugh … me!" said Simon. "You don't know how difficult they are!"

at
for
out of
about
to
into
after

Looking at the UK: Theatre groups

1. This is a school drama group. They have practices every week.

2. Children often act in Christmas plays at church.

3. Big towns sometimes have a puppet theatre. This one is in London.

4. This is a professional theatre for children.

1 Theatre in Germany

1. Is there a drama group at your school?
   Or at your church or at a club in your town?
2. Did you act in a play at school last year?
   Or at your first school? What play was it?
3. Have you got puppets at school or at home?
   What are they like? What are their names?
   Do you sometimes act plays with them?
4. Where is your nearest theatre?
   Do you sometimes go there?
   What play did you see there last?
   Did you like it?
   Say why or why not.

Step C

Don't worry, Jenny!

On the day of the junior play, Shabina doesn't come to school.
Soon everyone knows why. She is ill.
"No problem," says Mrs Mason. "Jenny can take Shabina's part.
She knows all the words by heart. – Come on, Jenny!"

Jenny: But I can't act! I …
Mrs Mason: Yes, you can! Don't worry, Jenny. I'll help you. We'll go through your part at lunch time.
Jenny: But there's another thing, Mrs Mason. I can't be the prompter when I'm on the stage.
Mrs Mason: Never mind, Jenny. We'll find another prompter.

1 I'll help you

These Maths exercises are difficult. Oh dear, there's no milk in the house. I can't find my pen. Oh, I haven't got my purse! The dogs are making a terrible noise. I don't understand this computer game.	–	Wait. Don't worry. Just a minute. It's OK.	I'll	show you how it goes. lend you £5. go to the shops. help you with them. give you my biro. feed them.

2 Listening practice: The Canterville Ghost

a) *What do you already know about the play 'The Canterville Ghost'?*

b) *Now listen to the dialogue. What new information can you find out about the play?*
Find out about – Mr Otis and the ghost; – Virginia and the ghost; – the children and the ghost; – what happens at the end of the story.

3 ⟨A song: Five hundred miles⟩

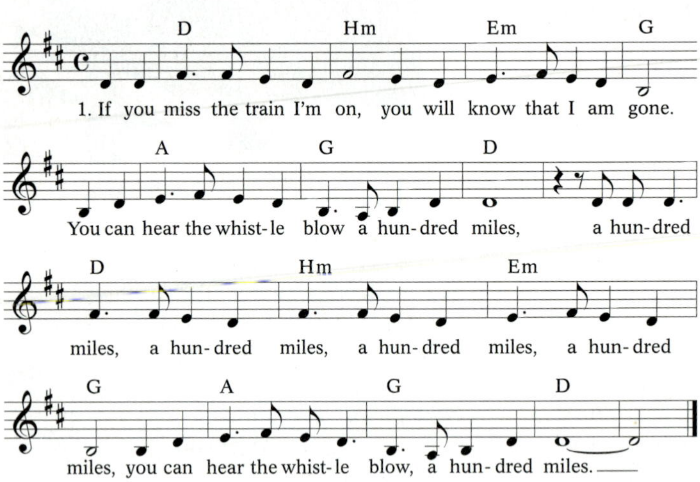

2. Lord, I'm one, Lord, I'm two,
Lord, I'm three, Lord, I'm four,
Lord, I'm five hundred miles
from my home.
Five hundred miles, (four times)
You can hear the whistle blow a
hundred miles.

3. Not a shirt on my back,
Not a penny to my name,
Lord, I can't go back home
this-a-way.
This-a-way, (four times)
No, I can't go back home
this-a-way.

Step D

On the stage

"Good evening, everybody. We hope you will all like our play, 'The Canterville Ghost.' I'm sorry to say that Shabina Ismaili can't be with us this evening because she's ill. So Jenny Leinert will play the part of Virginia."

Everybody clapped, and Mrs Mason left the stage. Jenny was behind the scenes. She felt very nervous now.

"Don't worry, Jenny!" said Robert. "You know all the words by heart. Not much can go wrong!"

"But I can't act like Shabina. And now I can't be the prompter – and I can't do the sound effects for the first scene!" said Jenny.

"I can do those jobs," said Robert. "I won't be on the stage in the first scene. Mrs Mason will do the sound effects when we're both on the stage together."

In the first scene Jenny didn't have much to say. Soon she felt fine on the stage with the others. It was the Americans' first evening at Canterville Chase. All the family sat round the table, and Mrs Umney, the housekeeper, gave them tea. Jenny thought about the sound effects.

"I hope Robert won't forget to play the cassette at the right time!" she thought.

The first sound effect was thunder. Before that there was lightning. Then Mrs Umney said, "Terrible things happen in this house!"

Now it was time for the thunder. "Come on, Robert!" Jenny thought. "What are you waiting for?" But nothing happened. Then it came – the sound of pop music. Really loud!

"Oh no!" thought Jenny. "He's got the wrong side of the cassette!" The music stopped. Now it was Jenny's turn to speak. "Listen to the thunder!" she said. And – of course everybody laughed.

Robert felt really terrible. "What an idiot I am!" he thought. "Well, I hope I'll be OK on the stage. I'll be on in a minute now. Oh dear – if people laugh at me, I'll die!"

When Robert came on the stage, everybody was very quiet. In his long white shirt and the white beard, he looked really good as the ghost. Nobody laughed.

"That's good, then," thought Robert.

He felt fine now. So everything was OK!

Then came the scene when Mr Otis and his two younger sons first see the ghost. The boys aren't scared of the ghost, and they throw pillows at him.

"Silly old ghost!" the boys shouted and threw their pillows. Everybody laughed. That was all right. But then one of the pillows hit Robert's face and his beard came off! People laughed even more then.

"Hey, it isn't a ghost, Mum! It's Robert!" called a child in the first row. It was Mark. "Hello, Robert!"

But after that everything was fine. People laughed in the right places and everybody clapped a lot at the end.
"Well done, everyone!" said Mrs Mason.
"You were great, Virginia!" she said to Jenny.
"Yes, what you said was right, Robert!" said Jenny.
"Oh? What did I say?" asked Robert.
"Not much can go wrong!" said Jenny.

1 The text

Look at the text again.

How many parts are there in the text?
Can you find a title for each part? Why is it a good title?

Start like this:
Part one is from line 1 to line 14.
You can call it 'Behind the scenes', because Jenny and Robert are talking behind the scenes at the beginning of the play.
'Before the play' is a good title, too, because ... *Go on.*

2 After the play

After the play, Jeff Dickens from 9GN talked to Robert and Jenny. He wanted to write about the play for the school magazine.

Here are his questions. *Can you give their answers?*

1. How did you feel before you went on the stage, Jenny?
2. And later, when you were on the stage?
3. Why was there pop music in the first scene?
4. How did you feel then, Robert?
5. You were very good as Virginia, Jenny! When did you learn the words?

3 What Jeff wrote

What did Jeff Dickens write for the school magazine?

You can start like this:
"There were many people in the school hall. It was the evening of the junior play. Everyone was surprised when Mrs Mason came on the stage before the play. Shabina Ismaili was ill. So Jenny Leinert took her part ..." *Go on.*

4 Looking at English

Jenny's father **will** be in London **next week**. "Next week" is a signal for the future.

What other signals can you find? Write a list in your exercise book.
Then write short sentences with five of them.

Step E

Let's check

1 I hope …

Make sentences with 'will' or 'won't'. Start your sentences with 'I hope …'.

Example: 1. *Robert:* I feel so nervous! (I – forget – words) → I hope I won't forget my words!

2. *Jenny:* Listen to the thunder! (it – rain)
3. *Becky:* I've got some new dog food for Maxi and Mini. (they – like it)
4. *Mark:* Here's Grandma! (she – play – a game with me)
5. *Mrs Croft:* Shabina is ill. Oh dear! (Robert – get ill, too)
6. *Sarah:* This jacket is nice. (Mum – buy it for me)
7. *Simon:* I'm going to Mike's house. (his brother Barry – be at home)

2 The weather tomorrow

	morning	afternoon	evening
Nottingham			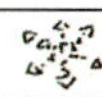
London	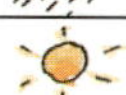		
Berlin			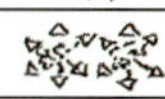

 = wet  = warm  = cold

 = sunny   = very cold

Talk about the weather with a partner.

Examples:

What will it be like in Nottingham tomorrow?
– It'll be wet in the morning.
But it'll be sunny in the afternoon.

Will it be cold in Berlin tomorrow?
– Yes, it'll be cold there in the morning, and very cold in the evening.

3 The Maths book

It is Wednesday afternoon. When Robert gets home and opens his schoolbag, he finds David's Maths book. "Oh dear," he thinks …

Example: 1. I'll take it to his house now. Then he'll have it right away.
– If I take it to his house now, he'll have it right away.

2. But maybe he'll be at his grandma's house. Then he won't be at home.
– If he is at …
3. But his dad will probably be at home. Then I'll give *him* the book.
4. But maybe Mr Penrose will be out with Mark. Then nobody will be there.
5. I'll phone the Penroses in the evening. They'll all be at home then.
6. But maybe David won't need the book today. So I'll give it to him at school tomorrow.

4 WORD POWER

a) What can they be like? Find as many adjectives as you can.

Example: Houses can be big or small.
Some houses are very tidy.
Others are … Go on.

houses clothes films
people school subjects games

b) *Have you collected all the words for your 'drama list'?*
(Remember exercise 2 on page 33.)

In town

Step A Something for everyone

WELCOME TO

In the shopping centre

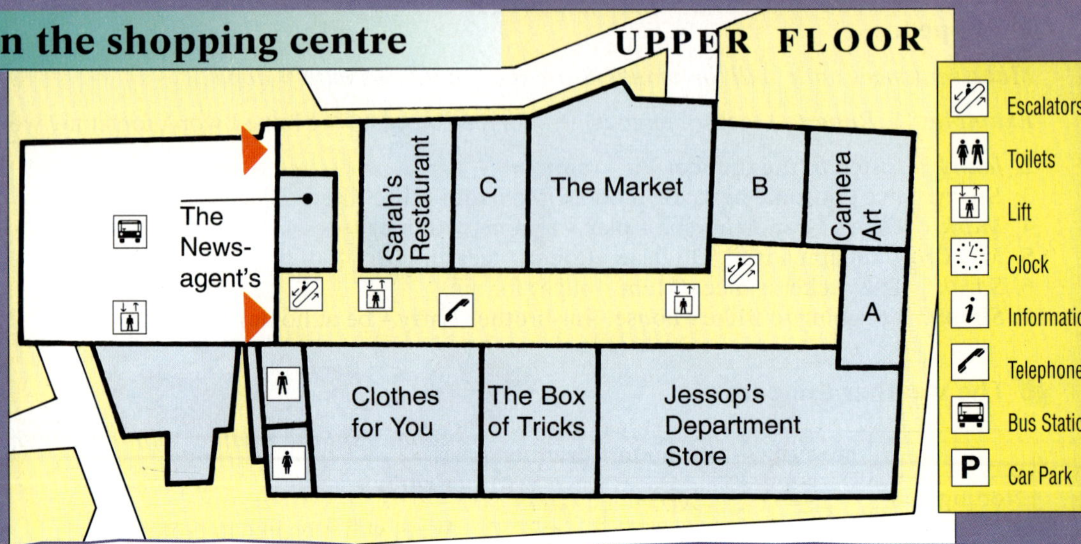

1 Let's look

1. What shops are there in the shopping centre? What else can you find there?
2. What do you think you can buy or do there?

2 Where is it?

Where's	the Biscuit Box? the bus station? Camera Art? …	–	It's	on the upper floor on the lower floor	between opposite next to in the middle of above …	…

THE SHOPPING CENTRE *Something for everyone*

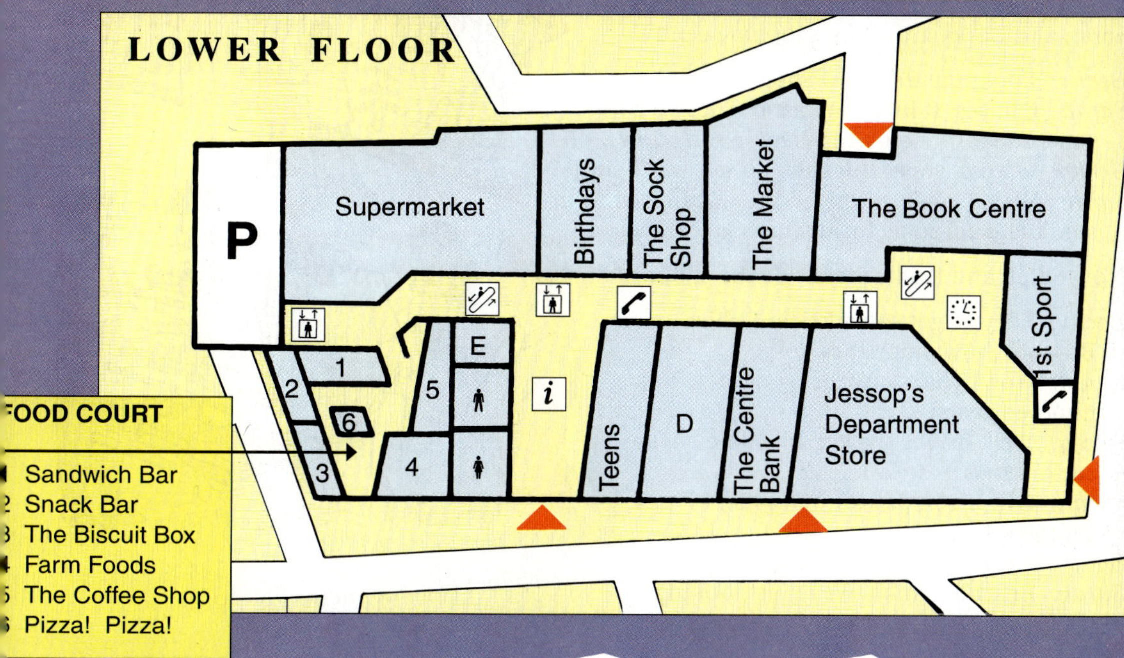

3 Listening practice: Which shop is which?

People often ask where things are in the shopping centre. There are people near the clock on the lower floor now.

They want to find these places:
1. Sue's Tea Shop 2. Broadwood's Bank 3. the Taj Mahal Indian Restaurant
4. the Post Office 5. the Sweet Shop

Listen to the text and find out where the people want to go.
In the plan of the shopping centre you can find the letters A, B, C, D, E.
Which places are they?

4 WORD POWER

What can you do in a shopping centre?

Start like this:
You can look at nice clothes.
You can eat … .

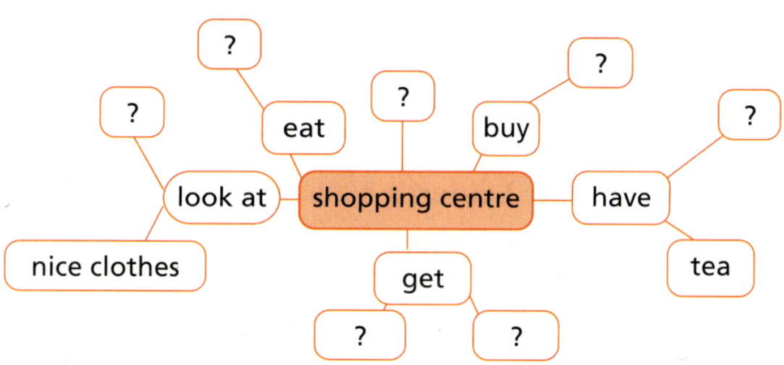

Step B

Just looking

Sarah and Becky are at the shopping centre.

Becky: Look, there's a new shop, "Teens".
Sarah: Oh, yes. It looks fantastic. They've got some super trainers over there in the corner.
Becky: Oh yes, great. But can you see any T-shirts?
Sarah: Well, I can't see any in the window, but I'm sure there are some inside. Let's go in.

Now Sarah and Becky are inside the shop.

Becky: They've got some lovely T-shirts here. But look how much they cost.
Sarah: Wow! That's my pocket money for a hundred years!
Becky: Well, maybe they've got some cheap socks for us.
Sarah: OK. If you pay for one sock, I'll pay for the other sock.
Shop assistant: Do you need any help?
Sarah: Er – no thanks. We're just looking.

There are **some** trainers in the window.
I can't see **any** T-shirts.
Do you need **any** help?

Unit 5

1 Do you need any help?

Put in 'some' or 'any'.

1. *Customer:* Have you got … warm tights, please? I didn't see … tights in the window.
   Assistant: We've got … lovely tights, but we haven't got … for this cold weather.
2. *Customer:* I'm looking for … socks for my brother. Have you got … red socks?
   Assistant: I can show you … nice socks for boys, but I think there aren't … red ones.
3. *Customer:* Have you got … crayons, please?
   Assistant: Yes, we've got … big boxes of crayons. They're in eight different colours.
4. *Customer:* I'm looking for … table tennis balls.
   Assistant: I'm sorry, we haven't got … table tennis balls at the moment.

2 *Watch out:* 'some' or 'any'?

Example: 1. She doesn't like tennis. She never watches **any games.**
2. Mike and Simon went to the newsagent's and looked at … .
3. I can't make a sandwich because there isn't … .
4. Mike isn't a bully. Bullies haven't got … .
5. The coconut shy is great. There are … .
6. I've got two cats and a dog. Have you got …?

some **any**

computer magazines
great prizes
pets
bread
games ✔
friends

3 Listening practice: Mr Leinert's busy day

Mr Leinert and Jenny are thinking about what they must do.
Listen to the cassette and take notes.
Can you finish Mr Leinert's list?

Things to do — Things to buy
repair Jenny's bike — eggs

Something silly

One Saturday morning something silly happened to Jenny and her father at the sports centre. First they went swimming. Then they had something to drink, but they didn't have anything to eat, because it was nearly time for lunch. They went to the top floor of the car park and looked round.
"That's funny," said Mr Leinert. "I can't see the car anywhere. It must be somewhere. Come on," he said and went down to the second floor.
"Oh, wait a minute," Jenny answered and ran after him.
But Mr Leinert didn't listen and said "We must ask somebody, but I can't see anybody here."
"But Dad!" Jenny shouted at him. "We didn't come by car!"

4 Looking at English

a) *Collect all the compounds with 'some' and 'any' in the text. Make two lists. You will find more compounds with 'some' and 'any' later in the book. Then you can put them on the list, too.*
b) *Write a little dialogue with each compound.*
Example: Can you hear anything? – Yes, I can hear something outside.

Some-	any-
something	anything

5 At the sports centre

Jenny and her father are telling Mrs Leinert about their day. Put in compounds with 'some' and 'any'.

1. *Jenny:* We went by car last time, but we couldn't find a place to park … .
2. *Mrs Leinert:* Well, I usually find a place for the car … on the top floor.
3. *Mr Leinert:* Jenny was hungry, but I didn't buy her … to eat, only … to drink.
4. *Mrs Leinert:* So that's why she didn't want … to drink at lunch.
5. *Mrs Leinert:* What was it like? Did you meet … from your tutor group?
6. *Jenny:* Yes. Anna was there. She was with … from our school.

6 Did you really do that?

a) *Ask five people in your class about their weekend. Make a list.*

Did you
- go anywhere special at the weekend?
- do anything useful at the weekend?
- meet anybody from school at the weekend?

pupil	somewhere special	something useful	somebody from school
Ken	Berlin	tidied his room	no
Sue	no	repaired her bike	met Anna in town

b) *Write about the information on your list. Start like this:*
Ken went **somewhere** special: He went to Berlin. The others didn't go **anywhere**. *Go on.*

7 What about your next weekend?

Talk to a partner. Ask and answer questions about your plans for the weekend.

Are you going to do anything interesting on Saturday?

- Yes, I am. I'm going to see a film with my friends.
- No, I'm not. I'm going to stay at home.

Sarah's favourite

Sarah: Hey, Becky. Do you know who'll be in Nottingham on Saturday?
Becky: No, who?
Sarah: Jack Ripple! You know, from 'Two'n'Two'.
Becky: So what?
Sarah: Oh Becky, he's fantastic! He'll be at the sports centre at 10 o'clock. I'm going to see him. Do you want to come, too?
Becky: Well, not really.
Sarah: Oh, come on, Becky. I'm going to get his autograph. I've already got a super poster of him.

He'll be at the sports centre tomorrow.
I'm going to get his autograph.

8 Little dialogues

Put the little dialogues together.

1. Why have you got your guitar with you?
2. I haven't got time to wash this table.
3. My cousin wants a photo of me.
4. Mike's bike is broken. He can't get home.
5. Why are you leaving the party so early?
6. Hey, what are you doing with that camera?
7. Why did you put a bucket of water on the table?

- I'll take him home. That's no problem.
- I'm going to take a photo of you. Say 'cheese'.
- I'm going to take my friend home now.
- I'll take a photo of you. Give me the camera.
- Because I'm going to wash it.
- Don't worry! I'll wash it.
- Because I'm going to play it soon.

9 In the future

Make a list: What are people planning and what will happen?
Then complete the sentences with 'will' and 'going to'.

Example: 1. Jack Ripple: be in Nottingham on Saturday **(will happen)**
Sarah: get his autograph **(plan)**
Jack Ripple **will be** in Nottingham on Saturday. Sarah **is going to get** his autograph.

2. Jenny: be 13 on 7th February – have a big party.
3. Weather: be good on Monday. – Simon: play football.
4. Mr Leinert: be away next weekend – Jenny and her mother: visit the Penroses.
5. Next year: be Kim's last year at school. – She: look for a job.
6. Next Friday: be a holiday. – The Penroses: go to the seaside.

10 *Watch out:* 'will' or 'going to'

1. *Becky:* I can't come with you to see Jack Ripple, Sarah. I ... any time. (not have)
   Sarah: Why not?
2. *Becky:* I ... my dad in the bike shop on Saturday. (help)
3. *Sarah:* All day? Can't you come in the afternoon? Oh, Becky. I'm sure you ... it. (love)
4. *Becky:* Hm, maybe Kim ... with you, too? (go)
5. *Sarah:* No, she just laughs at 'Two'n'Two', and she ... at 'Just Jeans' on Saturday. (be)
6. *Becky:* I'm sure the sports centre ... full. (be) It's always full when famous people come.
7. *Sarah:* I know. So let's go early, or we ... anything. (not see)

Looking at the UK: Things to do

This is Twycross Zoo in Nottingham.

At weekends many people go to the ice rink or to the swimming pool.

You can visit the Lace Museum, too.

If you don't understand all the words on the signs it doesn't matter. But the pictures will help you to understand them.

1 Find out what the words mean

You don't know some of the words on the signs:

adults *non-swimmers* *hire* *skates* *smoke*

Talk about the words.

Example:

What do you think "adult" means?

Look at the sign. It says "adults" and "children". And it costs more for adults.

So adults aren't children. It must mean "older people".

2 Signs

Make English signs for your classroom or your school.

Step C

Something different

1 Role play: Shopping

Play the parts of shop assistant and customer.

Hello. Can I help you? → I'd like some ..., please./ Could you show me some ...?

Sorry, we haven't got any ... . Would you like some ...? → No, thank you./ Yes, please.

Here you are. → Thank you very much.

2 Clap 'n' Rap

Groups A and B read this in rhythm. Group C must clap on 'what' and 'do' and so on.

A What are you going to do today?
B What did you say? What did you say?
A What are you going to do today? Today, today, TODAY!
B I'm going to go into town today.
A What did you say? What did you say?
B I'm going to go into town today. Today, today, TODAY!
A What are you going to do on the way?
B What did you say? What did you say?
A What are you going to do on the way? The way, the way, THE WAY!
B I'm going to throw all the bottles away.
A What did you say? What did you say?
B I'm going to throw all the bottles away. Away, away, AWAY!
A I'll give you some bottles, you'll take them, I'm sure.
B No, I won't!
A Yes, you will!
B No, I won't!
A Well, if you don't take them, my brother will break them.
B He won't!
A Yes, he will!
B No, he won't!

Step D

A present from Robert

Last Saturday it was cold and wet, so Robert didn't want to play outside. "Becky and Simon are going to go to the shopping centre, Mum. I'd like to go, too," he said.

"All right," said Mrs Croft."I'll give you some money for a haircut. Your hair looks a mess."

"Oh, Mum," said Robert.

"And don't forget," Mrs Croft added, "it's Great Uncle Arthur's birthday tomorrow. I've got a present for him already. Are you going to give him anything?"

Robert and Mrs Croft visited Great Uncle Arthur every year and always took him a birthday present. Robert didn't like these visits because there were never any young people there. It wasn't any fun for him.

"Mum, it's so boring," Robert said.

"Well," his mother answered, "he doesn't know anyone else your age. His birthdays were fun when he was younger, and he often played funny tricks on people. Maybe you can find a nice present for him. I'll pay for it. Here's some money – and don't forget the haircut."

"Well," Robert thought. "Great Uncle Arthur is lucky. He never really needs a haircut because he hasn't got any hair."

Robert met Becky and Simon at the shopping centre. They looked everywhere for a nice present for Great Uncle Arthur, but they couldn't find anything.

"I must get a haircut," Robert said to the others. "I'll meet you here in half an hour."

"OK," said Becky. "If we see a good present, we'll tell you later."

When Robert met the others again they were very excited.

"Robert, there's a great new shop here, the Box of Tricks," said Simon. "Come on, we'll show you."

It was a wonderful shop. There were a lot of interesting tricks and funny clothes and jokes. They looked at everything and tried some of the clothes on.

When they came out of the shop they all looked very silly. They went up and down the escalators ten times and a lot of people laughed at them.

They went back to Robert's house together. Robert went into the living-room first and the others waited behind the door.

"Robert!" his mother shouted. "You can't go to school on Monday with pink and yellow hair. What will your teachers think? They'll probably put you in the zoo."

Then Robert took off his wig and the others came into the room. Mrs Croft laughed. "You're a great actor, Robert," she said. "Well, what did you get for Great Uncle Arthur then? Did you find anything nice?"

"Oh, Mum. It was so difficult," Robert said. "We couldn't find anything. And then we found this joke shop and, well, I forgot Great Uncle Arthur's present, but maybe, well … ."

The next day Mrs Croft and Robert drove to Great Uncle Arthur's house. It was a long way, but it wasn't boring this time. Robert was a bit nervous about his present. When they arrived Mrs Croft gave Great Uncle Arthur a book and Robert gave him a big box. Great Uncle Arthur opened it, looked into it and said "What on earth …?"

He took out the pink and yellow wig. He looked at Robert, smiled and put the wig on. When he looked in the mirror, he laughed.
"Oh, dear," he said. "What do I look like? It's fantastic. Oh, I've got an idea. I'll wear it at the 'Over 60s' party next week. Thank you, Robert."
"And after that you can use it as a tea-cosy," said Robert.

1 Ask about the text

a) *How many parts has the text got? Make groups. Group A takes part 1, group B looks at part 2 and so on. Write 3 or 4 questions for your part.*
Ask: Who? When? What? Where? Why?

b) *Ask all the questions in class and write down the answers.*

2 Can you tell the story?

Now put all the answers from exercise 1 in the right order and tell the story again. Are all the important things in your story?

3 Write a story

These are some words from this unit.

Write five of the words on a piece of paper and give it to a partner. Then take your partner's list. Now write a little story with the words on that list.

zoo lift escalators
lovely adult boring
skate to pay for opposite
wig exciting cheap
tea-cosy haircut pool
away useful trick ice rink

4 Sound practice

Harry had a hat on his head.
Sally said she sat on the bed.
Barry fed a fat cat with bread.
Jenny's dad met a vet in red.

a) *Listen to the rhyme. Make two lists of the words with* [æ] *like 'sat' and* [e] *like 'vet'.*

[æ]	[e]
sat	vet

b) *Listen again.* Is there a [t] or a [d] sound at the end of the words in your lists?
Make four new lists.
Read the words again, then say the rhyme.

[æt]	[æd]	[et]	[ed]
sat		vet	

Step E

Let's check

1 WORD POWER

Where can things be?
Collect prepositions like 'between', 'in' etc.
Make sentences with five of them and draw little pictures.
Example: The dog is between the trees.

2 A present for Jenny

What is the right word?

some **something** **somebody** **somewhere** **any** **anything** **anybody** **anywhere**

1. *Sarah:* Kim, it'll be Jenny's birthday soon. I can't think of … for her.
2. *Kim:* Well, I'm going to go to the shopping centre now. Maybe you'll find … for her there.
3. *Sarah:* That's a good idea. Can you see my purse …, Kim?
4. *Kim:* I think it's … in the hall.
5. *Sarah:* Ah, here it is. Oh. There's nothing in it. Just 5p and … stamps.
6. *Kim:* Well, don't look at me, Sarah. I can't lend you … money because I want to buy the new 'Ghosts' CD today.
7. *Sarah:* But Kim. I've got that CD already. … gave it to me for Christmas.
8. *Kim:* Oh, you never tell me …, Sarah. Now I needn't go to the shops.
9. *Sarah:* But *I* still want to go. Is … else coming with me?

3 In the future

Make sentences with the going to-future or the will-future.
Example: 1. Simon/feed/Maxi and Mini. Then they/not be hungry.
Simon **is going to** feed Maxi and Mini. Then they **won't** be hungry.

2. Mr Leinert/wash his car. Then it/look/much better.
3. Jenny/be 13 soon. She/have/a big party with all her friends.
4. Great Uncle Arthur/wear/his wig at the Over 60's party next week. Robert hopes he/not forget it.
5. Mrs Leinert/buy/Jenny/a sweatshirt. Then Jenny/be/very happy.
6. David/save/his pocket money. He hopes he/have/enough for a skateboard soon.

4 Don't forget: Be polite

In this dialogue the customer and the shop assistant aren't very polite.
Write the dialogue again and make it more polite.

Shop assistant: What do you want? Can I help you?
Customer: I want some green socks. I'd like …
Shop assistant: We haven't got any. Do you want pink socks? *
Customer: Yes. please
Shop assistant: Here. you are
Customer: They're not cheap enough, but I'll take them. *
Shop assistant: OK. Thank you

*a bit expensive
*sorry but… would you like

Here you are.
Can I help you?
Sorry, but …
Yes, please.
I'd like …
Thank you.
Would you like …?
They're a bit expensive.

Food, food, food

Step A

Letters to a magazine

YOUR CORNER

Last month we asked you for letters about

FOOD.

Here is what some of you told us …

I love Chinese food. Last year someone gave me a book of Chinese recipes for my birthday. Now I often cook nice meals for my family.

Tim Price, 14, Belfast

I don't eat any meat or fish because I don't think it's right to kill animals. Fruit and vegetables are better for you anyway.

Emma Martin, 16, Leeds

British food is the best. Roast beef with roast potatoes – that's my favourite meal. But I can't stand cabbage.

Lee Brown, 13, Truro

I grow carrots and beans in our garden. It's fun. And when vegetables come straight from the garden they taste much nicer.

Becky Burton, 12, Nottingham

LUCKY magazine

Here are some useful words for this exercise. You can ask your teacher for more words.

1 Let's talk about food

Talk to a partner. Ask and answer questions about food.

Example: Do you like fish?
– No, I don't. I can't stand fish.
or: – Yes, I love fish fingers with potato salad.

What's your favourite fruit/meat/…? Do you like …?
What do you usually have for breakfast/…?
Do you cook meals for your family? Do you grow …?

peas	[pi:z]	Erbsen
garlic	[ˈgɑ:lɪk]	Knoblauch
cucumber	[ˈkju:kʌmbə]	Gurke
tomato	[təˈmɑ:təʊ]	Tomate
orange	[ˈɒrɪndʒ]	Apfelsine
pear	[peə]	Birne
pork	[pɔ:k]	Schweinefleisch
rice	[raɪs]	Reis

2 More letters

Here are sentences from more letters.
Put in the right words.

some · any · somewhere · something · anything · somebody · anybody · anywhere

1. … in my class brought … German sausage to school. It was OK.
2. Can … give me a quick recipe for bread, please? I can't find one … .
3. I like it when we go … new for our holidays. Then the food is new, too.
4. When my sister and I come home from school, … strange happens. Suddenly there aren't … biscuits in the house!
5. … people eat frogs' legs. Ugh! I can't think of … worse!

3 My English folder

Write a letter to LUCKY magazine about food. What do you like, what don't you like? Look at all the ideas on this page. Start like this: Dear Lucky magazine, … .

Sunday morning

It is 12 o'clock.
Mrs Penrose is busy in the kitchen.
David is helping her. He is making a fruit salad. He is cutting the fruit into little pieces.

Now it is 12.15. Here is Mr Penrose.

Mr Penrose: How are things in the kitchen?
David: Fine. We've finished all the big jobs. Lunch is almost ready now.
Mrs Penrose: David has helped a lot. He's made the fruit salad.
Mr Penrose: Oh, you've been very busy, you two. Your fruit salad looks good, David!
David: It *is* good. I know because I've just tasted it. Mmm. Let's taste it again.
Mrs Penrose: Hey, you've had enough! What about our guests?

I/you/we/they **have** help**ed**
he/she **has** help**ed**

to be → **have/has been**
to make → **have/has made**
to have → **have/has had**

1 Kitchen partners

Which sentences go together?

1. The Penroses have invited guests for lunch.
2. Mrs Penrose and David have finished all the big jobs.
3. David has helped a lot.
4. David has made the fruit salad.
5. He has tasted the fruit salad.

- Lunch is almost ready now.
- And he wants to taste it again.
- It looks good!
- So they are busy in the kitchen.
- His mother is happy with him.

2 Jobs at home

a) *Say what the people are doing.*
Example: 1. Jenny is collecting the dirty clothes.

open **wash** **repair** **cook** **collect**

b) *Now say what they have done.*
Example: 1. Jenny has collected the dirty clothes.

Unit 6

3 Sound practice

Sometimes the letters in irregular forms are the same, but the sound is different.

a) *First listen to the sentences, then read them.*
1. Do you want to **read** this book? – No, thank you. I've already **read** it.
2. Let's d**o** our homework together. – Oh, I've just d**o**ne it.
3. I'll dr**i**ve now. – Thanks. I've dr**i**ven a long way.
4. Why don't you want to h**ea**r that joke? – Because I've h**ea**rd it so often!

b) *Now listen and say these sentences. What are the infinitives? Compare the sounds.*

1. I've just wr**i**tten a letter.
2. He has g**o**ne to the cinema.
3. They've already s**ai**d goodbye.
4. Where have you h**i**dden my pen?

4 At the Burtons'

a) *Which of these verbs are irregular?*
Check in the list on page 182.
and write down the past participles.

to cook **to eat** **to work** **to take** **to throw** **to tidy up** **to walk**

b) *Put in the right forms of the verbs.*
1. *Simon and Becky:* We**'ve tidied up** the living-room for you. It looks OK now. (*tidy up*)
2. *Becky:* Dad, Simon **has** … my CD player, and he doesn't want to give it back! (*take*)
3. *Simon:* Oh, Mum. You … my comic. Now I can't read it. (*throw away*)
4. *Mr Burton:* Look at the floor! Someone … into the house with dirty shoes on. (*walk*)
5. *Mrs Burton:* Hm. I … too many sausages. But we can eat them cold tomorrow. (*cook*)
6. *Simon:* Where's my piece of cake? Oh no! Maxi and Mini … it! (*eat*)
7. *Becky:* I … in my vegetable garden all morning. Now I'm very tired. (*work*)

5 Dialogues

You look …

Yes, I've just …

Use the ideas and make little dialogues.
Example: "You look happy." – "Yes, I've just heard some good news."

scared
excited
angry
tired
happy
miserable …

–

win a prize
hear some good/bad news
see a ghost
remember a nice/terrible dream
find some money under my bed
cut my hand/…
run a long way
have a nice surprise
start/finish my homework
…

6 Listening practice: On the telephone

It is 12 o'clock at the Dixons' house.
Kim hears the telephone.
First read the questions.
Then listen to the cassette and answer the questions.

1. Who is on the telephone?
2. Where is she phoning from?
3. Why won't she be home for lunch?
4. What is she going to have for lunch?
5. What does she know about German food?
6. When will she come home?

A guest from Karlsruhe

The Penroses' two guests are here now: Grandma Penrose and a young German. His name is Andreas Berger and he comes from Karlsruhe, Nottingham's twin town. He has just arrived in Nottingham.

Mark: Have you heard of Robin Hood, Andreas?
Andreas: Oh yes, I have, Mark. I've read a lot of exciting stories about him.
David: Have you visited the Tales of Robin Hood yet? It's very good.
Andreas: No, I haven't. I haven't had time yet.
Mrs Penrose: You want to work in Nottingham. Is that right, Andreas?
Andreas: Yes. I want to work here for a year.
Mr Penrose: Has my mother found a good job for you?
Andreas: Yes, she has. In a bookshop.
Grandma: But he hasn't started his job yet.
Andreas: No. Tomorrow will be my first day. I hope my English will be OK. If I don't know a word, I'll look for a dictionary in the shop!

7 Have you done it yet?

a) *Find out what your partner has or hasn't done today.*
Example: "Have you had breakfast yet?" – "Yes, I have."

Have you | had breakfast / looked at a magazine / watched TV / listened to music / made your bed / talked to your friends | yet? – Yes, I have./ No, I haven't.

b) *Make more questions like this for your partner.*

have lunch? buy anything? do the washing-up? ...?

8 Questions and answers

Make questions and answers about these people.

Example: 1. Grandma and Andreas/come for tea?
Have Grandma and Andreas come for tea?
No, they haven't. They have come for lunch.

2. Andreas/hear of Robin Hood?
3. the Penroses and their guests/have lunch yet?
4. David and Mark/visit the Tales of Robin Hood?
5. Andreas/see a film about Robin Hood?
6. Grandma/find a good job for Andreas?
7. Andreas/start his job yet?
8. the other shop assistants/make plans for a welcome party?

Yes, ... No, ... I'm not sure.

9 Grandma's jobs

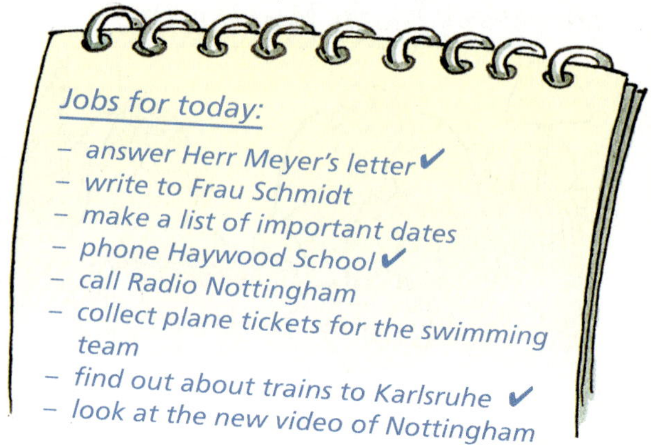

Grandma Penrose has got a lot of jobs to do at the Twinning Office today. But a lot of people have phoned her, and now someone from Karlsruhe is on the phone, too. So Grandma hasn't done many of her jobs yet!

She has answered Herr Meyer's letter.
But she hasn't … to Frau Schmidt yet.
And she hasn't … yet.
She … *Go on.*

10 Looking at English

Practise the present perfect.

a) *Take your exercise book and write –*
1. a sentence with 'just'.
2. a question with 'yet'.
3. a sentence with 'not … yet'.

b) *Now write your sentences on a piece of paper. Cut between the words and make a puzzle. Can your partner put the words back in the right order?*

Example:

Unit 6

11 In the classroom

Make dialogues. Ask about your things. Start with these ideas, and find answers.

– What has happened to my …?
– Where have you put my …?
– Has anybody seen my …?
– What have you done with my …?
– Have you taken my …?

Examples:

Has anybody seen my pen?

Yes, I've seen it. It's under your chair.

Where have you put my book?

I haven't put it anywhere.
I don't know anything about your book.

12 ⟨Just for fun⟩

"What's this?"
– "It's bean soup."
"I don't want to know what it has **been**.
I want to know what it is now!"

Step C

Something to drink

1 WORD POWER

a) *Read this little dialogue.* The words in yellow are new.
But they aren't difficult. Some words look a bit like German words.
And sometimes the other words in the sentence can help.

Would you like some biscuits?

– No, thank you. I'm not hungry, but I'm thirsty.
Can I have something to drink, please?

Yes, of course. What about a cup of tea?
Or some coffee, maybe?

– Thanks, but just a glass of water will be fine.

b) *Show you have understood the words in a).*
Finish these sentences with them.

1. A lot of Germans drink … for breakfast.
2. You usually drink lemonade from a … and tea from a … .
3. You drink something when you are … .

2 Role play: Would you like something to drink?

Practise with a partner. Ask for different things to drink.

– Would you like – Can I get you – What about	something to drink? a cup of …? a glass of …? some …? …

– Yes, please.	I'd like … . I'm very thirsty. …
– No, thanks.	I'm not thirsty. But can I have …, please? …

3 WORD POWER

Can you find all the words?

1. Think of four different vegetables.
2. What comes from milk? Find two things.
3. What is the name for things like apples and bananas?
4. What do chickens give us?
5. What is the name of the meat from a cow?
6. It's a word for a meal, and you can drink it, too. What is it?

HV

4 Listening practice: At the table

a) *You will hear four dialogues. Find out what meals the people are having.*

Start: 1. They are having … BREAKFAST? LUNCH? TEA?

b) *Listen again. The people in the dialogues try to be polite.*

What do they say when they …
1. … don't want any carrots?
2. … want the milk?
3. … don't want anything else?
4. … like the coffee?

Unit 6

Looking at the UK: Nottingham 'takeaways'

Fish and chips has always been a popular meal in the UK. (Of course! Fish comes from the sea, and there is sea all around the UK.) But a lot of people don't cook their fish and chips at home. They buy it from a chip shop.

Chip shops were the first 'takeaways' in Britain. But today you can find other kinds of 'takeaways' too – Chinese, for example. When you go to a Chinese or Indian 'takeaway', it is sometimes difficult to choose.
You can get so many different meals there!

1 The food in the photos

I think … looks/tastes nice.

I like … .

I can't stand … .

I think I'd like … .

…

Your turn 2 What about your town?

Have you got any 'takeaways'?

Step D

Saturday lunch

A

Sarah picked up her fork and looked at her plate. “Mince and potatoes is boring,” she said. Her mother wasn’t very happy about that. “I’ve been busy all morning,” she told Sarah. “And mince is quick and easy to cook.”
“Well, Sarah,” her father said. “You haven’t helped your mother. Why don’t you cook lunch next Saturday? Show us your idea of a good meal.”
“Well – er – OK,” Sarah answered. “I’ll try.”

B

Next Saturday morning Sarah showed her mother a shopping list. “I’ve found a great recipe for a curry, Mum. But I need some chicken and these other things. Can I have some money, please?”
“Yes, of course. A chicken curry is a nice idea, Sarah.”
Just then the telephone rang. It was Jenny.
“Hi, Sarah. Do you want to come swimming with Becky and me?”
Sarah didn’t want to say no because they always had great fun when they went swimming together. But this morning there was no free time for fun with friends. “Oh, I – I can’t,” she told Jenny.

Unit 6

C

The shops in Mansfield Road were full. So it was late when Sarah arrived back home. She went into the kitchen and put everything on the table. But she dropped some cream.
“Oh no! What a mess!” she thought. Then she had an idea. “Tabby!” she called. “Look, cream! Good cat!” And while Tabby cleaned the floor, she started with the curry.

First she cut the vegetables into pieces. It wasn’t difficult really, but Sarah didn’t often do jobs like that, so she wasn’t very quick. Tabby was quicker with the cream. And when the floor was clean, the cat was still hungry.

D

At last the vegetables were ready. Sarah looked at the recipe again. Time for the chicken now. She turned round for it. But there were only three pieces of chicken on the table. The fourth was under the table. Tabby was there, too. “No!” Sarah shouted at Tabby – just in time. She opened the back door, and Tabby ran out. Mrs Dixon heard the noise and put her head round the door. “Is everything OK?” she asked. “Oh, you’ve dropped some chicken. But it looks all right. Let’s clean it and put it back on the plate.” “But – er – thanks, Mum. – Yes, everything is fine. No problem.” But it was already twelve o’clock, and there was still a lot to do. While she worked hard in the hot kitchen, Sarah thought of Jenny and Becky at the swimming pool.

Step D

E

The Dixons usually had Saturday lunch at one o'clock. That day Sarah brought her curry to the table at quarter to two. "Sorry it's so late," she said. "But I've tasted it and I think it's OK. I hope you'll like it." Her parents tried it. "It's great! You can be proud of it," her father told her. "I've never tasted anything so good," her mother said. "Do you want to make lunch again next Saturday?" Sarah smiled. "No thanks, Mum. Mince will be fine! Or maybe you'd like to cook next week, Dad?"

1 Questions about the pictures

Picture A: – Why isn't Sarah happy about her lunch? – Who has made the lunch? – What is Mr Dixon saying about next Saturday?

Picture B: – What has Sarah got in her hand? – What does she want to cook? – What is her mother giving her, and why?

Picture C: – Where has Sarah been? – What has happened? – What is Tabby doing?

Picture D: – Where is Sarah working? – What is on the floor? – How has it got there? – What does Mrs Dixon think has happened?

Picture E: – What time is it? – Why are Sarah's parents happy with her? – What does Sarah think about lunch next Saturday?

Unit 6

2 How does Sarah feel?

tired proud excited angry happy nervous sorry …

Say what you think? Can you explain?

How does Sarah feel when …

1. … her father says "Why don't you cook lunch?"
2. … she finds the recipe for the curry?
3. … Jenny phones?
4. … Tabby takes the piece of chicken?
5. … her mother puts the chicken back on the plate?
6. … she has finished the curry?

Example:

1. I think she feels happy because it is a good idea.

or:

I think she feels a bit nervous. But she wants to try.

3 Let's talk about it

1. What does Sarah find out when it's her turn in the kitchen? *Collect ideas.*
2. Do you feel sorry for Tabby? *Explain why or why not.*

4 On the telephone again

The next day Jenny phoned Sarah again. *Put in the verbs – in the simple past.*

Hi, Sarah. You know Becky and I … (*want*) to go swimming yesterday? Well, we … (*meet*) in Mansfield Road and … (*wait*) at the bus stop. But we … (*not get on*) the bus because David's grandma … (*see*) us there and … (*take*) us in her car. Well, when we … (*arrive*) there, we … (*get out*) and David's grandma … (*drive away*). Then Becky suddenly … (*remember*) – her swimming things … (*be*) still in the car, so she … (*not have*) anything to wear! David's grandma … (*find*) her things and … (*bring*) them to her house. But that … (*be*) later, of course. – Anyway, because we … (*not go*) swimming yesterday, we want to go this morning. Have you got time today?

Step E

Let's check

1 WORD POWER

a) *Can you find the words? They are all new in this unit.*

1. It tells you how you can cook something.
2. You usually drink tea or coffee from this.
3. Carrots and cabbage are examples of this.
4. You feel like this when you've done something difficult.
5. You put meat in your mouth with this.

b) *Now try to explain these words:* CHICKEN GLASS FRUIT THIRSTY PLATE

2 David's room

Read what David thinks.
The picture shows his room 20 minutes later. What has or hasn't he done?
Start like this: He has made his bed. And he has … . But he hasn't … yet. *Go on.*

Unit 6

3 Has your friend done it yet?

A friend tells you:

1. "I can't *find* my purse."
2. "I must *write* to my cousin."
3. "I want to *try* my new computer game."
4. "I must *talk* to my tutor."
5. "Maybe I can *repair* that broken chair."
6. "I want to *make* a cake for my mum's birthday."

The next day you ask:

– "Have you … your purse yet?"
– "Have you … yet?"
– "Have you …?"
– "…?"
– "…?"
– "…?"

4 Dialogues

Put questions and answers together, and make four little dialogues.

What would you like?
Oh yes, please.
Can you pass me the sugar, please?
Do you like this fruit salad?
Yes, here you are.
Yes, it tastes very good.
I'd like a cup of coffee, please.
Would you like some cheese?

Looking at the UK: Beautiful Britain

Spend a long weekend in London – one of the most exciting cities in the world. You'll love it! Shops, theatres, museums – the best in Britain!

ADVENTURE holidays

12-16

Wales

Do you love horses? Then you'll enjoy this holiday out on the hills every day! If you can't ride, you can learn here.

What about a caravan holiday at the seaside?

The Isle of Wight, with its lovely beaches, is great for holidays. And it's so small that you can travel round the island in one day!

Scotland

Scotland is great for an adventure holiday. Do you like mountain bikes, hill walks, climbing? You can choose different activities every day!

1 Find out where

Look at these pictures from holiday brochures. Now find the places on the map at the front of the book. Say where the places are – and what you know about them.

Example: The Isle of Wight is in the south. It is a small island. It has got beautiful beaches.

Your turn 2 Different places – different holidays

Have another look at the pictures.

Say where YOU would like to go – and why. (Say where you would NOT like to go, too!)

Example: I'd like to go to Scotland. I think holidays in the mountains are great.
– I wouldn't like to go to London, because I don't like big cities. *Go on.*

A week in Scotland

Step A

At the travel agent's

Jenny and her father are at a travel agent's in Nottingham. The Leinerts want to go to Scotland for a week in the Easter holidays – and David is going to go with them.

Travel agent: Good afternoon. Can I help you?
Mr Leinert: We'd like some brochures about holidays in Scotland, please.
Travel agent: How do you want to travel? By coach or train?
Jenny: Oh, we want to go by car.
Mr Leinert: Have you got any details about bed and breakfast places where we can stay?
Travel agent: No, I'm sorry, I haven't. You could try the bookshop opposite. I think they've got books with addresses and phone numbers.
Mr Leinert: Thank you very much.

1 Role play: At the travel agent's

Good morning/afternoon. Can I help you?
Yes, please?

I'd like / Can I have / Can you give me | some brochures / details | about holidays in … ?

Do you want to | go by coach/car/ … / stay at a hotel/ … ?

Yes, we do. / No, we don't. We'd like to … .

OK, here are some brochures/details about … .

Thank you very much.

2 Where did you go?

Talk about one of your holidays. Say where you went and what you did there.

Last year Last spring/… Two/… years ago	I we	went to … . stayed at/in … . visited … . spent … days/weeks at/in … . travelled round … .

caravan, beach, forest, farm, lake, castles, mountains, museums, hotel, churches, hills

Example: Last summer we went to Sylt. We went there by train. We stayed at a holiday cottage on the island. We went swimming every day. The beaches were beautiful.

3 My English folder

Write about your nicest holiday.
Say where you went and who went with you.
What did you see? What did you do?
Maybe you can put in a photo, too.

Step B

From Jenny's travel diary

April 3rd

We've arrived! We're staying at a bed and breakfast place on Loch Lomond. It was a long drive. We left Nottingham after breakfast, and drove up the M6. Dad drove in the morning (Mum read the map), and Mum drove in the afternoon (Dad read the map, and we went wrong twice!). But we got here in the end.

David and I can see Loch Lomond from our windows. Mum and Dad have taken the big room. But they can only see the garages from their window!

The loch looks really beautiful. We haven't been out on it yet. But Mr and Mrs MacTavish have got a boat for the guests. Dad can row (well, he says he can!). So we are going to go out in the boat tomorrow!

1 In Scotland

arrive | take/bags out of car | make/tea | write/postcard | go/bed

a) It is the Leinerts' first day in Scotland. *Say what has just happened.*
Example: 1. Here you can see the Leinerts. It is five o'clock. They **have just arrived.**

b) *Now it is the next day. Say what happened yesterday. Use the simple past.*
Example: 1. It was five o'clock when the Leinerts **arrived.**

2. Before they went in, Mr Leinert and David … . 3. First Mrs MacTavish showed them the rooms. Then she … . 4. After tea Jenny … . 5. The Leinerts were tired after their long day, and at half past ten … .

2 At home

Robert and his mother are at home in the Easter holidays.

Examples:

1. *Mrs Croft:* put bike away? — *Robert:* yes – two minutes ago
   – Have you put your bike away, Robert? — – Yes, I have, Mum. I put it away two minutes ago.
2. *Robert:* see my new comic? — *Mrs Croft:* no – sorry.
   – Have you seen my new comic, Mum? — – No, I haven't, Robert. Sorry.

3. *Mrs Croft:* make your bed? — *Robert:* yes – after breakfast.
4. *Mrs Croft:* eat the last apple? — *Robert:* yes – yesterday evening.
5. *Robert:* buy a new film for the camera? — *Mrs Croft:* yes – last week.
6. *Mrs Croft:* take the letters to the post? — *Robert:* no – sorry.
7. *Robert:* do the washing-up? — *Mrs Croft:* yes – half an hour ago.

3 Listening practice: Out on Loch Lomond

a) *Listen to the three scenes on the cassette.*
Say where the Leinerts and David are in each scene.

b) *The Leinerts and David are telling Mrs MacTavish about their day.*
Can you answer her questions?
1. Have you been out on the loch yet? *David:* … 2. Did you all go? *Jenny:* … 3. Who rowed the boat? *Mr Leinert:* … 4. Did you row out far? *David:* … 5. Oh, that was a good idea. Did you get back before the thunderstorm started? *Mrs Leinert:* …, because … .

Have you ever …?

Mrs MacTavish is talking to the Leinerts and David at breakfast time.

4 What about you?

Have you ever	travelled by plane? ridden a horse? stayed at a farm? heard the bagpipes? been to Britain?	–	Yes, I have. I	travelled by plane to … … rode …/…	last year/… . two/… years ago.
			No, I haven't/No, not yet.		

5 Looking at English

Has it happened?		When did it happen?
… ever …? … never … . … not … yet. … often … . … already … .	do play make eat see	… yesterday. … two years ago. … on Monday. … last week. … at the weekend.
I've already seen the film.		I saw the film at the weekend.

Make four more sentences with the present perfect – and four with the simple past. Use the time signals. Write the sentences in two lists in your exercise book.

At Fort William

It is the Leinerts' and David's third day in Scotland. Now they are staying at the Campbells' house – near Fort William.

Mr Leinert: I've got an idea for tomorrow. Let's climb Ben Nevis.
Jenny: The highest mountain in the UK! Great idea, Dad!
David: But what about Loch Ness? I want to see that, too.
Mrs Leinert: We can go there the day after tomorrow.
Mr Leinert: Right. If the weather forecast is good, we'll climb Ben Nevis tomorrow. And we'll go to Loch Ness the day after. Everybody happy now?

1 What are we going to do?

Make dialogues with a partner.

What are we going to do tomorrow?
What plans can we make for tomorrow?
Have you got any ideas for tomorrow?

Let's … .
Maybe we can … .
I'd like to … .

take photos
look round the museum
look at the shops
write postcards
climb a mountain
go to … .
… .

Well, let's listen to the weather forecast.

If it's	good, bad,	we'll we won't let's	do that/… . go there. … .

OK then.
All right.
Then maybe we can … the day after tomorrow.

2 Listening practice: In the deep waters of Loch Ness

Listen to the cassette. Are these sentences right or wrong?

1. Loch Ness is a big lake in Scotland. 2. There aren't any photos of the Loch Ness monster. 3. The first stories about the monster started 500 years ago. 4. Some people think that the monster looks like a snake. 5. We know what the monster eats. 6. Everyone can see the monster when they visit the loch.

3 ⟨A song: The rolling hills of the border⟩

2. I have travelled far and wide,
Seen the Hudson and the Clyde,
I've courted by Loch Lomond's side
But I dearly love the border
Chorus: When I die …

3. There's a certain peace of mind,
Bonny lassies there you'll find,
The men are hard, but yet so kind,
Among the hills of the border.
Chorus: When I die … *(2x)*

Step D

On Ben Nevis

"Be careful out on the hills," said Mr Campbell. The Leinerts were ready to leave the house now. "The weather forecast is all right. But we always warn people: don't go on if the weather changes. Get back as soon as you can."

"We'll be all right," said Mr Leinert. "Ben Nevis isn't very high. Not like the mountains in the Alps."

"Well, it can still be dangerous," said Mr Campbell. "There was a bad accident up there last year. It was in April, too. The path was slippery, and –"

"Oh dear, don't tell us about that now, Mr Campbell," said Mrs Leinert. "You'll make us scared! But don't worry, we'll be careful."

It was sunny and warm when they got out of the car.

"Have you all got your anoraks?" asked Mr Leinert. "We'll need them when we get higher up."

The path was easy at first. It wasn't steep yet.

"Look at those people behind us," said David. It was a young man and woman. They had T-shirts on, and the woman wore tennis shoes without socks. "I don't think they'll get far!"

After a time the path got steeper, and the stones on the path got bigger.

"I'm tired!" said David. "Let's have our sandwiches now."

So they sat down at the side of the path. It wasn't so warm now, and they all had their anoraks on.

When they went on ten minutes later, it started to rain.

"This isn't much fun!" said Mrs Leinert.

"It'll stop in a minute," said Jenny. "Come on, Mum."

But it didn't stop. It got wetter and wetter. The path was wet now, and slippery in places, and they all felt cold. But they went on, although they were the only people on the path now.

Mr Leinert stopped and looked at the others. Nobody looked very happy.

"Let's turn back," he said. "We can't go on in this!"

He was right. Nobody wanted to go on. So they turned back down the path.

"Oh, Judy, this is terrible! I can't get up!"

"I'll help you, Kevin. You'll be all right."

It was the young man and woman.

"Oh dear, what's happened?" asked Mrs Leinert when she saw them at the side of the path.

"I've hurt my foot," said Kevin. "The stones are so slippery, and I fell."

They all tried to help him, but his foot hurt so much that he couldn't stand on it.

"Maybe it's broken," said David. "If it is, you can't walk on it."

"We'll get help," said Mr Leinert. "You two stay here together. We'll tell the Mountain Rescue people where you are. They'll come as soon as they can. – Here. Take our anoraks. You'll need them."

"Why are weather forecasts always wrong?" asked David. It was really terrible now.
They didn't see anyone else on the path when they went down.
"Forget the weather. We must hurry," said Mrs Leinert. "Come on."
"Hey, Dad, where are you going?" called Jenny. "The path doesn't go that way."
"I know, but this is a short cut. It's on our map here. Look. If we go this way, we'll be back at the car sooner."

But Mr Leinert was wrong. An hour later they were still on the path. But which path was it? And where was the car? They couldn't ask anyone. There were only sheep on the hills here.
They went on until at last they came to a small farm. It was almost half past six.
"We can probably phone from here," said Mrs Leinert. "At last! Poor Kevin and Judy!"

"Yes, Leinert is the name. I'm calling from Green Farm. – Yes. – Yes, we're all OK, but there are two people – What? *What* did you say? You've already rescued them? But how did you know –? – Oh, I see."
"What's happened, Mum?" said Jenny when her mother put the telephone down. "What did the Mountain Rescue people say?"
"They've already rescued Kevin and Judy, and taken Kevin to hospital."
"But how did they know?" said David. "Who told them?"
"Mr Campbell! When the weather got so bad and we didn't come back, he sent them out to look for us!"

1 What happened?

Finish the sentences. *Example:* 1. Before the Leinerts left their bed and breakfast place, Mr Campbell warned them about Ben Nevis.

2. He wanted to tell them about an accident on Ben Nevis, but … . 3. Everything was all right at first, because the weather … and the path … . 4. But when it started to rain, … . 5. They still went on, although … . 6. But after a time they turned back because … . 7. When they were on their way down, they saw … . 8. Kevin's foot was so bad that … . 9. The Leinerts and David hurried down the path, but Kevin and Judy … . 10. Mr Leinert tried a short cut down the mountain, but … . 11. They walked on until … . 12. As soon as they were in the farmhouse, …

2 Rules for the mountains

This list of 'rules' is in the hall at the Campbells' house.

a) 1. *Go through the list. Say what the Leinerts and David did right – and what they did wrong.*
Example: They told Mr Campbell where they planned to go.
And they probably told him when they … .
2. What did Kevin and Judy do wrong?

b) *Can you say why the rules are important?*
Example: It's important to say where you plan to go.
If you don't come back, someone will get help.
Maybe you'll get lost.
Maybe you'll have an accident.

3 *Watch out:* When or if?

1. I – see – Loch Ness monster – tomorrow – take – a lot of photos.
   If I see the Loch Ness monster tomorrow, I'll take a lot of photos.
2. I – get up – tomorrow – put new film in my camera.
3. the weather – good – tomorrow – we – go – Loch Ness.
4. it – rain – all day – we – go there – day after tomorrow.
5. we – arrive – at the Loch – I – look for – monster – right away.
6. I – get – a really good photo – send it to – school magazine.
7. we – go back – Nottingham – I – tell – Mrs Croft, too.
8. she – talk about it – Radio Nottingham – I – be – famous!

4 Sound practice

a) *Listen to the cassette and speak these sentences.*

Be careful with the [v] sound in 'of'.

1. David watches TV every evening.
2. We often visited Fred when he lived in the Grove.
3. Don't leave your van in front of Alan's car.
4. Our visitors arrived at half past eleven.
5. Have you had enough to eat?
6. I often dream of lifts.
7. Have you finished the fruit cake? – No, we've only had half of it.
8. I've never laughed so much in all my life!

b) *Now listen to the words on the cassette. Listen to the [f] and [v] sounds. Write each word down.*

5 WORD POWER

a) *In each group one word is 'wrong'. Find it and write it down.*

1. behind – in front of – so that – between.
2. always – although – sometimes – never.
3. bigger than – as quiet as – earlier than – as soon as.
4. beautiful – because – nice – lovely.
5. until – down – out – up.

b) *Now look at the five 'wrong' words from a). They are all conjunctions. Can you use them in these sentences?*

1. We stayed inside yesterday afternoon ... the weather was so wet.
2. We didn't go to the cinema ... there was a good film on.
3. Mum said, "We'll go for a walk ... the rain stops."
4. Mr Campbell gave us a big box of games ... it wasn't so boring.
5. We played cards ... it was time for bed.

Let's check

1 They've already done it

Example: 1. *Mrs Leinert:* Jenny! Please make your bed now. (after breakfast)
Jenny: I**'ve already made** it, Mum. I **made** it after breakfast.

2. *Mrs Penrose:* Colin! Can you repair Mark's cupboard, please? (last week)
3. *Mr Penrose:* David! Please do your homework now. (before tea)
4. *Becky:* Simon! Please take Maxi and Mini out. It's your turn! (an hour ago)
5. *Robert:* Mum! Can you wash my black jeans today, please? (yesterday)
6. *Sarah:* Kim! Can you buy that CD for Mum's birthday? (on Saturday)
7. *Mrs Dixon:* Sarah! Please feed Tabby now. She must be hungry! (after tea)

2 Holidays at home

Which is right? Simple past or present perfect?

1. *Sarah:* Isn't David at home, Mr Penrose?
   Mr Penrose: Didn't you know?
   He … to Scotland with the Leinerts last week. (go)
2. *Kim:* Mm! Can I try that fruit salad, Mum?
   Mrs Dixon: Wait, I … it yet. (not – finish)
3. *Mrs Penrose:* Where's Mark?
   David: He … into the garden. (just – go out)
4. *Robert:* This bread is good!
   Mrs Croft: I … it at that new shop in Mansfield Road yesterday. (buy)
5. *Mike:* Let's watch "Adventure Island"!
   Barry: No, I … it. (already – see)
6. *Becky:* Do you know where Mini is, Simon?
   Simon: I … her in the garage five minutes ago. (see) … you … there? (look)

3 WORD POWER

Collect as many words as you can.

Example: 1. There is water in the **sea**, and in … .
– a **lake**, a **pond**, a **river**.

2. You can stay the night at a **hotel**, or at … .
3. You can travel by **bus**, or … .
4. On a map of Scotland you can see **islands**, and … .
5. When you are on holiday, you can look round **museums**, or … .
6. When you walk in the mountains, take a **map**, … .

4 After an adventure holiday

Here are some sentences from young people's letters in a British 'Adventure Holiday' brochure.
Put the parts together with the right conjunctions.
(Sometimes there is more than one right answer!)

1. We all had a great time	as soon as	it rained every day.
2. I really enjoyed the holiday	and	I made so many new friends.
3. I felt at home	although	I arrived.
4. I'd like to try a holiday in Wales next year	until	I can learn to ride.
5. I didn't know anything about climbing	so that	I went on this holiday.
6. It was a fantastic holiday	when	I enjoyed every minute!
7. I felt really sorry	because	the holiday was over.

Help

Step A

The champion skater

Last Wednesday Robert, Becky and Simon were outside with their skateboards. Barry Jenkins was on the other side of the road. When Mrs Croft came home, she watched them for a minute. Then she said, "Hey, not bad! Let me try!"
"No, it's too dangerous, Mum," Robert said. And Becky warned her, "You haven't got a helmet, Mrs Croft."
"No problem," said Mrs Croft. "I was a champion skater when I was younger."
Then she jumped on Becky's skateboard – and tripped and fell.
The children were worried and ran towards her.
"Are you OK, Mum?" Robert asked.
"I'll be all right," she said. "I'll just go in and lie down."
"Wow, what a champion!" Barry laughed.
"Go away, Barry!" Robert said and ran into the house.

1 Role play: Are you OK?

Someone has had an accident: *Ask what is wrong. Work with a partner.*

Have you *hurt your arm*? → No, I haven't. It *doesn't hurt*.

What about your head? Does it hurt? → *It hurts a bit, but I'll be OK.*

broken your leg/hand /...?

isn't broken.

I'm all right./Don't worry.

How is

2 WORD POWER

Cut out a picture of someone in a magazine and write in the parts of the body.

3 Listening practice: Becky's dream

Becky is telling Simon about the monster in her dream.

a) 1. *Write this list in your exercise book. Then listen to the cassette and take notes. What does the monster look like?*
   2. *Try to draw the monster.*

b) *What does Simon think of Barry? What does Becky think of him?*

The monster

head:	ears:	colour:
eyes:	arms:	T-shirt:
mouth:	hands:	shoes:

Step B

The next morning

In the morning Mrs Croft got up at seven o'clock. But she didn't feel well and had to lie down again.

Robert: Do you have to go to work today, Mum?
Mrs Croft: Well, yes, I do, but first I'll make breakfast.
Robert: You don't have to do that, Mum. I'll do it.
Mrs Croft: Let's do it together, Robert, or you'll be late for school … . Oh, I feel ill and I've got a terrible headache.
Robert: Why did you have to go on that skateboard?
Mrs Croft: I don't know. Oh, I think I'll have to call the doctor.

1 What do they have to do?

It's Thursday morning. Today Mrs Croft can't go to work, but usually the Crofts are busy in the morning.

Usually	Robert Mrs Croft both of them	has to have to	go to work. make tea. go to school. have breakfast. leave the house at … . …

She **has to** go.
She **had to** go.
She **will have to** go.

2 Things to do

Say what Robert and his mother 'have to do' now and what they 'don't have to do'.

	call Radio Nottingham	do the washing-up	tidy up the living-room	make a sandwich for school	make the beds	go to work
Robert		✔		✔		
Mrs Croft	✔					✗
Robert & Mrs Croft			✗		✗	

Example: 1. Mrs Croft has to call Radio Nottingham.

✔ = have to/has to ✗ = don't/doesn't have to

3 At school

Today the history teacher is telling the pupils from 8MD about his school days.

a) *What questions do the pupils ask him?*

Example: 1. Wear – a uniform?
Did you **have to** wear a uniform?
2. When – get up?
3. Do – any homework?
4. Pay – for school books?
5. Learn – French?
6. Go – to assembly?

b) *Can you finish Mr Lee's answers?*

1. Yes, I did. (wear – a black and white uniform)
Yes, I did. I **had to wear** a black and white uniform.
2. Very early. (get up – at seven o'clock)
3. Of course. (do – a lot of homework, too)
4. No, we didn't. (use – old books from the school)
5. Yes, we did. (learn – Greek, too)
6. Yes, of course. (go – there every day)

The doctor's visit

Later that day Dr Patel came to the Crofts' house.

Dr Patel: Hello, Robert. Where's the patient?

Robert: Hello, Dr Patel. She's here – in the bedroom.

Dr Patel: Thank you, Robert. Good morning, Mrs Croft. No, don't sit up. Robert told me what happened.

Mrs Croft: I feel terrible, doctor. I tried to get up this morning but I really wasn't able to make breakfast. So I had to lie down again.

Dr Patel: Well, you hit your head, so you have to be careful. I'd like to do some tests. I think I'll send you to hospital. They'll be able to examine you and do the tests there.

They **are able to** do the tests.
They **were able to** do the tests.
They **will be able to** do the tests.

4 What happened?

1. Dr Patel sent Mrs Croft to hospital because they … (do the tests there).
   Dr Patel sent Mrs Croft to hospital because they **were able to** do the tests there.
2. The people from the Mountain Rescue found Judy and Kevin. So they … (help them).
3. David got some money from his grandma. So … (buy a new song book).
4. Mr Leinert found a job in Nottingham. So the Leinerts … (come to England).
5. Mr Cooper was ill yesterday. So he … (go to school).
6. Becky left her German book at school. So she … (do her German homework).

5 What about you?

When I was younger Last year Two years ago	I wasn't able to …	but now I can … .

write — read — play tennis — work with a computer — ride a horse — ride a bike — speak English — …

6 Sound practice

[t]	[l]	[d]
You mustn't listen to the radio. Mark often makes sandcastles.	It's half past four. Walk! Don't talk!	On Wednesdays we have sandwiches.

Here are some more words.
Say each word.
Which letters haven't got a sound?

two — knuckle — answer — know — autumn — biscuit — hour — grandpa — climb — guest

Step B

Mrs Croft in hospital

ⓐ Mrs Croft is in hospital now. She wants to do a lot of things but she isn't allowed to do them.

7 No, you aren't allowed to do that!

Here is what Mrs Croft wants to do:

look at magazines   watch TV
write some letters   phone a friend …

But here is what the nurse thinks:

have to rest   not good for you
have to sleep now   …

You **are allowed to** go home.
You **were allowed to** go home.
You **will be allowed to** go home.

Write little dialogues between Mrs Croft and the nurse.

Mrs Croft: I'd like … .
Nurse: I'm sorry. You … .

8 Happy or unhappy?

Do you think they are happy or unhappy? Why? Make sentences with 'be allowed to'.

Example:

1. *Doctor:* You can go home tomorrow, Mrs Croft.
   Mrs Croft is happy because she **will be allowed** to go home tomorrow.
2. *David:* No, Mark, you can't see this film with us.
   You have to be 12 for this film.
   Mark is unhappy because he **won't** … .
3. *Mrs Penrose:* You can go to London with me this weekend, David.
4. *Mr Burton:* No, children, you can't watch TV this evening.
5. *Kim:* No, Sarah, you can't wear my new sweatshirt to school tomorrow.
6. *Mrs Leinert:* Yes, you can go camping for a week this summer, Jenny.

Unit 8

ⓑ While Mrs Croft is in hospital, Robert is staying with the Penroses. He and David are getting ready for school.

It isn't **my exercise book**.
= It isn't **mine**.

Robert: I can't find my English exercise book.
David: Here's one. It isn't mine, so it must be yours. Why haven't you got your name on it?
Robert: I have, look. Are those your trainers?
David: No, mine are much smaller. These are Dad's.

my → **mine**	its → **its**
your → **yours**	our → **ours**
his → **his**	your → **yours**
her → **hers**	their → **theirs**

9 In the classroom

1. *Jenny:* Hey, this isn't my pencil case. Is it …, Robert?
2. *Robert:* No, it isn't. … is blue and yellow. Ask Becky. I think it's … .
3. *David:* What about these books? Are they …, girls?
4. *Sarah:* No, they aren't. … are on Mrs Dane's desk. Hey, isn't this Simon and Mike's computer magazine?
5. *Robert:* No, it's not … . It must be John's. … are always on the floor.

Step C

At the doctor's

1 Role play: Good morning, doctor

Act a scene at the doctor's with a partner.

– Good morning, … . What's wrong with you?
– Hello, … . What's the problem?

– I don't feel very well.
– I feel terrible / ill / tired.
– My … hurts.
– I've got a bad headache / stomach-ache / …
– I think I've got a temperature.

– Let me look at it / your arm / … .
Does that hurt?
– Please open your mouth and say 'aah'.
Let's have a look. / Let me examine you.

– Ouch! Yes, it hurts. / No, it doesn't.
– Aah!

Hm, I see.

– Will I have to go to hospital?
– Will I have to stay in bed?
– Can I go to school?

No, – you needn't stay in bed,
but you must stay at home.
– you mustn't work too much./
You mustn't use that arm. / … .
Yes, but you'll have to take some medicine.
Take this prescription to the chemist's.

Happy Helpers

hey would you like to know hey would you like to know hey would you like to know

Haywood Herald

News and information for pupils, parents and friends of Haywood

Happy Helpers

Don't let your mother get on a skateboard – at least not without a helmet. Robert Croft did, and his mother had to go to hospital. Her head hurt, and she had to have some tests.

When Robert and I went to visit her we also met a lot of other patients and talked to them. Some of them had problems. We couldn't help them all, but at least we were able to do something.

Shopping

An old lady was allowed to go home the next day. But she still wasn't very well and she couldn't go to the shops. That was no problem. She told us what she needed and we went to the supermarket for her.

Reading

Another lady had a letter, but she wasn't able to read it after her operation. So I started to read it to her. But then something funny happened. "That letter isn't for me," the lady said, and her neighbour said, "I know, it's mine." We all laughed.

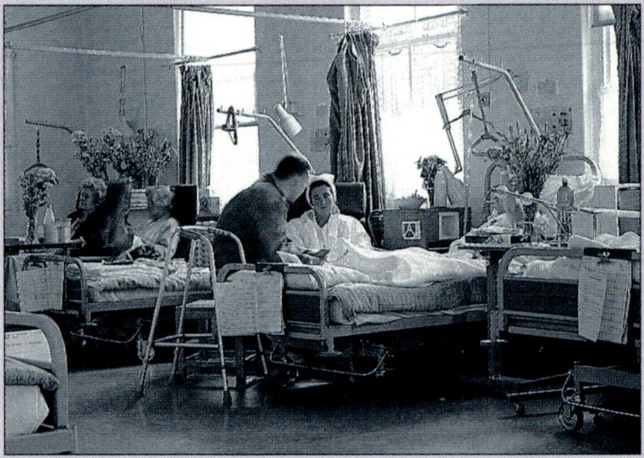

So then I read the right letter.

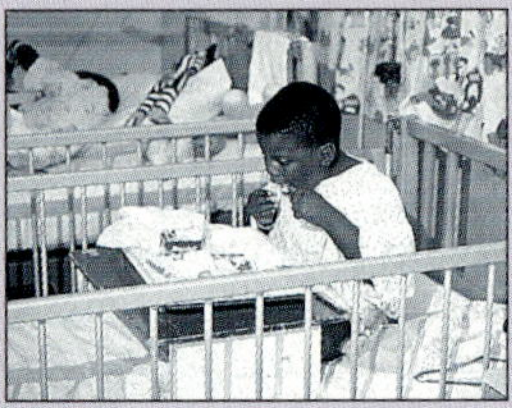

One of the nurses saw me. "Have you got a little more time?" she asked me and took me to the children's ward. There was a little girl there with a story book. She was only four and she couldn't read yet. I read one of the stories to her and played with her for half an hour. She was really sweet!

A surprise

And who else do you think was in the children's ward? Barry Jenkins from 8ES! Robert and I didn't know that he was in hospital. He had a stomach-ache last week and had to go to hospital. They took his appendix out but he'll be home soon, so watch out everyone! We wanted to help him. So we took *all* his homework to the hospital for him. He was *really happy*!

The Happy Helpers

It is really great to help other people. Some people go to the hospital every week to help the patients. They're the Happy Helpers. We've joined them, but they need more young people. So come and join us, too!

Mrs Croft is at home again now. "I'll never get on a skateboard without a helmet again," she says. So don't forget to wear your helmet, or you'll need a Happy Helper, too.

Becky Burton (8MD)
Photos: Robert Croft (8MD)

Unit 8

1 Looking at the report

a) *Answer these questions.*

1. Why did Becky and Robert go to the hospital?
2. How were they able to help people?
3. Did anything funny happen?
4. Why was Barry Jenkins in hospital?
5. How did they help him?

b) *What do you think?*

1. Do you think that Barry was happy when the friends helped him? Say why.
2. Would you like to join the Happy Helpers? Say why.

2 In Germany

Jenny is telling the others about her life in Berlin.
Some things are different, some are the same.

		go home from school at one o'clock.
	I had to	wear school uniform.
In Germany	I didn't have to	speak German with all my friends.
	I was allowed to	have lunch at school.
Like in England	I wasn't allowed to	get up at half past six.
	I was able to	go to school by bike.
	I wasn't able to	talk to my neighbours in lessons.
		…

3 At home

1. What **do you have to** do at home? What **don't you have to** do?
   What **are you allowed to** do? What **aren't you allowed to** do?

Example: "Do you have to go to the shops?" – "No, I don't usually have to go to the shops."

2. What about your brother/your sister/your best friend?
3. What will or won't *your* children have to do/be allowed to do?

4 WORD POWER

1. You can get medicine at the … .
2. You must usually have a … for medicine.
3. When your head hurts, you've got a … .
4. I feel hot all over. I've got a … .
5. It hurts when I eat and I can't speak. I've got a … .
6. Your knee hurts? Let me … it.
7. For tests a doctor will send you to … .
8. Please, open your … and say 'aah'.
9. If you eat too much, you'll get a … .

5 Listening practice: Mrs Croft on the radio

Mrs Croft is on Radio Nottingham again. She is talking about the Happy Helpers and their work.

a) *Listen to Mrs Croft and take notes.*

– What is Mr Davis's problem?
– What about the neighbours?
– How does Becky help?

b) *Now write a report about Mr Davis, Sniffy and Becky. You can start like this:*

There was another patient in hospital. His name was Mr Davis and he had … .

6 ⟨A song: Help⟩

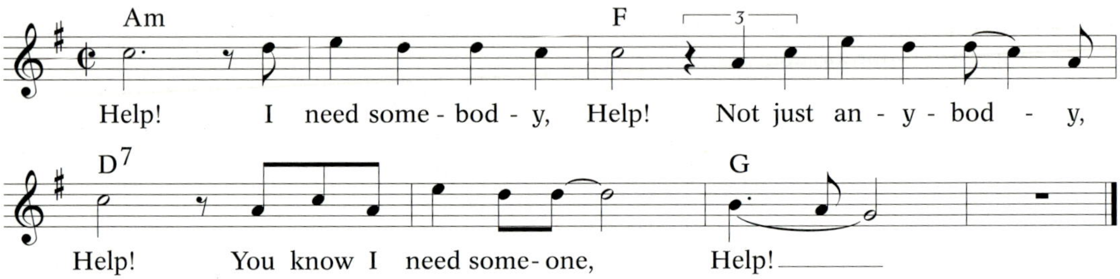

When I was younger, so much younger than today,
I never needed anybody's help in any way.
But now these days are gone, I'm not so self-assured,
Now I find I've changed my mind I've opened up the doors.

Help me if you can, I'm feeling down,
And I do appreciate you being round.
Help me get my feet back on the ground.
Won't you please, please help me?

Unit 8

7 In the children's ward

Becky and Robert are drawing pictures with some of the children in the ward.

mine · yours · his · hers · ours · theirs

1. *Anna:* Can I use your red crayon? I can't find … .
2. *Robert:* Sure, here you are. But look, … is under the table.
3. *Anna:* No, that's not … . I think Becky dropped it. It must be … .
4. *Jack:* Have you got a blue pen?
5. *Becky:* No, but Robert has. You can use … .
6. *Pat:* Could I have a biscuit, please?
7. *Robert:* I don't know. Do you see those girls over there? The biscuits are … .
8. *Helen:* No, Barry gave them to Anna and me. So they're … .
9. *Robert:* Barry? Really? Well, if they are …, you can give me one, too.

8 ⟨A joke⟩

Patient: Doctor, you have to help me.
I always forget everything.
Doctor: When did this start?
Patient: When did what start?

Step E

Let's check

1 What a mess!

Say what they 'have to do' or 'don't have to do'.

1

1. Robert has to clean the kitchen.

2

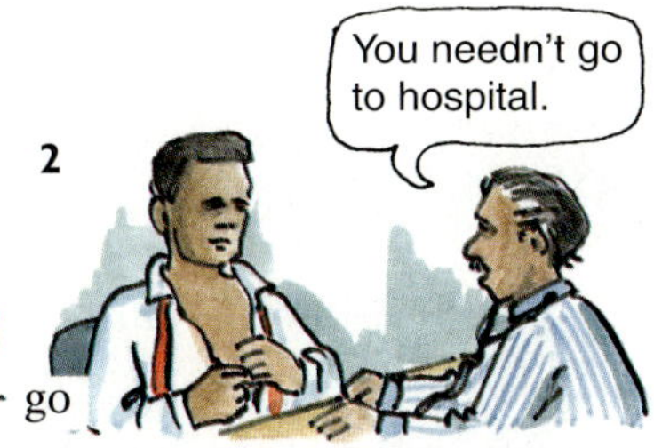

2. Mr Dixon ... .

Go on, please.

3

4

5

2 Hospital signs

Say what you are not allowed to do.

1 take

Example: You are not allowed to take pets to the hospital.

2 play

3 open

4 play

5 smoke

3 Were they able to?

Ask questions about the stories in this book and give the answers.

Example: 1. Becky and Robert – help Barry in hospital.
Were Becky and Robert able to help Barry in hospital? – ...

2. The Leinerts – climb Ben Nevis.
3. Sarah – cook a good meal.
4. Becky – hit the coconut.
5. Robin Hood – save Will Scarlet.
6. Shabina Ismaili – act in the play.
7. Robert – find a present for his great uncle.

4 Oh no! Where's my ...?

mine | his | hers | yours | ours | theirs

1. *Sarah:* Oh no! I've forgotten my biro.
   Mr Cooper: Well, Robert has got one on his desk. Maybe you can use ... or ask Mary for ... .
2. *David:* Where are my crayons?
   Mrs Dane: Look, Becky and her neighbour have got some. I'm sure you can use ... .
3. *Suvina:* I can't find my biscuits.
   Jenny: Sally and I have got a big box of biscuits. You can have some of ... .
4. *Becky:* Oh, I've left my apple at home.
   Barry: I've got one here. You can have ... .
   Becky: You want to give me ...? Thank you, Barry! That's very nice of you!

Unit 8

Animal world

Step A

Pets

This is Snowy, my rabbit. She lives in our garage. Sometimes I play with her in the garden.
Kevin, 12

My mouse, Tom, is very quiet. I have to clean his cage twice a week.
Mike, 15

Our hamster's name is Mr Bloggs. He's really sweet. He lives in a cage in my room and he runs around at night, so I can't sleep.
Yasmin , 14

I've got a fish tank with ten fish in my bedroom. They're all beautiful colours.
Peter, 14

Our budgies Jill and Jackie fly around our living-room when they're not in their cage. Then we have to keep all our windows closed.
Nina, 15

I haven't got a pet, but I go to the riding school every weekend. My favourite pony there is Belle.
Susan, 13

1 What is it?

1. It lives in a cage and runs around at night.
2. It sometimes plays in the garden.
3. It's very small and quiet.
4. They live in a cage and they can fly.
5. They're beautiful colours and can swim.
6. You can ride this animal.

2 My English folder

Write about your pets. If you haven't got a pet, say what pet you would like. Find photos for your text, too.

I'd like a budgie. I like budgies because they can talk and they can

Step B

Sarah's video diary

Last Saturday Sarah got up early because she wanted to start a new hobby. She wanted to make a video diary with her dad's camcorder. First she filmed her dad while he was going into the bathroom.
"Ugh, put that thing down, Sarah," said her dad and closed the bathroom door.
When Sarah went downstairs, her mother and Kim were sitting in the kitchen. Mrs Dixon was making a sandwich and Kim was eating cornflakes. Sarah wanted to film them while they were having breakfast.
"Oh, Sarah. Don't film me. I look terrible in the morning," said her mum.
"Gosh, what a boring family!" thought Sarah.

Then she heard the milkman and went to the front door. The milkman was just leaving with the empty bottles.
"Hello!" Sarah shouted. "Smile!"
The milkman turned round and smiled at Sarah.
"Morning!" he said. But as he was turning back, Tabby ran between his legs and he fell over.
"At last!" Sarah said. "Some action!"

1 What were they doing when Sarah saw them?

1. Mr Dixon **was going** ...
2. Mrs Dixon and Kim ...
3. Mrs Dixon ...
4. Kim ...
5. The milkman ...

He **was** just leav**ing.**
They **were** hav**ing** breakfast.

2 Sarah's friends

Sarah wanted to film other people on Saturday. What were they doing when she found them?

Example:
1. When Sarah found Robert, he **was playing football**.

3 A game: How good is your memory?

Work with a partner. Ask what he/she was doing at different times yesterday?

Example: What were you doing **at 7.20 yesterday morning**?
– I **was waiting** for the bus.

4 Looking at English

Write these sentences in your exercise book and colour them in with the right colours:

simple past

past progressive

Example: I was watching TV | when Mum came home.

When Sarah came in, Tabby was sleeping on her bed.
Mrs Jones was going to the shops when the accident happened.

5 Tabby, the video star

This is what happened last Saturday.
Can you tell the story? Use the right verb form.
Read the sentences before you start.
Go on like this:

1. Last Saturday Tabby **was sitting** *(sit)* in front of the TV. She … *(watch)* football when Sarah … *(come)* into the living-room.
2. Sarah … *(want)* to film Tabby with the camcorder. "Come on, Tabby," she … *(say)*. But Tabby … *(think)* that the football was more interesting.
3. Sarah … *(get)* Tabby's mouse. While she … *(try)* to film Tabby, she … *(begin)* to play with the mouse. That was difficult.
4. Then Kim … *(help)* Sarah. But while Kim … *(play)* with the mouse, Tabby … *(go)* away.
"Oh Tabby!" Sarah … *(say)*.
5. "Let's go and find Mum," Kim … *(say)*. They … *(go)* out to the kitchen. When Kim … *(turn)* round, Tabby … *(play)* with the mouse.

HV 6 Listening practice: There's nobody at home

Jenny tried to phone her friends last night. But they weren't at home. *Listen to the cassette. What were David, Becky, Robert and Sarah doing when she called?*
Example: When Jenny called, David was … .

Hard work

Sarah wanted to film the park. Jenny and Robert were with her. They had to say something about the park while Sarah was filming. First they went to the children's playground. But the children there were all shouting loudly and Jenny's voice was too quiet.

"We'll have to do it again," said Sarah. "You were speaking too quietly." So Jenny had another go. It was hard work.

Then they went to the big pond.

"What on earth can you say about a pond?" asked Robert.
"Er … what about this: This pond is one of the most interesting ponds in Nottingham. It …"
"That's too fast!" said Sarah. "Please don't speak so fast, Robert."
"All right," laughed Robert. "This – pond – is – "
"That's too slow!" said Jenny. "You mustn't speak *too* slowly, Robert. Come on, you're really good at Drama. You'll have to try really hard. But if we do this well, our video will be great."

quiet → quiet**ly**
careful → careful**ly**
tidy → tid**ily**

good → **well**
fast → **fast**
hard → **hard**

7 How do they do it?

1. Grandma Penrose has got a headache, so Mark must play … .
2. Yesterday David ran to school very … but he still arrived late.
3. Becky's clothes are usually on the floor, but today she is putting them … in the cupboard.
4. Simon heard a funny noise outside the back door. He opened the door … .
5. Robert laughed … at Sarah's new joke.
6. Maxi is in the kitchen and she is looking … at the meat on the table.

hungry
nervous
tidy
fast
quiet
loud

8 Looking at English

a) *Which adjectives do these adverbs come from:*
terribly, nicely, angrily, sweetly?

b) *Make adverbs from these adjectives and then make sentences with them:*
untidy, loud, correct, beautiful, slow.
Example: My brother always writes **untidily**.

9 Sound practice

a) *All these words have got the [ʌ] sound in them. Which letters do you have to put in? Write these sentences in your exercise book.*

1. My ■ncle l■ves c■rry for l■nch every S■nday.
2. M■ther's favourite c■lour is red.
3. We m■st h■rry! The b■s is c■ming.

b) *You can change the meaning of a sentence when you make different words important.*

Practise:
1. "Was Jenny with Robert?" – "No, **Sarah** was in the park with Robert."
2. "Was Sarah alone?" – "No, Sarah was in the park with **Robert**."
3. "Were they in the garden?" – "No, Sarah was in the **park** with Robert."
4. "I didn't see Sarah." – "But Sarah **was** in the park with Robert."

Unit 9

Looking at the UK: Animals at the zoo

A

B

C

D

E

F

1 Which animal is which?

How many of these animals do you know?

I think	picture A ...	is a picture of shows	a some	... .

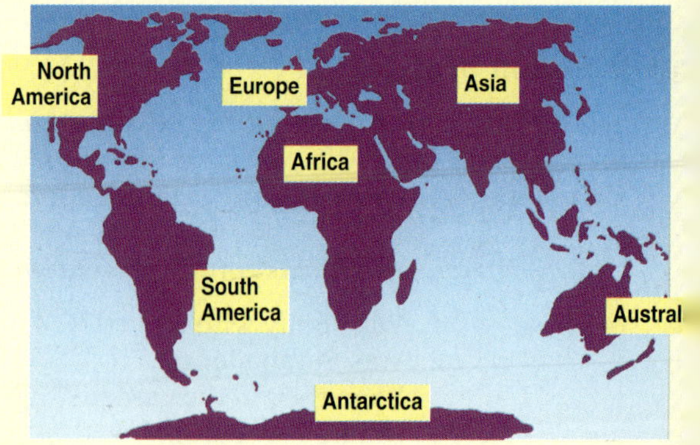

Your turn 2 My favourite animals

1. Where do these animals come from?
2. What other animals can you see when you are at the zoo?

Step C

Escape!

David and Becky were visiting Twycross Zoo last summer when something funny happened. A monkey escaped! This picture shows what everybody was doing when it happened.

1 What was happening?

What were the people in the picture doing when the monkey escaped?
Example: An old man was reading a book. Two boys were …

HV 2 Listening practice: Who is who?

Five people say what they were doing when the monkey escaped.
Can you find them in the picture?
Example: Number one must be …

3 A game: What were you doing when I phoned last night?

What were you doing when I phoned last night?
Work with a partner. You need six pieces of card or paper.
Draw an activity on each card.
Put the cards on the table (so you can't see the pictures).

Now you can make dialogues.

Example:
You: What were you doing when I phoned last night?
Partner (takes a card): I was listening to music.

Unit 9

4 WORD POWER

a) *Can you think of more words?*

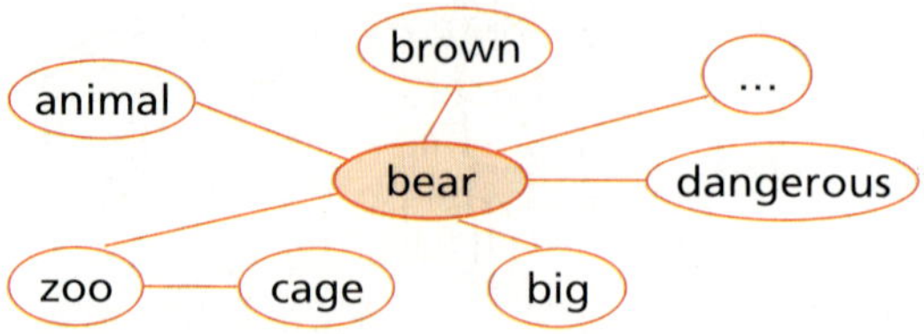

b) *Write words like these for your favourite animal.*

5 ⟨Just for fun⟩

A man was walking through the park when he saw a monkey.
"What can I do with this?" he asked a policeman.
"Take it to the zoo," the policeman answered.
The next day the policeman was walking down the road when he saw the man with the monkey again.
"Why didn't you take it to the zoo?" he asked.
"I did," said the man, "and today I'm taking it to the cinema!"

6 ⟨A song: Going to the zoo⟩

© Tom Paxton; Cherry Lane Music Ltd.

2. See the elephant with the long trunk swingin'
   The great big ears and the long trunk swingin'
   Sniffin' up the peanuts with the long trunk swingin'
   We can stay all day.
   (Chorus)
3. See all the monkeys scritch, scritch, scratchin'
   Jumpin' all around and scritch, scritch, scratchin'
   Hangin' by their long tails and scritch, scritch, scratchin'
   We can stay all day.
   (Chorus)
4. Well, the big black bear he's a-womp, womp, wompin'
   Coat's too heavy, he's a-womp, womp, wompin'
   Don't get too near the womp, womp, wompin'
   Or you won't stay all day.
   (Chorus)

5. Well, the seals in the pool they're honk, honk, honkin'
   Catchin' fish and honk, honk, honkin'
   Little seals are honk, honk, honkin'
   We can stay all day.
   (Chorus)
6. Well, we stayed all day, we're gettin' sleepy
   Sittin' in the car gettin' sleep, sleep, sleepy
   Home already, we're sleep, sleep, sleepy
   We have stayed all day.
   Chorus: We've been to the zoo, zoo, zoo
   So have you, you, you
   You came too, too, too
   We've been to the zoo, zoo, zoo.
7. Daddy's taking us to the zoo tomorrow
   Zoo tomorrow, zoo tomorrow
   Daddy's taking us to the zoo tomorrow
   We can stay all day.
   (Chorus)

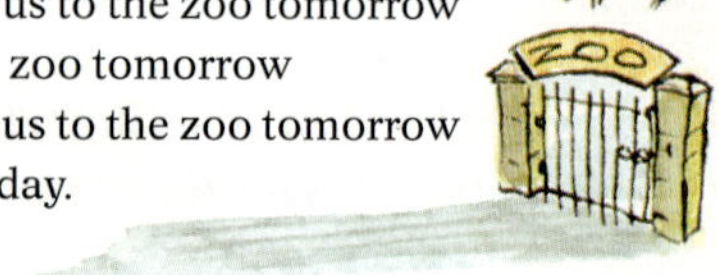

Unit 9

Step D

Rabbits for sale

"For sale ...," Becky bent down so that she could read the notice at the bottom of the newsagent's window, "... five sweet, brown rabbits. Phone ... ."

Becky wrote the phone number down and ran home. When she got there, her mother was reading a book in the garden. It seemed a good moment, so Becky began slowly, "Mum, do you like rabbits?" "Yes, dear. They're very sweet!" It was going well, so Becky went on. "Can I have one as a pet?" "No, you can't!" came the answer. "But, Mum ...," said Becky. "No, Becky, you can't have a rabbit. Think of our dogs."

Every day Becky looked in the newsagent's window. Every day she read the notice. It was still there on Saturday when she took Maxi for a walk. As she was looking at the notice, Robert came out of the shop. "Hello, Becky. What are you doing here?" Robert asked. "I'm just taking Maxi for a walk," Becky said. "Do you want to come?" "Yes," said Robert. "Let's go to the park."

They got to the park and they were going towards the pond when Becky said, "Hey, what's that man doing over there?" "Which man?" Robert asked. "That man over there, under the trees," Becky answered. Robert looked at the man. He was at the side of the pond and he had one hand in the water. Becky and Robert walked towards him. He was holding something under the water. "Excuse me," Becky said. "What are you doing?" "Me?" the man said. He stood up, but he didn't look at Becky and Robert. "What? Oh – nothing!" he said. Suddenly he turned and ran away quickly. Robert looked down. There was something in the water. "What is it?" Becky asked excitedly. "Can you get it?" It was a bag. Together they pulled it out of the water and opened it carefully. Inside there were five little, brown, and very wet rabbits. "Oh no!" Becky shouted angrily. "He wanted to drown them!"

When Robert and Becky walked into the Burtons' kitchen with the rabbits, Mrs Burton was not happy. "I said no rabbits, Becky! You have to take them back," she said. Becky explained to her about the man at the pond. "How terrible," said Mrs Burton, "but we can't keep them." "Oh, Mum!" Becky said miserably. "Poor little things!" "What about the pet shop?" her mother asked. "Maybe they could sell them."

There were a lot of brown rabbits in the window of the pet shop. "Oh, dear!" Robert said. "I don't think they'll want any more rabbits." They went in and asked. "No, sorry," the man in the pet shop answered. "Oh, no!" said Robert. "Now what are we going to do?"

Then Becky had an idea. "It's the summer fete at school soon. We could sell them there. But they need a home now." "That's OK," Robert said. "I can look after them at home. Mum won't mind. – Well, I hope not."

Unit 9

1 Robert's story

Robert comes home with the five baby rabbits. He has to explain to his mother
- where they came from
- why he has got them
- what will happen to them.

What does Robert say? Start like this:
This morning I met Becky outside the newsagent's. She was reading a notice about some rabbits. She wanted to take Maxi … .
Go on.

2 In the newsagent's window

People put notices in the newsagent's window when they want to buy or sell something or when they want to find work.
Write three notices for the newsagent's window. Choose something from each list.

Example:

WORK	***FOR SALE***	***WANTED***
babysitting ✓	old comics	music magazines
help with homework	baby hamsters	Two'n' Two CDs
work in garden	computer magazines	games
shopping	games for small children	stamps from Asia and Africa
take dog for a walk	…	…
…		

3 What a morning!

Put the verbs in the right form – simple past or past progressive?

Last Friday was a bad day for Robert. He … (wake up) at eight o'clock, … (get) out of bed and … (go) into the bathroom. While he … (sit) in the bath, Jenny … (phone). So Robert … (go) to the telephone, all wet. While he … (talk) to Jenny, his mother … (bring) him a cup of tea. "Thanks, Mum!" Robert said, but the cup was too hot and he … (drop) it on the floor. Then Robert … (leave) the house. While he … (go) down the street, he … (see) Sarah. Robert … (call) her, but she … (listen) to some music, so she couldn't hear him. When Robert … (walk) into the classroom, he remembered that his homework … (lie) on his desk at home. What a morning!

4 The adventure park

Last summer the Leinerts visited an adventure park. It was terrible.
What were/weren't they allowed to do? What did/didn't they have to do?

Step E

Let's check

1 WORD POWER

a) *Make rhymes with animals.*

Example: 1. cake → **snake**

2. meal
3. hair
4. of course
5. house
6. wig
7. hat

b) *How many animals do you know?*

pets	farm animals	zoo animals
dog	sheep	elephant

2 What were they doing?

What was everybody doing when David arrived at school yesterday?

Example: 1. Sarah eat a sandwich.
Sarah **was eating** a sandwich.

2. Robert read a book.
3. Becky watch a bird.
4. Jenny look in her bag.
5. Mrs Dane talk to a boy.
6. Two girls hide behind a tree.
7. Three boys play cards.

3 Something happened

Example: 1. Sarah – film her mum / she – drop the camcorder.
While Sarah **was filming** her mum, she **dropped** the camcorder.

2. Becky – visit the zoo / Jenny – try to phone her.
3. The Penroses – watch TV / David – eat two bars of chocolate.
4. Robert – make tea in the kitchen / his mother – come in.
5. Mark and his friends – play in the garden / Mark – fall over the ball.
6. Jenny and Sarah – have lunch in a restaurant / somebody – take Jenny's purse.

4 Choose carefully

These sentences need an adverb.
Choose the right adjective and use its adverb form.

careful hard easy quiet good fast

1. *Sarah:* Our German homework is very difficult.
   Jenny: Oh, but I can do it … .
2. *Sarah:* Mum, can I use your bike today?
   Mrs Dixon: Yes, OK, but don't ride too … .
3. *David:* Can I play my guitar in here, Dad?
   Mr Penrose: OK, but do it … because I'm writing a letter.
4. *Robert:* Do you want to play football?
   Jenny: No, you always kick the ball too … .
5. *Simon:* Do you know this song?
   Becky: Yes, it's great! I know it very … .
6. *Mark:* Can I write in your diary, Becky?
   Becky: OK, but write … .

The end of the school year

Step A

The summer fete

The last part of the summer term is usually great fun at Haywood School. There are often games during lessons, and the school always has a summer fete, with a bring-and-buy sale and other games and competitions. Half the money from the fete is for the school, and half goes to a charity.
This year there are some girls and boys from Karlsruhe in Nottingham. They are members of a brass band, and the Twinning Office has invited them to play in a big concert. Some of them are staying with the families of pupils at Haywood, and so they are happy to play at the school fete, too.

1 WORD POWER

Make a 'word map'.
Start with the word 'fete'.
How many words can you find?

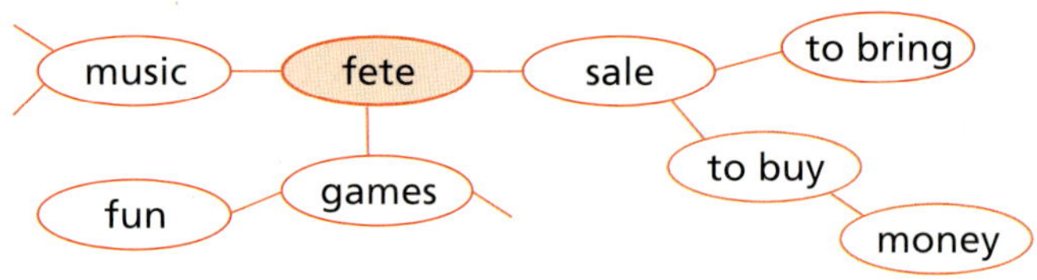

2 Problems!

The school needs things for the bring-and-buy sale.
Put in the right forms of the verbs. Simple past or present perfect?

1. *Mrs Croft:* Look. I (*just – find*) … this old puppet for the bring-and-buy sale.
   Robert: Oh, I don't want to give that away. I (*play*) … with it when I was little.
2. *Mr Dixon:* Where's my pullover? I (*put*) … it with some other clothes in the hall yesterday evening. But now they're all gone.
   Kim: They were clothes for the school sale! Sarah (*already – take*) … them there!
3. *Mrs Leinert:* Jenny can have this book for the sale. Somebody (*give*) … it to us years ago – I can't remember who.
   Mr Leinert: Wait a minute. I (*never – read*) … that book. It looks interesting!
4. *Becky:* Oh, look! Some idiot (*eat*) … a piece of my cake! Now I can't take it to school.
   Simon: Sorry, Becky. I (*not know*) … the cake was for the bring-and-buy sale.

3 Listening practice: What's it like in England?

The members of the German band are talking on Radio Nottingham.

Listen to the cassette. You can take notes while you're listening. Find out what is different in England. Is anything the same?

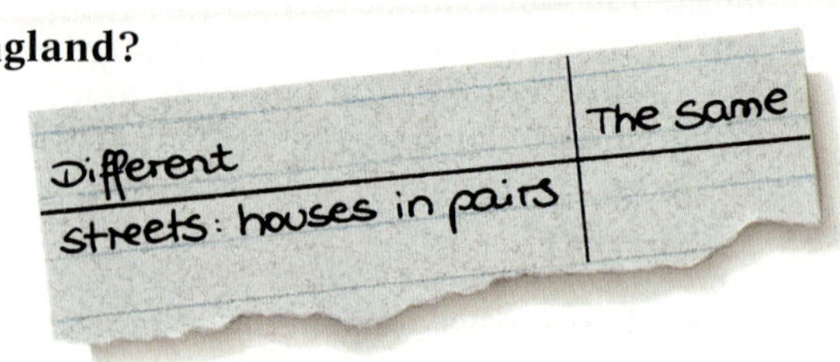

Before the fete

It is Saturday morning, and the girls and boys are getting things ready for the fete in the afternoon. David is counting sweets into a big bottle for the "How many sweets?" competition. It is a slow job, but he is working hard – much harder than his friends. They are looking at things on the bring-and-buy stalls.

Becky: Here's a skateboard, Sarah. Just the thing for you.
Sarah: I don't want a skateboard. I can go faster on my bike.
Jenny: Who wants a new pen? You, Robert? Mr Stevenson always says that you write most untidily.
Robert: Very funny, Jenny. – Oh, a toy trumpet! Let me try it.
Becky: No, let me have a go.
Jenny: No, give it to me. I can play it best.
David: Hey, can't you all talk more quietly?
Sarah: Oh, sorry. – Poor David! He always works hardest. Right, David?
David: Don't be silly. But I'm trying to count these sweets, and … Oh dear, where was I? Now I'll have to start again!

quiet**ly** – **more** quiet**ly** – **most** quiet**ly**

well – **better** – **best**
badl**y** – **worse** – **worst**

hard – hard**er** – hard**est**
fast – fast**er** – fast**est**

1 Crazy competitions

a) *What do you think you have to do in these competitions?*
Example: 1. You have to eat crisps **more quietly than** everyone else.
2. You have to walk on flowerpots … everyone else. *Go on.*

1

2

3

4

5

6

b) *Have you got more ideas for crazy competitions? Say what you have to do.*

2 They all do something best

a) *Make sentences about the friends.*
Example:
1. Robert – play cards – cleverly.
   Robert plays cards **most cleverly**.
2. Sarah – ride her bike – fast.
3. David – play the guitar – beautifully.
4. Becky – do puzzles – quickly.
5. Jenny – speak German – well.

Your turn
b) *What can you say about your friends – or family?*
Make more sentences like these.

cook, talk, sing, run, work, play …

hard, carefully, quietly, badly, well …

Looking at the UK: Charities

◄ In the UK a lot of people collect money for different charities. Nobody pays them for their time. They do it because they want to help other people – at home and in other countries, too. Children aren't allowed to collect money in the street. But they can make money in different ways – and have fun, too!

▲ Some children swim or run or ride their bike a long way. Family and friends pay them for their "work". Then the children give the money to a charity.

Schools or youth groups often organize sales, or they make money from concerts, plays and discos.
The photo shows some pupils from Haywood School. They are doing a car wash for charity. ►

Sometimes there are charity programmes on TV. A lot of children send their pocket money. Even a few pence can help when everybody works together.
▼

1 Charity activities

1. How can you make money for charities?
   What ideas can you find on this page?
   Have you got more ideas?
2. What can you say about Germany?
   Do a lot of people organize charity activities?
   Are there sometimes charity programmes on TV?
3. (Your turn) Have you ever helped a charity?
   What did you do?

Step C

Let's have fun

They look great – and they sound great!

Yes, a brass band is fun. I think we should start a brass band at Haywood.

1 At our school

What do **you** think is fun? *Collect and talk about ideas for your school.*

I think we should	start have organize …	a disco. a climbing club. a charity bike ride. a visit to … . …	–	Yes, that sounds fun. No, I don't think that's … . What about …? But … . …

2 Listening practice: At the fete

a) *Listen to what David tells his grandma. Then put the pictures in the right order. Start:* The right order is picture …, then … .

b) *Now match these words to the pictures. Who said the words, do you think – and why? Explain what the situation was.*

1. Don't laugh – it isn't for me!

Example: 1. I think David said, "Don't laugh – it isn't for me!" It was when he was buying the toy trumpet for Mark. Becky was laughing because she thought it was for David.

2. There she is!
3. I'm not going to tell you!
4. Wow! I've done it!
5. Oh!!

3 Sound practice

a) Some English words are easy to understand when you see them – because they look almost the same as German words. But you say them differently. *Please say these sentences, then listen to the cassette:*

- The **concert** was great.
- I loved the **music**.
- I've never heard this on the **radio**.
- Let's **organize** a charity walk.
- That's a good **idea**.

b) *Can you find more words like these? Write them down and show them to your partner. Can he/she say the words correctly?*

Unit 10

4 A game: Everything must go!

People often buy old or strange things at school fetes, even when they don't really want the things. That's because they know the money will go to a charity. Of course, for the pupils it's fun to try and sell something "different" to a customer!

What can you say about these things? Try to 'sell' them to your partner.

5 ⟨A song: We are the world⟩

© Text und Musik: Michael Jackson, Lionel Richie;
Arrangement: Margot Kroner

1. There comes a time when we heed a certain call, when the world must come together as one. There are people dying and it's time to lend a hand to life, the greatest gift of all.
2. We can't go on pretending day by day that someone somewhere will soon make a change. We are all a part of God's great big family and the truth you know, love is all we need.
   Chorus
3. Well, send them your heart so they'll know that someone cares and their lives will be stronger and free. As God has shown us by turning stones to bread, so we all must lend a helping hand.
   Chorus
4. When you're down and out there seems no hope at all, but if you just believe there's no way we can fall – whoa. Let's realize, that a change can only come when we stand together as one.
   Chorus

Step D

Lucky weather

Sarah and Robert were in the school car park. They were trying to make money at the summer fete. Although it was early, a lot of people – and cars – were already there. It was a good afternoon for the job, dry but not too sunny.

Just then Mr Stuart, one of the teachers, drove into the car park and jumped out of his car. Robert and Sarah stopped him.
"Your car is very dirty, Mr Stuart. Can we wash it, please?" asked Robert. "It only costs £1."
"Don't bother me now," Mr Stuart answered quickly. "I haven't got time to look for money. I'm already late for the fete."
But Sarah was quick, too. "You can pay us later," she said.
"Do what you want. Wash the car if you like. Oh dear, I'm *very* late now!" And with that he hurried away into the school.
"Hm. He got out of bed on the wrong side today," said Robert.
"Oh, he's always grumpy. Poor Kim is in his tutor group," laughed Sarah. "Come on, Robert. Let's start with these cars."

The car wash was fun, but hard work, too. After an hour or so Robert felt a bit tired.
"I'm going to have a break now," he told Sarah.
"Why do boys always get tired more quickly than girls?" she laughed.
"You shouldn't say things like that, Sarah Dixon! Now you'll have to pay for it!"
Robert picked up a bucket of water and threw it at her.
"Help!" she shouted, and jumped out of the way.
The water fell on the car behind her.
It was Mr Stuart's car. But when she and Robert looked at the car, they got a shock.
The water wasn't only outside.
It was inside, too – all over the front seats.
"Oh no, look! He left the sunroof open," said Sarah.
"What are we going to do now?"
"Well, we'll have to tell him what we've done," Robert answered. "These seats will never be dry before he comes back. Oh dear, he'll be *very* grumpy now!"

Sarah and Robert left the car park and looked for Mr Stuart.
They didn't feel very happy. Even the weather wasn't so friendly now. There was a big black cloud over the school.
They found Mr Stuart in the playground. He was organizing pupils and parents. They were carrying stalls from the playground into the school.
"Er – excuse us, Mr Stuart," Sarah said. "We … ." But she wasn't allowed to go on.
"Not now!" Mr Stuart answered. "Can't you see we're all busy here? Look at that cloud. We have to get everything into the school before it rains. Oh dear, here come the first drops now. Faster, everybody! Don't just stand there, you two. Help with these stalls!"
A few minutes later everything was inside. Just in time. It was raining hard now.

"What terrible weather – how unlucky! – But the fete will go on in the school," Mr Stuart told everyone. "Don't forget, the brass band is going to play again in the Assembly Hall in five minutes."

Then he saw Robert and Sarah. "Ah yes. You two should learn to wait for the right moment. Now, what did you want?"

Robert and Sarah thought of the wet seats in the car – and of the rain.

"We wanted to tell you, Mr Stuart … ."

"You left your sunroof open."

1 Mr Stuart's story

a) *How do you think Mr Stuart tells the story? Look at the ideas in the box. Try to use other words, too.*

You can start: "When I arrived at school, two pupils from Year 8 were in the car park.
They wanted to … . Well, I was already late for …, but … ."

arrive at school – two pupils from Year 8 – car park – want to – already late but say 'Yes' – go into school – help with the fete – later in the afternoon – the weather change – big black cloud – pupils and parents – get the stalls into the school just in time – rain hard – then – the two Year 8 pupils – want to tell me sunroof open – too late, of course – car seats – wet!

b) *Why do you think the title of the story is "Lucky weather"?*

2 Should they?

Sarah and Robert tell Mr Stuart about his sunroof. But what don't they tell him? Should they tell him everything? Say what you think.

– Yes, they should because … .

– No, they shouldn't because … .

his/their mistake – (not) important – wrong to hide things – too grumpy – angry – …

3 Looking at English

You can use a lot of words as verbs or nouns.
Example: park – Please **park** your car in the car **park** behind the school.
a) *Use the right words as verbs and nouns in these sentences.*

answer – help – rain – wash – smile – stay

1. We'll … your car at our Superclean Car …!
2. Try to … when I take your photo. Yes – that's a nice …!
3. That's a good …! I can never … difficult questions so quickly.
4. Oh dear. I've just felt a drop of … . Why does it always … at the wrong time?
5. Parents give a lot of … at the fete. They always … with the bring-and-buy sale.
6. The Germans are going to … in Nottingham for two weeks. I hope they enjoy their … .

b) *Now make sentences with these words as verbs and nouns.*

laugh – work – film – plan – jump – bully

Step E

Let's check

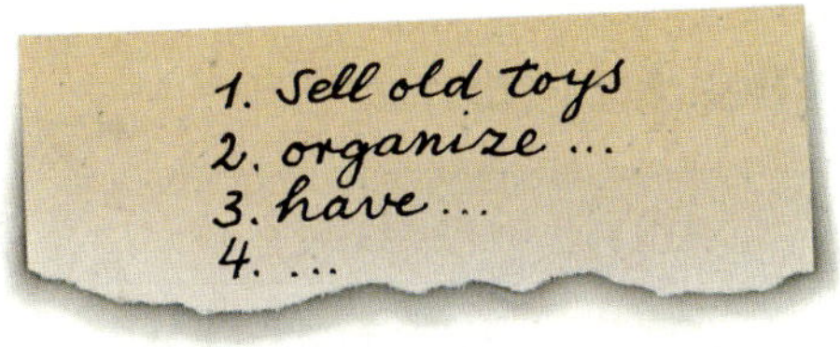

1 WORD POWER

How can you make money at a fete?
Write down a list of ideas.

How many ideas can you collect?

2 Who's the winner?

1. They all eat quickly. But Maxi eats most quickly.
   She eats … than Mini and Tabby.
2. They all run fast. But Sarah runs … . She … than … .
3. They all write untidily. But Mark … . He … .
4. They all sing very badly. But … . …

3 Fun with words

Sometimes words can "hide" in sentences.
For example, you can find "a little bit of water" in the sentence:
"You need rope when you go climbing." – The word is 'drop'!

Now look for:	*in:*
1. – you can play with it:	Happy Birthday to you!
2. – a part of the school year:	Run after me, Maxi!
3. – this group makes music:	The drama club and the computer club are fun.
4. – something with rain in it:	Isn't that music loud?
5. – you can sit on it:	I left my purse at home.
6. – a place with music:	This food is cold!

4 ⟨Time for a joke⟩

What pets
make the most noise?

The noisiest pets
are trum-pets, of course.

Unit 10

⟨Extra line⟩

⟨Reading corner⟩

Carol[1] singing[2]

(after unit 3)

"Hey, Mum," Nicola[3] said. "You know Roger[4], in our class? Well, his sister is in hospital. It's her leg."
"Oh dear, and it's nearly[5] Christmas[6]," said Mrs Davis[7].
"Well," said Nicola's sister Paula[8]. "You can send her a nice card."
"We can go carol singing," Nicola said, "and collect money for her."
"Don't be silly!" Paula answered. "She doesn't need money. But the hospital does. They're collecting money for a special machine[9]."
"Yes," their mother said. "We can get a collecting tin[10] from the hospital and go carol singing next week. Oh, and we must tell the police, too."

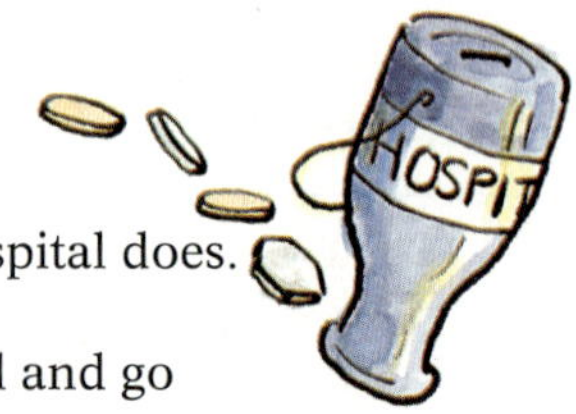

They decided[11] to go on Thursday evening. There were five singers[12]: Roger, Nicola, Paula, and Mrs Davis. – There was also Dean.
"But he can't sing!" said Paula. "We don't want him."
"But he's nice and he wants to come," answered Nicola. "And anyway, he *can* sing!"
"Well, he can have the collecting tin," said their mother.

Dean was outside the video shop. The other four arrived. Dean smiled at[13] Nicola.
"Where are we singing?" he asked.
"You aren't singing," said Paula.
"Can you take the tin?" said Mrs Davis. "We are going to the streets behind the supermarket."

Mrs Davis, Roger and the two girls stood[14] under a lamp-post[15] and sang[16]:

The holly[17] and the ivy[18]
When they are both full grown[19]
Of all the trees that are in the wood[20]
the holly bears[21] the crown[22].

Dean went along the road with the collecting tin. He knocked[23] on the door of the first house: a woman came to the door and looked at him. Then she looked at the collecting tin.
"Yes?" she asked.
"We're carol singing and collecting money for the hospital," Dean answered.
"No, thank you," the woman said and closed the door.
"And happy Christmas to you!" called Dean, and went to the next house.
"We're carol singing for the hospital," he said to an old man.
"Carol singing? But you're not singing," the old man said.
"No," answered Dean. "They're over there."
"Oh," said the man. "Well, here you are." And he put something in the tin.

[1]carol ['kærəl] *Weihnachtslied* – [2]carol singing ['kærəl sɪŋɪŋ] *Weihnachtslieder singen* – [3]Nicola ['nɪkələ] *weibl. Vorname* – [4]Roger ['rɒdʒə] *männl. Vorname* – [5]nearly ['nɪəlɪ] *fast* – [6]Christmas ['krɪsməs] *Weihnachten* – [7]Davis ['deɪvɪs] *Familienname* – [8]Paula ['pɔ:lə] *weibl. Vorname* – [9]machine [mə'ʃi:n] *Maschine* – [10]tin [tɪn] *Dose, Büchse* – [11]to decide [dɪ'saɪd] *sich entschließen* – [12]singer ['sɪŋə] *Sänger* – [13]to smile at ['smaɪl‿ət] *jmd. anlächeln* – [14]to stand, stood [stænd, stʊd] *stehen, stand* – [15]lamp-post ['læmppəʊst] *Straßenlaterne* – [16]to sing, sang [sɪŋ, sæŋ] *singen, sang* – [17]holly ['hɒlɪ] *Stechpalme* – [18]ivy ['aɪvɪ] *Efeu* –[19]full grown [ˌfʊl 'grəʊn] *groß gewachsen* – [20]wood [wʊd] *Wald* – [21]to bear [beə] *hier: tragen* – [22]crown [kraʊn] *Krone* – [23]to knock [nɒk] *klopfen*

"That sounds[24] funny," thought[25] Dean when he shook[26] the tin.
Dean knocked on another door and then another. Nobody came.
He went back to the singers. "Sorry," he said. "I'm not very lucky."
And then it started to rain.

"Give *me* the tin," said Paula. "You're useless![27]"
They all went to the next street. Nicola, Roger, Dean and Mrs Davis stood under a lamp-post and sang *Oh, little town of Bethlehem*[28]. Paula knocked on the first door.
A friendly woman came to the door. "What a terrible night!" she said.
"Hello," said Paula. "We're collecting for the hospital."
"Oh, isn't that nice. Here's five pounds."
"Thank you very much. Merry[29] Christmas!" called Paula.

Before she knocked on the next door it opened. A man looked out.
"Where's that singing coming from?" he asked. "It's very good. You've got nice voices[30]."
"Hm," thought Paula. "Nicola was right[31]. Dean really *can* sing."
The man put a lot of money in the tin.
Paula went to the next house and the next and everyone said "What beautiful[32] singing!"
They all gave a lot of money for the hospital.

When Paula told the others about all the money, it was a surprise for Mrs Davis, too.
And Dean was upset[33]. "You were just lucky," he said.
"Well, maybe," Paula said. "They were all very friendly to me."
Just then[34] a man came out of one of the houses.
"Hello," he said. "Your carols sound lovely[35]."
"You see," Nicola said to Paula. "I told you so[36]. Dean can sing."
"What are you collecting for?" the man asked them.
"The hospital," Mrs Davis answered.
"Well, here's ten pounds for the tin," he said.
"Wow!" said Roger.

"I'm so cold and wet," Dean said. "My grandma lives here. Let's go to her house."
"What a good idea," Mrs Davis answered.

Inside the house it was nice and warm. They had a cup of tea[37] and some mince pies[38] and Roger and Mrs Davis counted the money from the collecting tin.
"Forty-four pounds, sixteen pence, and two buttons[39]!" said Mrs Davis.
"I know who gave the two buttons," Dean shouted.
"Forty-four pounds, that's very good," Dean's grandma said. "Let me give you six pounds to make it fifty."
"Super!" everyone shouted.
"Carol singing is OK," said Dean. "Can I have another mince pie?"

[24]to sound [saʊnd] *klingen, sich anhören* – [25]to think, thought [θɪŋk, θɔ:t] *denken, dachte* – [26]to shake, shook [ʃeɪk, ʃʊk] *schütteln, schüttelte* – [27]you're useless ['ju:slɪs] *du taugst nichts* – [28]Bethlehem ['beθlɪhem] *Stadt* – [29]merry ['merɪ] *fröhlich* – [30]voice [vɔɪs] *Stimme* – [31]to be right [raɪt] *Recht haben* – [32]beautiful ['bju:təfʊl] *schön* – [33]upset [ʌp'set] *verletzt* – [34]just then [ˌdʒʌst 'ðen] *in dem Moment* – [35] lovely ['lʌvlɪ] *schön* – [36]I told you so. [ai 'təʊld‿ju: ˌsəʊ] *Das habe ich dir gesagt.* – [37]cup of tea [ˌkʌp‿əv 'ti:] *Tasse Tee* – [38]mince pie [ˌmɪns 'paɪ] *gefülltes Weihnachtsgebäck* – [39]button ['bʌtn] *Knopf*

⟨Extra line⟩

The Canterville Ghost

(after unit 4)

Characters:

Mr and Mrs Otis
their daughter Virginia Otis
their sons: Washington, Tom, Tim
Mrs Umney, the housekeeper
Speakers 1, 2, and 3
Ghost

Dieses englische Theaterstück ist nach einer Geschichte von Oscar Wilde geschrieben.
Ihr könnt es gut bei einem Klassen- oder Schulfest aufführen. Eure künstlerischen Fähigkeiten und Ideen sind dabei natürlich gefordert.
Viel Spaß und gutes Gelingen!

Virginia: Hello. My name is Virginia Otis. I'm American, but I live in England. That's because my father works in England now. Our new home is a beautiful[1] old English house. It's like a castle, it's so big! It's called Canterville Chase.

Speaker 1: Before we start, we must tell you a bit about Canterville Chase. – Well, it all happened over a hundred years ago: the Otis family came to England in 1885. Mr and Mrs Otis looked for a house. They found Canterville Chase, and decided[2] to buy it. But they soon heard some *very* strange stories about the house.

Speaker 2: People said to them: "*Don't* buy Canterville Chase! It's haunted[3]! Didn't you know?" – Haunted?! Well, Mr Otis just said,

Mr Otis (steps forward): "We're Americans. *We* don't believe in[4] ghosts! We want to buy Canterville Chase – and we want to live there. If there's a ghost in the house, well – OK, we'll buy the ghost, too!"

Speaker 3: So they bought the house – and they all arrived at Canterville Chase on a lovely July evening. Virginia with her parents, her big brother Washington, and her two little brothers, Tom and Tim … .

Scene I: *The living-room at Canterville Chase. In the middle of the room, there is a table, with tea things on it. Mrs Umney is standing at the door. Mr Otis, Mrs Otis and Virginia come in first. Washington and the two smaller boys come in with bags.*

Mrs Umney: Welcome to Canterville Chase! Please come in!
Mr Otis: Thank you, Mrs Umney. Well, here we are – in our new home!
Mrs Otis: What a fantastic[5] house! – What do you think of it, Virginia?
Virginia: I think I'll like it very much, Mother.

(Tom and Tim are running round the table now. Tom is running after Tim. They are laughing and having fun.)

⟨Extra line⟩

[1]beautiful ['bju:təfʊl] *schön* – [2]to decide [dɪ'saɪd] *sich entschließen* – [3]it's haunted [ɪts 'hɔ:ntɪd] *es spukt da* – [4]to believe in [bɪ'li:v‿ɪn] *glauben an* – [5]fantastic [fæn'tæstɪk] *fantastisch*

Mrs Umney: Tea is ready, madam[6].

Mrs Otis: Thank you, Mrs Umney. – Come to the table, all of you. – Stop it, you two boys! That's enough! Now come and sit down, so we can have tea together.

(They all sit down. Mrs Umney goes out and comes back with a big teapot[7]. She gives them all tea. They take biscuits and cake, and start to eat and drink. Mrs Otis looks round the room. Suddenly she sees a red stain[8] on the floor. She points to[9] it.)

Mrs Otis: Oh look, Mrs Umney! There's a very bad stain on the floor!

(Tom gets up from his chair. He runs round the table. Tim runs after him. They look at the stain.)

Tom: Ugh! A big red stain! It looks like blood[10]!

Tim: Blood! Ugh! It's a bloodstain!

Mrs Umney: Yes, that's right, dear. It's blood.

Mr Otis: Blood? Well, we don't want blood on the floor. Please clean it up, Mrs Umney.

Mrs Umney: Sorry, sir, but I can't. It's the blood of Lady[11] Eleanore Canterville. She died in 1575. Her husband[12], Sir Simon Canterville, murdered[13] her here – in this room.

Mrs Otis: Murdered his wife[14]? In this room? How terrible!

Mrs Umney: Yes, madam. I think you all know about the ghost here at Canterville Chase.

Washington: Well, we know there are *stories* about a ghost, yes!

Mrs Umney: They aren't just stories, young man. It is the ghost of Sir Simon Canterville. He murdered Lady Eleanore in this room – and he lived in this house for nine years after that. Then he suddenly disappeared[15]. Nobody knows what happened to him. They never found his body[16]. But his ghost is still here, at Canterville Chase!

Tim: A ghost! A ghost! Come on, Tom! Let's go and look for the Canterville Ghost!

Tom: Yeah! Let's look through all the rooms. Ghost! Ghost! We're coming!

Virginia: The poor ghost! Why must he haunt the house for so many years?

(They run out of the room. They make a lot of noise.)

Mrs Umney: And that old blood stain is still on the floor here. Nobody can clean it up[17].

Washington: Wait. Let me try. We've got a bottle of stain remover[18] in one of our bags.

(He gets the bottle from a bag and wipes[19] over the stain with the stain remover.)

Washington: You see? This American stain remover is very good. The stain is gone[20] now!

Mrs Umney: Ah – but it will be there on the floor again tomorrow morning!

[6]madam ['mædəm] *gnädige Frau* – [7]teapot ['ti:pɒt] *Teekanne* – [8]stain [steɪn] *Fleck* – [9]to point to ['pɔɪnt‿tu:] *zeigen auf* – [10]blood [blʌd] *Blut* – [11]Lady/Sir ['leɪdɪ/sɜ:] *engl. Adelstitel* – [12]husband ['hʌzbənd] *Ehemann* – [13]to murder ['mɜ:də] *ermorden* – [14]wife [waɪf] *Ehefrau* – [15]to disappear [ˌdɪsə'pɪə] *verschwinden* – [16]body ['bɒdɪ] *hier: Leiche* – [17]to clean up ['kli:n‿ʌp] *wegputzen* – [18]remover [rɪ'mu:və] *Entferner* – [19]to wipe [waɪp] *wischen* – [20]gone [gɒn] *weg*

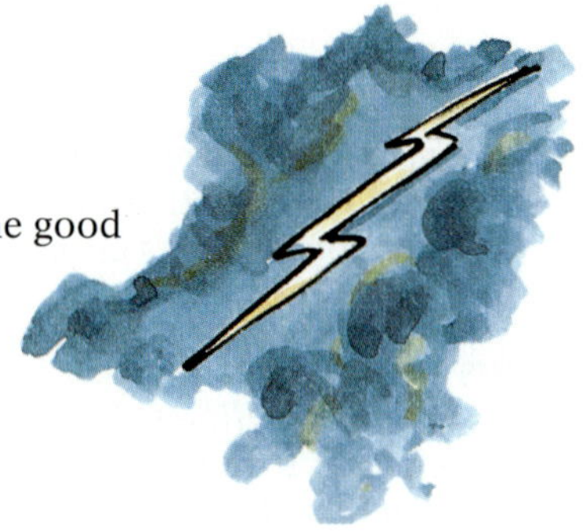

(There is lightning at the window.)

Mrs Otis (not afraid): Oh, lightning! Maybe that's the end of the good weather.

Mrs Umney: I sometimes see terrible things here. So I often can't sleep at night. Terrible things happen in this house!

(There is a loud noise of thunder.)

Virginia: Listen to the thunder.

Speaker 1: Well, they didn't see the ghost that night. But the bloodstain was on the floor again the next morning. Washington cleaned it up. But every morning the terrible red stain was there again! Washington said, "Well, it really must be the ghost!" Then, on the third night, the ghost appeared[21] … .

Scene II: *Upstairs at Canterville Chase. There are two doors. One is Mr and Mrs Otis's bedroom door. The other one is the little boys' bedroom door. Moonlight[22] from a small window is the only light. On the left the ghost appears. He is a terrible old man, with long white hair and an untidy beard. He is wearing a long white shirt. Heavy[23] chains[24] are hanging[25] from his arms and legs. He is very slow[26] – but with every step[27] there is a loud noise from the chains. Mr Otis opens his door and comes out with a candle.*

Mr Otis: What's that terrible noise? – And who is this? Ah, it must be Sir Simon Canterville. But my dear sir, you really *must* oil[28] those chains! They're making a terrible noise out here. You woke me up with it! – Look what I've got for you. *(He takes a small bottle and puts it on a table.)* Here's a bottle of very good hair oil[29]. It's American! Try it! I'm sure it'll help. *(He goes back into his bedroom and closes the door.)*

Ghost (in an angry whisper[30]): Hair oil for my chains? Hair oil?! Pah!! Has he no respect[31] for me? No respect for the great ghost of Canterville Chase? Americans, eh? Pah! I'll show them! They'll be sorry[32] they ever came to this house! *(He walks towards the window, and gives a terrible laugh.)* Ha ha ha! Ha ha ha haaaaa!!

(Suddenly the door on the right opens, and Tim and Tom come out. They have both got pillows in their arms.)

Tom: There he is, Tim!

Tim: Yeah!! Silly old ghost! We aren't scared of you!

Tom: Ready, Tim? OK – one – two – three – NOW!!

(They throw the pillows. One pillow hits the ghost. The ghost shakes his fist at[33] the two boys and runs off the stage.)

[21]to appear [ə'pɪə] *erscheinen* – [22]moonlight ['mu:nlaɪt] *Mondlicht* – [23]heavy ['hevɪ] *schwer* – [24]chain [tʃeɪn] *Kette* – [25]to hang, hung [hæŋ, hʌŋ] *hängen, hing* – [26]slow [sləʊ] *langsam* – [27]step [step] *Schritt* – [28]to oil [ɔɪl] *ölen* – [29]hair oil ['heər‿ˌɔɪl] *Haaröl* – [30]whisper ['wɪspə] *Flüstern* – [31]respect [rɪ'spekt] *Respekt* – [32]they'll be sorry [ˌðeɪl bi: 'sɒrɪ] *sie werden es bereuen* – [33]he shakes his fist at [hi: ˌʃeɪks hɪz 'fɪst‿æt] *er droht mit der Faust*

Speaker 2: I think all this was a big surprise for the ghost. Nobody in the family was scared of him – he just couldn't believe it! So he decided to take his revenge[34]. Again and again he tried to scare[35] them at night, but his tricks didn't work[36].

Speaker 3: Tim and Tom played a lot of tricks on him. Once they put pieces of string[37] across[38] the corridor – and he tripped and fell. Then they put butter at the top of the stairs[39], and he fell down again!

Speaker 1: But one day, when Virginia was upstairs, she saw that one of the doors was open. So she went in – just to see who was there. And there was the ghost! …

Scene III: *A room with a small chair at the window. The ghost is sitting there. He is looking out of the window.*

Virginia: Oh!! Mr Ghost – er Sir Simon! I didn't know you were here!

Ghost (in an unhappy voice): Oh, Miss Virginia, it's you! Oh, I am so unhappy! Please, help me, Miss Virginia! Everyone in your family laughs at me!

Virginia: I don't laugh at you.

Ghost: But your brothers! They have no respect for me! They play tricks on me. It's so unfair[40]!

Virginia: Unfair? But *you* wanted to scare people in this house. Wasn't *that* unfair? And you murdered your wife! How can you forget *that*?

Ghost: That was a long, long time ago. I'm sorry about it now, but I can find no peace[41]. I can never leave this house. I can never sleep! Three hundred years without sleep! And I'm *so* tired.

Virginia: Poor, poor ghost! How can I help you?

Ghost: Do you know the old Canterville rhyme?

Virginia: Yes, I know it by heart:

When a child gives its tears[42]
To charm away[43] the old, old fears[44],
Then will all the house be still
And peace will come to Canterville. –

But what does it mean?

Ghost: It means that if you are really sorry for[45] me, your tears will save me. And I will find peace – and death[46].

Virginia (with tears): Oh, poor ghost. Of course, I feel sorry for you. *(They go off the stage.)*

Speaker 2 (in a slow voice): Nobody ever saw the ghost again. The charm[47] was broken now, and the ghost was at peace.

[34]to take revenge [ˌteɪk‿rɪˈvendʒ] *sich rächen* – [35]to scare [skeə] *erschrecken* – [36]to work [wɜːk] *hier: funktionieren* – [37]piece of string [ˌpiːs‿əv ˈstrɪŋ] *Schnur* – [38]across [əˈkrɒs] *über* – [39]stairs [steəz] *Treppe* – [40]unfair [ˌʌnˈfeə] *ungerecht* – [41]peace [piːs] *Frieden* – [42]tear [tɪə] *Träne* – [43]to charm away [ˌtʃɑːm‿əˈweɪ] *wegzaubern* – [44]fear [fɪə] *Angst* – [45]to be sorry for [ˈsɒrɪ ˌfɔː] *jmd. bemitleiden* – [46]death [deθ] *Tod* – [47]charm [tʃɑːm] *Zauber*

Food in Britain

(after unit 6)

At the supermarket

If you go to a British supermarket, you will find most of the foods you can get in Germany, too. But of course, some things are different. You won't find so many cold meats[1] or so many different cheeses. You'll find a lot of different cereals[2], crisps, sweets and biscuits, a lot of instant coffee[3] and ready-made meals[4]. You'll see many Indian foods, too. The bread and the sausages are different and the butter has got salt[5] in it.

What you can find in a supermarket

You can find many of these words in German, too. Where do they come from?

grapefruit **steak** **avocado** **melon** **orange** **toast** **kiwi** **ketchup** **muesli** **broccoli** **baguette** **milk shake** **yoghurt** **salami** **mineral water** **pepper**

The English Breakfast

Is there a typical[6] English breakfast? Well, yes, it's a big meal. Most people don't have time for it in the morning. But a lot of people like a good English breakfast on Sundays. Of course, you can get it in hotels and cafés, too.

You can start with orange juice[7] or grapefruit. Some people start with cereal, yoghurt, fruit or porridge[8]. Then there is bacon[9] and eggs with things like sausages, baked beans[10], fried mushrooms[11] and tomatoes. You think that's all? Oh, no. Then there's toast and marmalade[12]. Marmalade is not as sweet[13] as jam[14] (that's *Marmelade* in German) and it's made from special oranges.

What do *you* have for breakfast? And what is a *typical* German breakfast?

[1]cold meats [ˌkəʊld ˈmi:ts] *Wurstsorten* – [2]cereal [ˈsɪərɪəl] *Getreideflocken* – [3]instant coffee [ˈɪnstənt ˌkɒfɪ] *löslicher Kaffee* – [4]ready-made meal [ˌredɪmeɪd ˈmi:l] *Fertiggericht* – [5]salt [sɔ:lt] *Salz* – [6]typical [ˈtɪpɪkl] *typisch* – [7]orange juice [ˈɒrɪndʒ ˌdʒu:s] *Orangensaft* – [8]porridge [ˈpɒrɪdʒ] *Haferbrei* – [9]bacon [ˈbeɪkn] *durchwachsener Speck* – [10]baked beans [ˌbeɪkt ˈbi:nz] *weiße Bohnen in Tomatensoße* – [11]fried mushrooms [ˌfraɪd ˈmʌʃrʊmz] *gebratene Pilze* – [12]marmalade [ˈmɑ:məleɪd] *Marmelade aus Zitrusfrüchten* – [13]sweet [swi:t] *süß* – [14]jam [dʒæm] *Marmelade*

⟨Extra line⟩

A recipe: Apple crumble[15]

g = gram[16]; tsp = teaspoon[17]; tbsp = tablespoon[18]

You need:
an ovenproof[19] dish[20] (for about 1.5 litres[21])
3 - 4 big apples (not too sweet)
30 g sugar
2 tbsp water

For the crumble:
150 g flour[22]
150 g oats[23]
150 g butter
100 g Demarara (brown) sugar
1/4 tsp ground[24] cinnamon[25]

Put the oven[26] on at 190°C.

Make the crumble first. Mix[27] the cinnamon with the sugar and then mix this together with the flour, oats and butter. (You can do this with your fingers or with a fork.)

Grease[28] the ovenproof dish with butter. Peel[29] and cut the apples into small pieces. Put the apples into the dish with the water and the sugar. Put the crumble on the apples.

Bake[30] in the hot oven for 30 - 40 minutes.

Eat it with cream or custard[31].

If you can't cook at school, cook it at home.

[15]apple crumble [ˌæpl 'krʌmbl] *Apfel-Streusel-Süßspeise* – [16]gram [græm] *Gramm* – [17]teaspoon ['ti:spu:n] *Teelöffel* – [18]tablespoon ['teɪblspu:n] *Esslöffel* – [19]ovenproof ['ʌvnpru:f] *feuerfest* – [20]dish [dɪʃ] *hier: Auflaufform* – [21]litre ['li:tə] *Liter* – [22]flour ['flaʊə] *Mehl* – [23]oats [əʊts] *Haferflocken* – [24]ground [graʊnd] *gemahlen* – [25]cinnamon ['sɪnəmən] *Zimt* – [26]oven ['ʌvn] *Ofen* – [27]to mix [mɪks] *mischen* – [28]to grease [gri:s] *einfetten* – [29]to peel [pi:l] *schälen* – [30]to bake [beɪk] *backen* – [31]custard ['kʌstəd] *heiße Vanillesoße*

⟨Extra line⟩

⟨Translation Practice⟩

Wie du ja weißt, kann man beim Übersetzen nicht alles Wort für Wort in die andere Sprache übertragen. Viele Wörter haben mehrere Bedeutungen:
z. B. *only* – nur, erst.

Auch die Wortstellung ist im Englischen oft anders als im Deutschen,
z. B. "He ran to school because he was late." –
„Er lief zur Schule, weil er spät dran war."

Ich habe hier einige Problemstellen mit Gelb angemalt um etwas zu helfen.

Unit 1

a) *John:* I've got three books for English. Two green ones and a red one. Which one do we need in the lesson today?
Becky: The red one. We only need the green ones on Wednesdays.

b) 1. Simon is with a new friend. He looks like Barry Jenkins's brother.
2. Becky is worried about Simon. She is looking for him in the playground now.
3. *Becky:* Quick, Robert! That bully is taking Simon's money. Look!
4. *Simon:* Hey, stop it, Becky! Don't look at Mike like that! We're both computer fans, and we want to buy a magazine together.

Unit 2

a) *Jenny:* Did you have a nice weekend, Robert?
Robert: Yes, I did. Mum and I went to Sherwood Forest. What did *you* do?
Jenny: Dad took me to the 'Tales of Robin Hood'. David and Mark came with us.
Robert: Did Mark like it?
Jenny: Yes, he did. But he was a bit scared of the Sheriff at first.

b) 1. One day the Sheriff's men caught Will Scarlet.
2. Robin was angry when he heard the news.
3. But soon he had a good plan. He played a trick on the Sheriff, and the outlaws saved Will from the gallows.

c) 1. Was hast du gestern gemacht?
2. Ich bin ins Kino gegangen.
3. Welchen Film hast du gesehen?
4. Einen guten: Robin Hood.

Unit 3

a) 1. When the girls arrived at the fair, everything went wrong right away.
2. Becky felt miserable when the other two laughed at her.
3. She remembered the fair last year. It was better than this year because Jenny wasn't with them then.
4. "Let's stay together," said Jenny. "That's the most important thing."

b) 1. Mein Vater ist drei Jahre älter als meine Mutter.
2. "Fußball ist nicht so interessant wie Tennis." – "Das stimmt nicht! Fußball ist viel interessanter."
3. Die teuersten Sachen sind nicht immer die besten.

⟨Extra line⟩

⟨Translation Practice⟩

Unit 4

a) 1. What are you looking at?
2. Who are you waiting for?
3. "I don't understand this exercise." – "Don't worry. I'll help you."
4. If there's a drama group next year, I'll join it.
5. If you don't give me my CD back, I won't lend you my other CDs.

b) 1. Wenn das Wetter morgen schön ist, gehen wir schwimmen.
2. Wir bleiben aber zu Hause, wenn es regnet.
3. Und wenn unsere Freunde kommen, spielen wir Karten. Aber wir werden nicht fernsehen.

Unit 5

a) *Assistant:* Hello. Do you need any help?
Customer: Have you got any black socks?
Assistant: Sorry, but we haven't got any black ones. But I can show you some very nice blue ones. Here you are.

b) "Excuse me. Is there a bookshop anywhere near here?"
– "Yes, there's a very good one on the lower floor, opposite the supermarket."

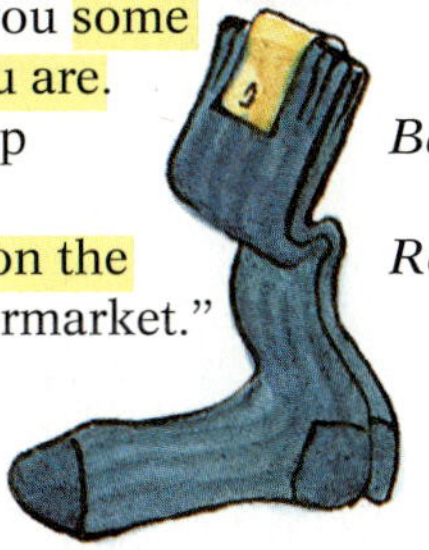

c) *Becky:* Where's Mini? I can't find her anywhere.
Simon: She's somewhere outside. Can't you hear her? She's barking, and I think someone's talking to her.
Becky: There must be someone at the door.
Robert: Hello! Is there anybody at home?

Unit 6

a) 1. What would you like to drink?
2. I'd like a glass of milk, please.
3. Would you like some coffee?
4. No, thanks. I don't like coffee.

b) 1. "Have your friends arrived yet?" – "Yes, they've just come."
2. "What's happened to the last piece of chicken?" – "I've put it on that plate over there."

c) 1. Ich habe meine Hausaufgaben gemacht. Aber ich habe mein Zimmer noch nicht aufgeräumt.
2. Hast du schon gefrühstückt?
3. Papa hat heute das Essen gekocht. Es ist jetzt fertig.
4. Aber er hat noch nicht den Tee gemacht.

Unit 7

a) 1. "Have you ever been to America?" – "Yes, I have. I went there with my parents two years ago."
2. "This is a good photo of Mum. When did you take it?" – "I took it when we were on holiday."
3. "Have you listened to the weather forecast?" – "Yes, I have. The weather will probably change at the weekend."

b) 1. Ich möchte im Sommer nach Schottland fahren. Könnten Sie mir bitte ein paar Broschüren geben?
2. „Hast du schon mal Sauerkraut gegessen?" – „Ja, das essen wir oft zu Mittag."
3. Letzte Woche haben wir meinen Onkel in Berlin besucht. Warst du schon mal in Berlin?

Unit 8

a) 1. "Have you hurt your hand?"
– "Well, my little finger hurts a bit. But I'll be all right!"
2. My mother had to go to hospital last week. But she'll be allowed to come home again tomorrow.
3. "What's wrong with you?"
– "I've got a sore throat and a temperature."

b) 1. "Du warst gestern nicht in der Schule."
– "Ich war beim Arzt. Als ich aufgestanden bin, hatte ich Bauchschmerzen. Aber jetzt geht's mir gut!"
2. Mark war traurig, weil er den Film nicht sehen durfte. Er musste zu Hause bleiben.
3. "Wo sind meine Turnschuhe?"
– "Ich weiß nicht, wo deine sind. Diese hier sind meine. Vielleicht hat Papa sie."

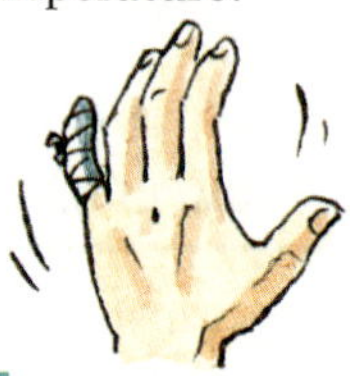

Unit 9

a) 1. "When we got home yesterday, a black cat was sitting in the kitchen."
– "How lucky!"
– "Not for us! It was eating our lunch!"
2. "I've lost my rabbit."
– "Why don't you put a notice in the newsagent's window?"
– "Don't be silly. He can't read."
3. "How do you get an elephant into a biscuit box?"
– "First, open the box carefully and take out all the biscuits."

b) 1. Meine Oma ist sehr langsam. Sie arbeitet langsam und sie spricht auch langsam.
2. "Spielst du Gitarre?"
– "Ja, aber ich kann noch nicht sehr gut spielen."
3. Wir saßen alle im Garten, als mein Onkel ankam. Er machte ein Foto von uns, während wir gerade Tee tranken.
4. "Die Kaninchen sind süß. Sind sie alle zu verkaufen?"
– "Nein, sie kosten nichts. Willst du eins mit nach Hause nehmen?"

Unit 10

a) 1. A girl from Karlsruhe is staying with the Dixons. She plays the trumpet.
2. Don't bother your dad just now! He's busy.
3. We arrived at the concert just in time. Next time we really should leave a bit earlier!
4. We aren't allowed to collect money in the street. But maybe we can organize a concert and make some money like that.

b) 1. Es regnet! Wir müssen die Stühle alle ins Haus tragen!
2. Dürfen wir beim Schulfest Jeans tragen?
3. Meine Schwester schwimmt langsamer als mein Bruder. Aber er wird schneller müde!
4. Bitte parken Sie nicht vor der Schule. Benutzen Sie den Parkplatz hinter dem Schulhof.

Grammar

Hallo, ihr wisst ja bereits, dass es in jeder Sprache Grammatikregeln gibt. Die folgende Zusammenstellung der englischen Regeln hilft dir beim Englischlernen.
Wenn du bestimmte Regeln suchst, dann schlage einfach die Übersicht auf Seite 127 auf. Dort ist das alphabetische Verzeichnis des Grammatikanhangs. Du kannst dort die deutschen und englischen Begriffe nachschlagen und findest Beispiele zu jeder Regel.

Unit 1 Step B

§ 1 What? – Which?

What subjects do you do at school?	**Which** do you like best?
What's the next lesson?	**Which** subject is it now? German or English?
What's for lunch today?	There's fish or sausages for lunch today. **Which** do you want?

What things can you see on the table?

Welche …

Which of them can you eat?

Welche …

- Mit *what* fragt man nach Dingen, deren Auswahl unbegrenzt ist (was, welche/r/s).
- Mit *which* fragt man nach Dingen, von denen eine begrenzte Auswahl vorhanden ist (welche/r/s).

§ 2 Das Stützwort one/ones The prop word one/ones

Becky has got three **pens**,	a black **one** and two blue **ones.**	… einen schwarzen und zwei blaue.
Which **poster** do you want,	the big **one** or the small **one**?	… das große oder das kleine?
Which **books** do we need?	– The blue **ones**.	– Die blauen.

- Wenn man ein zählbares Substantiv nicht wiederholen möchte, ersetzt man es durch das 'Stützwort' *one/ones*. Das Adjektiv kann hier nicht – wie im Deutschen – allein stehen.
- Auch nach *which*, *this* und *the* kann *one/ones* ein zählbares Substantiv ersetzen:

I've got two **Maths books** here. **Which one** do we need?
I don't usually like **plays**, but **this one** is really good.

Denk dran:
Man kann nicht alle Substantive zählen.
Man kann z. B. nicht 'one money' sagen.

Unit 2 Step B

§ 3 Die einfache Vergangenheit: regelmäßige Formen
The simple past: regular forms

Yesterday	I	helped	my father.
On Saturday	Becky	played	tennis with David.
Last Friday	it	rained	in the afternoon.
Last week	we	repaired	our skateboards.
Last night	my parents	watched	TV.

- Das *simple past* drückt Ereignisse oder Handlungen aus, die in der Vergangenheit stattgefunden haben und abgeschlossen sind. Deshalb benutzt man es z. B. um Geschichten zu erzählen oder über Erlebnisse zu berichten.

- Das *simple past* der regelmäßigen Verben wird gebildet, indem man die Endung *-ed* an den Infinitiv (ohne *to*) anhängt: *help + ed* → *helped*.
- Die Form des *simple past* ist für alle Personen gleich.
- Da das *simple past* Vorgänge ausdrückt, die vorbei sind, wird es häufig von Zeitangaben begleitet, wie z. B. *last year, on Saturday* usw.
  Solche ‚Signalwörter' zeigen, dass das *simple past* verwendet werden muss.

Man schreibt die regelmäßigen Verben im *simple past* mit *-ed*, aber man **spricht** sie nicht immer gleich:

call	→	called	[d]
help	→	helped	[t]
want	→	wanted	[ɪd]

Einige regelmäßige Verben werden im *simple past* besonders **geschrieben**:

1. *like + ed = liked*
2. *try + ed = tried*
3. *stop + ed = stopped*

Kannst du selbst Regeln hierzu aufstellen?

1. Das stumme End -e fällt weg.
2. Verben, die auf Konsonant + y enden, erhalten die Endung **-ied**.
3. Nach kurzem, betontem Vokal wird ein Endkonsonant verdoppelt.

§ 4 Die einfache Vergangenheit von ‚to be'
The *simple past* of 'to be'

Were you in London last Sunday?	No, I **wasn't**. I **was** in Nottingham.
Was your grandma with you?	Yes, she **was**. We **were** at the shopping centre.
Was it good?	No, it **wasn't**. There **weren't** many shops open.

- Im *simple past* gibt es zwei Verbformen von *to be*: *I/he/she/it* **was**, *you/we/they* **were**

§ 5 Die einfache Vergangenheit: unregelmäßige Formen
The simple past: irregular forms

Im Englischen gibt es – wie auch im Deutschen – regelmäßige und unregelmäßige Verben, z. B.

Infinitive	simple past	
to have	had	Yesterday I **had** breakfast at 8 o'clock.
to go	went	After breakfast I **went** to school.
to see	saw [sɔː]	On my way I **saw** my friend.
to do	did	We **did** five subjects at school.
to get	got	At school I **got** a new book.
to give	gave [geɪv]	Our teacher **gave** us a lot of homework.
to come	came [keɪm]	At 3 o'clock I **came** home.
to say	said [sed]	My mother **said:** 'Do your homework after tea'.

- Während die regelmäßigen Verben im *simple past* alle auf *-ed* enden, gibt es für die unregelmäßigen Verben keine Bildungsregeln. Man muss die einzelnen Formen lernen.
- Auf Seite 182 findest du ein Verzeichnis aller unregelmäßigen Verben, die in diesem Buch vorkommen. Alle anderen Verben in diesem Buch sind regelmäßig.
- Auch bei den unregelmäßigen Verben sind die Formen des *simple past* für **alle** Personen gleich. (Ausnahme: *to be* – siehe § 4).

§ 6 Die Verneinung der einfachen Vergangenheit mit ‚didn't'
Negative sentences in the simple past with 'didn't'

Subject	didn't	Infinitive				
I	didn't	play	football.	I	played	tennis.
He	didn't	like	the headmaster,	but he	liked	his new tutor.
Becky	didn't	do	her homework,	but she	did	a lot of other things.
We	didn't	go	to the supermarket.	We	went	to the cinema.

- Im *simple past* verneint man mit *didn't* (*did not*) + Infinitiv.
  Die Formen sind für alle Personen gleich. (Ausnahme: *to be* – siehe § 4).

Nach *didn't* steht der Infinitiv, nicht das *simple past*.

§ 7 Fragen mit ‚did/didn't' Questions with 'did/didn't'

Question word	did/ didn't	Subject	Verb/ Infinitive		Answer
	Did	you	watch	TV last night?	Yes, I did.
	Did	the girls	play	tennis yesterday?	No, they didn't.
What	**did**	Becky	do	yesterday afternoon?	She did her homework.
Where	**did**	the boys	repair	their skateboards?	In the garage.
How	**did**	Jenny	help	her mother?	She made the tea.
Why	**didn't**	you	take	a photo of me?	Because there was no film in the camera.

- Entscheidungsfragen werden im *simple past* mit *did/didn't* gebildet.
- Auch Fragen mit Fragewörtern werden im *simple past* mit *did/didn't* gebildet.

Unit 3 Step B

§ 8 Die Steigerung von Adjektiven mit ‚-er' und ‚-est'
The comparison of adjectives with '-er' and '-est'

Man kann Adjektive steigern um Dinge miteinander zu vergleichen. Die Steigerung von Adjektiven mit ‚*-er*' und ‚*-est*' ist ganz ähnlich wie die Steigerung im Deutschen: kalt – käl**ter** – der käl**teste**.

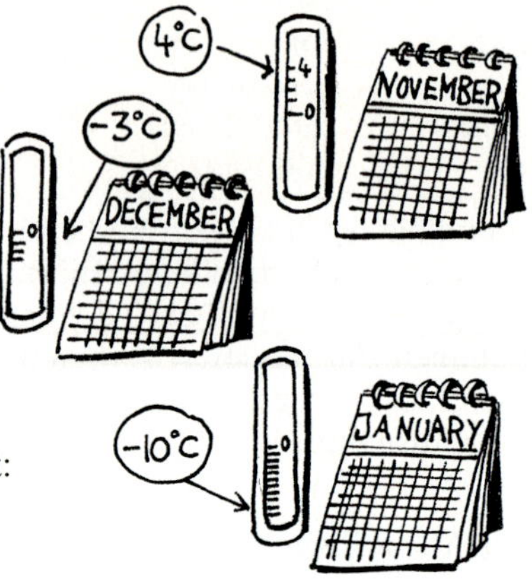

> November is a **cold** month.
>
> December is **colder**.
>
> And January is usually the **coldest** month of the year.

- Man bildet die 1. Steigerungsform (*comparative*), indem man **-er** an die Grundform (*positive*) anhängt: cold + **er** → cold**er**.
- Die 2. Steigerungsform (*superlative*) wird gebildet, indem man **-est** anhängt: cold + **est** → cold**est**.
- Mit ‚*-er*' und ‚*-est*' werden alle einsilbigen Adjektive gesteigert (z. B. *cheap*, *nice* usw.)
- Mit ‚*-er*' und ‚*-est*' können auch gesteigert werden:
  – zweisilbige Adjektive, die auf *-y* enden (z. B. *dirty*, *easy*, *sunny*, usw.)
  – die zweisilbigen Adjektive *clever*, *quiet* und *simple*.

Die folgenden Besonderheiten muss man beachten:

Beim Schreiben

big	→	bi**gg**er	→	bi**gg**est
nice	→	nic**er**	→	nic**est**
craz**y**	→	craz**ier**	→	craz**iest**

Es gelten hier die gleichen Regeln wie beim Schreiben des *simple past* (vgl. §3).

Bei der Aussprache

lo**ng**	[lɒŋ]
lo**ng**er	[lɒŋgə]
lo**ng**est	[lɒŋgɪst]

Ebenso: *young*

Unregelmäßige Steigerungsformen:

good	→	**better**	→	**(the) best**	–	gut – besser – der/die/das beste
bad	→	**worse**	→	**(the) worst**	–	schlecht – schlechter – der/die/das schlechteste

§ 9 Die Steigerung von Adjektiven mit ‚more' und ‚most'
The comparison of adjectives with 'more' and 'most'

Look at these pullovers. They aren't **expensive**.	teuer
No, they aren't. The white pullovers here are **more expensive**.	teurer
And these black ones are the **most expensive** in the shop.	die teuersten

- Alle Adjektive, die mehr als zwei Silben haben, werden mit **more** und **most** gesteigert: *difficult → more difficult → (the) most difficult.*
- Auch die meisten zweisilbigen Adjektive, die nicht auf *-y* enden, werden mit **more** und **most** gesteigert: z. B. *boring*, *careful*, *famous*, *nervous*.

§ 10 Der Vergleich im Satz Sentences with comparisons

Es gibt drei verschiedene Möglichkeiten Gleichheit oder Ungleichheit auszudrücken:

Gleichheit

1. 	The teddy is **as big as** the cat. It is **as expensive as** the cat, too.	… so groß wie … … so teuer wie …

Ungleichheit

2. 	The frog is **not as big as** the cat. And it is**n't as expensive as** the cat.	… nicht so groß wie … … nicht so teuer wie …
3. 	The cat is **bigger than** the frog. And it is **more expensive than** the frog.	… größer als … … teurer als …

- Man kann bei Ungleichheit auch **not so … as** verwenden: *Nottingham is **not so big as** London.*

Verwechsle nicht *than* mit *then* (= dann)!

Unit 4 Step B

§ 11 Das ‚will'-Futur
The will-future

Es gibt im Englischen mehrere Möglichkeiten, mit denen man zukünftiges Handeln oder zukünftiges Geschehen ausdrücken kann.

Du kennst bereits das *going to*-Futur, das man verwendet, wenn man über eine geplante zukünftige Handlung spricht:
I'm going to play tennis this afternoon. –
Ich habe vor heute Nachmittag Tennis zu spielen.

Man kann auch das *will*-Futur verwenden um auszudrücken, was in der Zukunft passieren wird.

Next year Robert **will be** 14.
His birthday **will be** on a Sunday.
It **won't rain** tomorrow, it'**ll be** fine.

- Man kann das *will*-Futur verwenden um etwas über zukünftige Ereignisse zu sagen, die nicht von eigenen Entscheidungen abhängen.

I think everyone **will like** the new play.
I hope people **won't laugh** at me.
I hope it'**ll be** OK. – Yes, it **will**.
Robert is sure he **won't be** nervous.

- Man kann das *will*-Futur auch verwenden um Vermutungen über die Zukunft zu äußern. Diese Vermutungen werden oft mit *I hope, I'm sure, I think* eingeleitet.

- Das *will*-Futur wird aus *will* + Infinitiv (ohne *to*) gebildet.
- *Will* ist in allen Personen gleich.
- Häufig wird statt *will* die Kurzform *'ll* verwendet.
- Die Kurzform der Verneinung *will not* ist *won't* [wəʊnt].

§ 12 Nebensätze mit ‚when'
Subordinate clauses with 'when'

Nebensatz mit *when* (*simple present*)	Hauptsatz (*will-future*)
When Robert **acts** in the new play,	he **won't be** nervous.
When Becky **is** 14,	she **will be** in year 9.

- In einem Satzgefüge (Hauptsatz + Nebensatz), das sich auf die Zukunft bezieht, steht im Hauptsatz das *will*-Futur und im Nebensatz das *simple present.*
- Das Satzgefüge kann, genau wie im Deutschen, auch mit dem Hauptsatz beginnen: *Robert won't be nervous when he acts in the new play.*

§ 13 Bedingungssätze
Conditional sentences

Ein Bedingungssatz besteht aus einem *if*-Satz und einem Hauptsatz.
Der *if*-Satz drückt eine Bedingung aus. Der Hauptsatz drückt aus, was passiert, falls diese Bedingung erfüllt wird.

If-Satz (*simple present*)	Hauptsatz (*will-future*)
If the weather **is** nice tomorrow,	we'**ll go** swimming.
But if it **rains**,	we **won't go**. We'**ll stay** at home and **play** a game.
If you **don't wear** your anoraks,	you'**ll get** wet.

- Der Hauptsatz wird mit dem *will*-Futur gebildet, der *if*-Satz steht dann immer im *simple present*. (Vgl. § 12, *when*-Sätze)
- Das *simple present* im *if*-Satz drückt aus, dass die Bedingung erfüllbar ist: d. h. es ist möglich, dass das Wetter morgen schön wird.
- Bedingungssätze können entweder mit dem *if*-Satz oder dem Hauptsatz beginnen:

If it rains, I'll get wet.
I'll get wet, if it rains.

If I go to the shops tomorrow, I'll get you a comic.
– Falls …

When I go to the shops tomorrow, I'll get you a comic.
– Wenn … (d. h. ich habe es fest vor).

Unit 4 Step C

§ 14 Das ‚will'-Futur (besonderer Gebrauch)
The will-future (special use)

Man kann das *will*-Futur auch verwenden, wenn man jemandem schnell Hilfe anbietet oder sich plötzlich entscheidet etwas zu tun:

It's cold in here.	– I'**ll close** the window. OK?
I'm so hungry.	– I'**ll make** you something to eat in a minute.
I've got so much to do today.	– Don't worry, we'**ll help** you.

Unit 5 Step B

§ 15 ‚Some' und ‚any'
'Some' and 'any'

Im Englischen drückt man eine unbestimmte Menge oder Anzahl (im Sinne von ‚etwas', ‚einige' oder ‚ein paar') mit *some* oder *any* aus.

Bejahte Aussagen mit **some**	Fragen mit **any**	Verneinte Aussagen mit **not any**
I'm going to make **some** sandwiches.	Have we got **any** bread?	No, there is**n't any** bread.
Ich möchte ein paar belegte Brote machen.	Haben wir (etwas) Brot?	Nein, es ist kein Brot (mehr) da.
OK, I'll get **some** bread.	Do we need **any** eggs?	Yes, we do. There are**n't any** in the kitchen.
Gut. Ich hole (etwas) Brot.	Brauchen wir (–) Eier?	Ja. In der Küche sind keine.

- In bejahten Sätzen verwendet man *some*, in Fragen und verneinten Sätzen meistens *any*.
- Im Deutschen bleiben *some* und *any* oft unübersetzt:

  Do you need any help?
  Brauchst du Hilfe?

§ 16 Zusammensetzungen von ‚some' und ‚any'
Compounds of 'some' and 'any'

Wie *some* und *any* werden auch ihre Zusammensetzungen verwendet.

Bejahte Aussagen	Fragen	Verneinte Aussagen
I want to buy **something** for Jenny's birthday.	Can you think of **anything**?	I'm sorry, I can't think of **anything.**
We must ask **somebody.**	Can you see **anybody**?	I'm sorry. I can't see **anybody.**
My purse must be **somewhere.**	Is it **anywhere** in the kitchen?	No, I can't find it **anywhere.**

§ 17 Das ‚going to'-Futur und das ‚will'-Futur
The 'going to'-future and the 'will'-future

Auf einen Blick

Du kennst schon die zwei Zukunftsformen ‚going to'-Futur und ‚will'-Futur (vgl. § 11 und § 14).
Welche Form man verwendet, hängt von der Sprechabsicht ab:
Hat man einen Plan oder möchte man eine Vorhersage machen oder einen plötzlichen Entschluss fassen?

1. **going to**
Pläne, Vorhaben
What **are** they **going to do** at the weekend? Sarah **is going to see** Jack Ripple. Simon and Mike **are going to play** football. They **aren't going to play** computer games.

2. **will**
a) **Vorhersagen, Vermutungen**
His birthday **will be** on a Sunday this year. I hope it **won't rain** then.
b) **schnell gefasste Entschlüsse**
I don't know the way to the bus station. – We**'ll come** with you and show you.

Während man im Deutschen oft die Gegenwart verwendet um auszudrücken, was in der Zukunft geschieht, ist dies im Englischen meistens nicht möglich. Vergleiche:

Am Sonntag besuchen wir unsere Oma.	Warte, ich helfe dir.
We**'re going to visit** our grandma on Sunday.	Wait, **I'll help** you.

Unit 5 Step C

§ 18 ‚Some' in Fragen
'Some' in questions

Im Englischen benutzt man *some* in Fragen, die eigentlich eine höfliche Bitte oder ein höfliches Angebot sind.

Could I have **some** sugar, please? Would you like **some** biscuits?	Könnte ich bitte etwas Zucker haben? Möchten Sie (ein paar) Kekse haben?

Unit 6 Step B

§ 19 Das Perfekt
The present perfect

Mit dem *present perfect* drückt man aus, dass eine Handlung oder ein Ereignis, das in der Vergangenheit stattgefunden hat, in der Gegenwart noch von Bedeutung ist.

The man is washing his car.

He **has washed** the car. It is clean now.

Hier ist die Handlung (das Waschen) vorbei, aber das Ergebnis ist in der Gegenwart noch sichtbar: Das Auto ist sauber.

Das *present perfect* verwendet man auch, wenn man über Handlungen spricht, die gerade erst abgeschlossen wurden (häufig in Sätzen mit *just*).

Handlung	Ergebnis
zuvor	jetzt
Mrs Penrose **has cooked** lunch. I'**ve** just **collected** all the dirty clothes. David **has taken** a photo of Jenny.	They can eat it now. We can wash them now. Here it is. She looks great.

- Das *present perfect* wird gebildet aus *have/has* und der dritten Form des Verbs, dem *past participle*: I **have** walk**ed.** He **has** walk**ed.**
- Bei regelmäßigen Verben wird das *past participle* aus dem Infinitiv (ohne *to*) und der Endung *-ed* gebildet: *cook + ed* ⟶ *cooked*. (Bei diesen Verben ist also die Form des *past participle* gleich mit der Form des *simple past*.)
- Für die Bildung der unregelmäßigen Formen des *past participle* (*made, had, been* usw.) gibt es keine Regel. Deshalb muss man diese Formen lernen. (Auf Seite 182 findest du eine Liste aller unregelmäßigen Verben, die in **Green Line New 1** und **2** vorkommen. Alle anderen Verben in diesen Büchern sind regelmäßig.)

Beachte beim Übersetzen:

Mini has eaten all the dog biscuits.
Mini **hat** alle Hundekuchen **gefressen.**

Maxi has come into the house because it is raining.
Maxi **ist** ins Haus **gekommen,** weil es regnet.

§ 20 Das Perfekt: Fragen, Verneinungen und Kurzantworten
The present perfect: questions, negative sentences and short answers

Frage					Kurzantwort/Verneinung				
	has/ have	Subjekt	*past participle*			Subjekt	*has/ have*	*past participle*	
	Has	David	made	the fruit salad?	Yes,	he	has.		
	Have	they	eaten	it yet?	No,	they	haven't.		
	Has	Andreas	tasted	it?		He	hasn't	seen	it yet.
Who	has		done	the washing-up?		Nobody	has.		
						They	haven't	finished	lunch yet.

- In Fragen und Verneinungen mit dem *present perfect* verwendet man häufig das Wort *yet* bzw. *not yet*:

Have you done your homework ***yet?*** – Hast du **schon** deine Hausaufgaben gemacht?
*No, I have****n't*** *done it* ***yet.*** – Nein, ich habe sie **noch nicht** gemacht.

Beachte die unterschiedliche Wortstellung im Deutschen und im Englischen:

Has she written ***the letter****?* – *Yes, she has. She has written* ***the letter.***

Hat sie **den Brief** geschrieben? – Ja. Sie hat **den Brief** geschrieben.

Unit 7 Step B

§ 21 Das Perfekt und die einfache Vergangenheit
The present perfect and the simple past

Auf einen Blick

present perfect	simple past
Robert **has tidied** up his room. It's tidy now. Jenny **has made** tea. We can have it now.	He **tidied** it up **after breakfast.** She **made** it **ten minutes ago.**
Have you **ever eaten** porridge? **I've never been** to Scotland.	Yes, I **ate** porridge **last year** in England. But I **was** in Wales **last June.**

- Mit dem *present perfect* kann man ausdrücken, dass sich etwas in der Vergangenheit abgespielt hat, was jetzt noch wirksam ist (vgl. § 19).
- Das *present perfect* wird auch verwendet, wenn man einen Zeitraum beschreiben will, der von der Vergangenheit bis in die Gegenwart reicht. Signalwörter sind *ever, never, already, often, yet.*

- Mit dem *simple past* drückt man aus, dass etwas in der Vergangenheit stattgefunden hat und abgeschlossen ist (vgl. §§ 3–7).
- Daher wird es häufig von Signalwörtern begleitet, die sich mit ‚wann' erfragen lassen, z. B. *yesterday, last week, the day before yesterday, on Monday* etc.

Ich **habe** gestern eine Pizza **gegessen.** – *I* ***ate*** *a pizza yesterday.*

Unit 7 **Step D**

§ 22 **Sätze mit Konjunktionen**
Sentences with conjunctions

They went on **until** they came to a small farm.	… bis …
It was a difficult walk **so that** they came home very tired.	… so dass …
Although it started to rain, they went on.	Obwohl …
They turned back **after** the weather changed.	… nachdem …
Before they left, Mr Campbell warned them about Ben Nevis.	Bevor …
Get back **as soon as** you can.	… sobald …
I felt really sorry **because** the holiday was over.	… weil …

- Diese Konjunktionen verbinden einen Hauptsatz mit einem Nebensatz. Man nennt sie auch Bindewörter.

Unit 8 **Step B**

§ 23 **‚Must' und ‚needn't' und die Ersatzform ‚have to'**
'Must' and 'needn't' and the substitute form 'have to'

Must (müssen) und *needn't* (nicht müssen) können nur im *simple present* verwendet werden. Für die anderen Zeiten verwendet man eine Form von *have to*.

simple present	simple past	future
must		
I must be there at one o'clock.		
have to	**had to**	**will have to**
She has to stay in bed.	I had to get up early.	I will have to go soon.
needn't		
You needn't come with me.		
don't/doesn't have to	**didn't have to**	**won't have to**
He doesn't have to work today.	They didn't have to pay for it.	We won't have to walk. There's a bus.

- Fragen und Verneinungen mit *have to* werden im *simple present* mit *do/does* und im *simple past* mit *did* gebildet.

  Do you **have to** work today?
  – No, I **don't have to** work all week.

  Did you **have to** stay in bed yesterday?
  – No, **I didn't have to** stay in bed. I could get up.

- Man benutzt die Form *have to*, wenn man ausdrücken möchte, dass ein Zwang von außen besteht: *You have to do your homework now!*
- *Must* verwendet man, wenn man ein inneres Bedürfnis ausdrücken möchte: *I must find a present for Mum's birthday!*

§ 24 ‚Can/could' und die Ersatzform ‚be able to'
'Can/could' and the substitute form 'be able to'

Can ist wie *must* ein unvollständiges Hilfsverb, mit dem man nicht alle Zeiten bilden kann. Für die Zeitformen, die mit *can* oder *could* nicht gebildet werden können, nimmt man eine Form von *be able to*.

simple present	simple past	future
can	**could**	
David can play the guitar.	Last year he could only play easy songs.	
can't	**couldn't**	
I can't go to work today.	I couldn't get up at six o'clock.	
am/is/are able to	**was/were able to**	**will be able to**
Jenny is able to write in German and English.	Last summer her parents were able to visit her.	Next summer they'll be able to visit Berlin.
am not/isn't/aren't able to	**wasn't/weren't able to**	**won't be able to**
She isn't able to sing this song.	I wasn't able to do my homework.	They won't be able to come. They're ill.

§ 25 ‚Mustn't' und die Ersatzform ‚be allowed to'
'Mustn't' and the substitute form 'be allowed to'

Auch *mustn't* (nicht dürfen) kann nur im *simple present* verwendet werden. Für die anderen Zeiten verwendet man eine Form von *be allowed to*.

simple present	simple past	future
mustn't		
You mustn't be late for school.		
am not/isn't/aren't allowed to	**wasn't/weren't allowed to**	**won't be allowed to**
We aren't allowed to eat sweets before lunch.	I wasn't allowed to go home early yesterday.	They won't be allowed to see the film tomorrow.
am/is/are allowed to	**was/were allowed to**	**will be allowed to**
You're allowed to go home after the test.	She was allowed to go to bed late last Saturday.	They'll be allowed to have an ice cream later.

Auf einen Blick

§ 26 Das Possessivpronomen
The possessive pronoun

Possessivbegleiter + Substantiv			Possessivpronomen		
Is that	my	crayon?	No, it isn't	mine.	
Is that	your	comic?	Is it really	yours?	
Robert can't find	his	books.	Well, these here aren't	his.	
Becky hasn't got	her	pencils.	These must be	hers.	
These are	our	posters.	And those are	ours,	too.
Are these	your	folders?	Or are	yours	green?
These aren't	their	schoolbags.	But they can't find	theirs.	

- Das Possessivpronomen gibt an, (zu) wem etwas gehört.
- Wie im Deutschen verwendet man ein Possessivpronomen, wenn man ein Substantiv nicht wiederholen möchte:
  *Is this **your book**? – Yes, it must be **yours**.*
  Ist das **dein Buch**? – Ja, das muss **deins** sein.

§ 27 Der bestimmte Artikel: besonderer Gebrauch
The definite article: special use

Barry had a stomach-ache and had to go	to		hospital.
Robert and I didn't know that he was	in		hospital.
The Happy Helpers work	at	the	hospital.
They took all his homework	to	the	hospital.

- Wenn man an den Zweck von *hospital* denkt (also an einen Ort, an dem Kranke gepflegt werden), verwendet man keinen Artikel.
- Wenn man nur an das Gebäude denkt (in das zum Beispiel auch Besucher gehen), dann verwendet man den bestimmten Artikel.

Das Gleiche gilt auch für *school*:

The children go to school every morning.
Look at the school over there!

⟨A joke⟩

"Doctor, my eyes are so bad.
I think I'll have to go to hospital!"

"You're right. This is a fish and chip shop!"

Unit 9 Step B

§ 28 Die Verlaufsform der Vergangenheit
The past progressive

Im Englischen gibt es zu jeder Verbzeit eine *simple form* und eine *progressive form*. So gibt es neben dem *simple past* (vgl. §§ 3–7) auch das *past progressive*:

- Das *past progressive* wird gebraucht, wenn man betonen möchte, dass ein Ereignis in der Vergangenheit längere Zeit dauerte.
- Das *past progressive* wird gebildet aus der Vergangenheitsform von *to be* (= *was/were*) und der *-ing*-Form:

  I/he/she/it **was working.**
  We/you/they **were working.**

- Häufig wird das *past progressive* mit *while*, das *simple past* dagegen mit *when* verbunden.

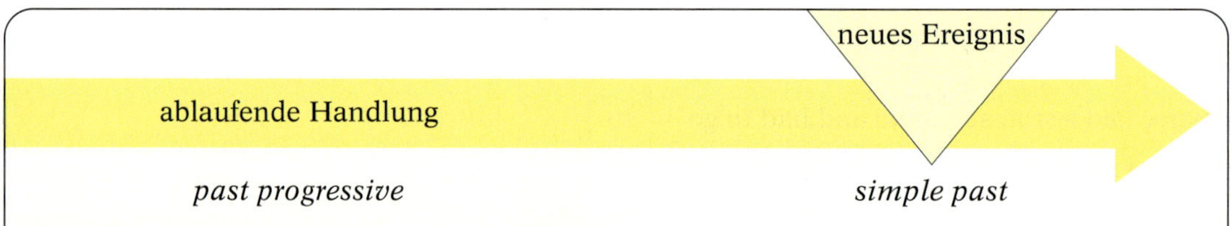

The Dixons **were** just **having** breakfast	**when** the milkman **came.**
Mrs Dixon **was eating** cornflakes	**when** Sarah **filmed** her.
While Becky **was working** in the garden,	she suddenly **saw** a rabbit.
While the boys **were playing** football,	it **started** to rain.

- In diesen Sätzen drückt das *past progressive* aus, dass etwas passierte und noch nicht abgeschlossen war. Man übersetzt die Zeit etwa mit: „… war gerade dabei, etwas zu tun."
  Das *simple past* drückt aus, dass ein neues Ereignis eintrat.

- Die Anordnung der Sätze ist dabei egal.
  Vergleiche:
  – *The Dixons were having breakfast when the milkman came.*
  – *When the milkman came, the Dixons were having breakfast.*

§ 29 Adverbien der Art und Weise
Adverbs of manner

adjective		adverb	
John is very **quiet.**	... ist sehr ruhig.	John speaks **quietly.**	... spricht ruhig.
John is a **quiet** boy.	... ist ein ruhiger ...		

- Adjektive geben an, wie eine Person oder Sache ist.
  ***What** is he **like**? – He is **quiet**.*
- Sie stehen vor einem Substantiv *(quiet boy)* oder nach dem Verb *to be (is quiet)*.

- Adverbien der Art und Weise *(adverbs of manner)* geben an, wie etwas geschieht.
  How** does he speak? – He speaks **quietly.
- Sie werden meistens aus Adjektiven gebildet, indem man *-ly* anhängt:
  quiet + ly ⟶ quietly
- Sie stehen meistens am Satzende.

- Im Deutschen haben Adjektive und Adverbien die gleiche Form.

Besondere Formen

adjective		adverb
good	⟶	well
fast	⟶	fast
hard	⟶	hard

Beachte beim Schreiben:

adjective		adverb
careful	⟶	careful**ly**
hungry	⟶	hungr**ily**
terrible	⟶	terrib**ly**

Unit 10 Step B

§ 30 Die Steigerung des Adverbs
The comparison of adverbs of manner

Die Steigerung dieser Adverbien wird nach den gleichen Regeln gebildet wie die Steigerung der Adjektive (vgl. § 8).

My brother plays the guitar **beautifully.**	... spielt schön.
My father can play it **more beautifully.**	... spielt schöner.
But my mother plays it **most beautifully.**	... spielt am schönsten.

- Adverbien mit der Endung *-ly* werden, so wie mehrsilbige Adjektive, mit *more* und *most* gesteigert.

I work **hard.**
My friend works **harder.**
But my dad works **hardest.**

- Einsilbige Adverbien werden wie die einsilbigen Adjektive mit *-er* und *-est* gesteigert.

Wie bei den Adjektiven gibt es bei den Adverbien zwei unregelmäßige Formen. Nur die Grundformen sind unterschiedlich, die Steigerungsformen sind gleich:

Adjektiv	good	better	best
Adverb	well	better	best

Adjektiv	bad	worse	worst
Adverb	badly	worse	worst

§ 31 Vergleiche mit Adverbien
Comparisons with adverbs

Wie bei den Adjektiven gibt es bei den Adverbien drei verschiedene Möglichkeiten Gleichheit oder Ungleichheit auszudrücken (vgl. § 10).

Gleichheit	
as … as	My mother works **as hard as** my father. Mark can do puzzles **as quickly as** Becky.

Ungleichheit	
… than …	Sarah plays cards **more cleverly than** Robert. My brother can run **faster than** everyone else.
not as … as	Robert can't play cards **as cleverly as** Sarah. No one runs **as fast as** my brother.

Grammar list

German	English	§
Steigerung von **Adjektiven** mit *-er/-est*	comparison of adjectives with *-er/-est*	**8**, 9
April is a warm month, June is warmer, but July is the warmest month.		
Steigerung von Adjektiven mit *more/most*	comparison of adjectives with *more/most*	**9**
Our homework isn't difficult. This exercise is more difficult. And that one is most difficult.		
Bestimmter **Artikel** besonderer Gebrauch	definite article special use	**27**
I didn't want to go to hospital, but when I saw the hospital I felt better.		
Adverbien der Art und Weise	adverbs of manner	**29**, 30, 31
She works very quickly.		
Steigerung des Adverbs	comparison of adverbs	**30**
But her sister works more quickly, and her friend works most quickly.		
Vergleiche mit Adverbien	comparisons with adverbs	**31**
Peter speaks German as well as John, better than Sarah, but not as well as Mr Cooper.		
Be able to*/can/could*	*be able to/can/could*	**24**
I can draw a dog. Last year I couldn't do that. Soon I'll be able to draw other animals.		
Be allowed to*/mustn't*	*be allowed to/mustn't*	**25**
We are allowed to eat in the playground, but we mustn't smoke.		
Bedingungssätze mit *if*	conditional sentences with *if*	**13**
If it doesn't rain tomorrow, I'll go swimming.		
Fragewörter *what/which*	question words *what/which*	**1**
What's for lunch?/Which do you want?		
Going-to-Futur und **will-Futur**	going-to future and will future	**17**
The weather will be nice tomorrow. I'm going to visit a friend at the seaside.		
Have to*/must/needn't*	*have to/must/needn't*	**23**
We have to wear a uniform, but the teachers needn't.		
Konjunktionen	conjunctions	**22**
before, so that, although, after, until, as soon as, because		
Nebensätze mit *when*	subordinate clauses with *when*	**12**
When I'm fourteen, I'll get a new bike.		
Some und any	*some* and *any*	**15**, 16, 18
Have you got any milk? – No, there isn't any milk here. But there is some milk in the kitchen.		
Some und *any* und ihre Zusammensetzungen	*some* and *any* and their compounds	**16**
I want to buy something for Mum. Can you think of anything?		
Some in Fragen	*some* in questions	**18**
Could I have some tea, please? – Of course, would you like some sugar with it?		

German	English	§
Perfekt	present perfect	**19**, 20, 21
He has done the washing-up. The plates are clean now.		
Perfekt: Fragen, Verneinungen und Kurzantworten	present perfect: questions, negative sentences and short answers	**20**
Has Grandma made a cake? – No, she hasn't. *Who has made it, then? – Nobody has. There isn't any cake.*		
Perfekt und einfache Vergangenheit	present perfect and simple past	**21**
Ben has done his homework. He did it yesterday evening.		
Possessivpronomen	possessive determiner	**26**
mine, yours, his, hers, its, ours, yours, theirs		
Stützwort *one/ones*	prop word *one/ones*	**2**
I've got three footballs. Two white ones and a brown one.		
Einfache Vergangenheit regelmäßige Formen	simple past: regular forms	**3**, 4, 5, 6, 7, 21
Yesterday I helped my father in the garden.		
Einfache Vergangenheit von *to be*	simple past of to be	**4**
I was there last week. And where were you?		
Einfache Vergangenheit: unregelmäßige Formen	simple past: irregular forms	**5**
My friend came last Friday. She gave me a nice present.		
Einfache Vergangenheit: Verneinung	simple past: negation	**6**
I didn't know this.		
Einfache Vergangenheit: Fragen mit *did/didn't*	simple past: questions with did/didn't	**7**
Did you see the film last night? What did you think of it?		
Vergleich im Satz	sentences with comparisons	**10**
Anna is as tall as my mother. But she isn't as tall as my father. *My father is taller than Anna.*		
Verlaufsform der Vergangenheit	past progressive	**28**
I tried to phone you last night. What were you doing?		
Will-Futur	will-future	**11**, 14, 17
I won't be fifteen, I'll be fourteen next year.		
Will-Futur: besonderer Gebrauch	will-future: special use	**14**
It's so warm in here. – OK, I'll open the window for you.		

Vocabulary

Englische Lautschrift

Vokale

[ɑː]	c**ar**, f**a**ther
[ʌ]	n**u**mber, b**u**s, m**o**ther
[e]	y**e**s, p**e**n, fr**ie**nd
[ə]	**a** sister
[ɜː]	g**ir**l, h**er**, t**ur**n
[æ]	b**a**g, c**a**t, th**a**t
[ɪ]	**i**t, a b**i**t, s**i**x
[iː]	sh**e**, s**ee**, pl**ea**se
[ɒ]	**o**n, d**o**g, wh**a**t
[ɔː]	d**oor**, f**our**, m**or**ning
[ʊ]	p**u**t, l**oo**k
[uː]	y**ou**, tw**o**, bl**ue**

Konsonanten

[j]	**y**es, **y**ou
[l]	**l**et's, b**l**ue, schoo**l**
[ŋ]	morni**ng**, si**ng**
[ŋg]	E**ng**lish
[r]	**r**adio, **r**ed
[s]	**s**ee, **s**i**s**ter, cla**ss**
[z]	i**s**, dog**s**, car**s**
[ʒ]	televi**s**ion
[dʒ]	**G**erman, **J**enny
[ʃ]	**sh**e, fi**sh**
[tʃ]	tea**ch**er, **ch**ild
[ð]	**th**e, **th**is, mo**th**er
[θ]	**th**ank you, **th**ing
[v]	**v**et, o**f**
[w]	**o**ne, **wh**at, sand**w**ich

Doppellaute

[aɪ]	n**i**ce, f**i**ve, b**ye**
[aʊ]	n**ow**, p**ou**nd
[eə]	th**ere**, ch**air**, th**eir**
[eɪ]	n**a**me, s**ay**, t**a**ble
[ɪə]	h**ere**, cl**ear**
[ɔɪ]	b**oy**
[əʊ]	n**o**, g**o**, sh**ow**
[ʊə]	**you're**

[ː]	bedeutet, dass der vorangehende Laut lang ist, z. B. blue [bluː]
[ˈ]	bedeutet, dass auf der folgenden Silbe die Hauptbetonung liegt, z. B. hello [həˈləʊ]
[ˌ]	bedeutet, dass auf der folgenden Silbe die Nebenbetonung liegt, z. B. washing up [ˌwɒʃɪŋ‿ˈʌp]
[‿]	zwischen zwei Wörtern bedeutet, dass man den letzten Laut des ersten Wortes zum nächsten Wort hinüberzieht, z. B. come on[kʌm‿ˈɒn]

Das englische Alphabet

a [eɪ]	g [dʒiː]	m [em]	s [es]	y [waɪ]
b [biː]	h [eɪtʃ]	n [en]	t [tiː]	z [zed]
c [siː]	i [aɪ]	o [əʊ]	u [juː]	
d [diː]	j [dʒeɪ]	p [piː]	v [viː]	
e [iː]	k [keɪ]	q [kjuː]	w [ˈdʌbljuː]	
f [ef]	l [el]	r [ɑː]	x [eks]	

a) Aufbau des Vokabulars

Das Vokabular ist genau wie in deinem Buch vom letzten Schuljahr aufgebaut:
In der linken Spalte findest du die englischen Wörter in der Reihenfolge, in der sie in der Unit vorkommen. Dahinter steht die Lautschrift in eckigen Klammern. Wie du die Lautschrift lesen musst, steht auf Seite 129.

In der mittleren Spalte stehen Beispielsätze oder kleine Zeichnungen sowie wichtige Hinweise, die dir beim Lernen helfen.

In der rechten Spalte findest du eine deutsche Übersetzung des englischen Wortes. Vergiss aber nicht, dass sich Wörter aus einer Sprache nicht einfach in die andere übersetzen lassen. Deshalb werden manchmal mehrere deutsche Übersetzungsmöglichkeiten angeboten.
Wie im Buch vom Vorjahr findest du Tipps zum Vokabellernen in den Kästchen vor den ersten Units. Außerdem findest du *vocabulary boxes*, die Wörter und Wendungen wiederholen und zusammenfassen. Du lernst sie am besten in Gruppen.

b) Abkürzungen und Zeichen

(pl) Plural, Mehrzahl
(sg) Singular, Einzahl

= ist gleich
←→ ist der Gegensatz von

° Bei Wörtern mit diesem Zeichen frag bitte deine Lehrerin oder deinen Lehrer, ob du sie lernen musst. (Erläuterungen hierzu finden sich auf Seite 165.)

Erinnerst du dich noch an meine Lerntipps vom letzten Schuljahr? Auch für das vor dir liegende Schuljahr sind diese Tipps gut zu gebrauchen:
Also denk dran:

- Du lernst Wörter schneller und leichter, wenn du sie dir in kleinen Lernportionen von 10–15 Wörtern vornimmst. Du lernst deine Wörter sicher schon so, indem du die englische oder deutsche Spalte abdeckst. Dies ist auch weiterhin sinnvoll.
- Die Vokabellernkartei kann auch in diesem Jahr als „Vokabellernmaschine" genutzt werden. Im Workbook findest du einen Bastelbogen, mit dem du dir eine Vokabellernkartei basteln kannst. Ansonsten kannst du auch einen Schuhkarton nehmen.
- Ganz schwierige Wörter kannst du dir auf Lernplakate oder Zettel schreiben und zu Hause an die Wand hängen. So wirst du bei jedem Hinsehen daran erinnert.
- Man kann Wörter auch mit einem Partner üben und wiederholen. Man kann sie gegenseitig abfragen oder man kann das „Remember-Spiel" zusammen spielen. Es geht so:
  Schreib die englischen Wörter, die du lernen willst, auf kleine Zettel. Auf die Rückseite jedes Zettels schreibst du in einer anderen Farbe die deutsche Bedeutung. Breite die Karten mit der deutschen Bedeutung nach oben aus. Wenn du den englischen Begriff nennen kannst, darfst du die Karte einsammeln. Wenn du beim Überprüfen feststellst, dass deine Antwort nicht richtig war, musst du die Karte wieder hinlegen.
  Das Spiel geht natürlich auch umgekehrt.
- **Und ganz wichtig:** Du behältst neu gelernte Wörter besser, wenn du sie dir mehrmals vornimmst und sie zusätzlich vor dem Einschlafen noch einmal ansiehst.

Unit 1 Welcome back

Step A **A new school year**

2 °**I spy** (with my little eye ...) [ˌaɪ ˈspaɪ]		Ich sehe was, was du nicht siehst (*Spiel*)
°to **spy** [spaɪ]		sehen, erspähen
something [ˈsʌmθɪŋ]		etwas
beginning with ... [bɪˈgɪnɪŋ wɪð]		was mit ... anfängt
to **begin** [bɪˈgɪn]		beginnen, anfangen

Step A **The wrong lesson**

Technology [tekˈnɒlədʒɪ]	Achte auf die Aussprache!	Computerunterricht, technisches Werken
timetable [ˈtaɪmˌteɪbl]		Stundenplan
which [wɪtʃ]		welche/r/s
subject [ˈsʌbdʒɪkt]	Technology or English? Which is your favourite *subject*?	Fach
Science [ˈsaɪəns]	Beachte die Aussprache und die Schreibung!	Naturwissenschaft(en)
break [breɪk]		Pause
Art [ɑːt]		Kunst
°**Humanities** (*pl*) [hjuːˈmænətɪz]		(*in der Schule*) Geschichte und Erdkunde
°**PE (Physical Education)** [ˌpiː ˈiː/ˌfɪzɪkl‿ˌedjuːˈkeɪʃn]		Sportunterricht
°**RE (Religious Education)** [ˌɑːr‿ˈiː/ rɪˌlɪdʒəs‿ˌedjuːˈkeɪʃn]		Religionsunterricht
Maths [mæθs]	*Maths* is my favourite subject.	Mathematikunterricht, Mathe
History [ˈhɪstrɪ]		Geschichte
Geography [dʒɪˈɒgrəfɪ]		Erdkunde, Geografie
5 b) **both** [bəʊθ]		beide

Step B **The junior play**

°**junior** [ˈdʒuːnjə]		Unterstufen-
play [pleɪ]		Theaterstück
notice board [ˈnəʊtɪs bɔːd]		Schwarzes Brett
meeting [ˈmiːtɪŋ]	*to meet* → meeting	Treffen, Besprechung
notice [ˈnəʊtɪs]	Achte auf die deutsche Bedeutung!	Aushang, Schild
the one at the bottom [ðə ˈwʌn]		der (Aushang) ganz unten
funny ones (*pl*) [ˈfʌnɪ wʌnz]		lustige (Aushänge)

Step B **The new pupil**

John [dʒɒn]		*männl. Vorname*
°**Chicago** [ʃɪ'kɑːgəʊ]		*Großstadt in den USA*
America [ə'merɪkə]	Achte auf die Schreibung!	Amerika
6 °**Stevenson** ['stiːvnsn]		*Familienname*

Step C **Activities**

°**bird watcher** ['bɜːd ˌwɒtʃə]		Vogelbeobachter/in
bird [bɜːd]		Vogel
club [klʌb]		Klub, Verein
piano [pɪ'ænəʊ]		Klavier
date [deɪt]		Datum, Termin
term [tɜːm]		Trimester, Schuljahresdrittel
climbing ['klaɪmɪŋ]	Achte auf die Aussprache!	Bergsteigen, Klettern
°**Patterson** ['pætəsn]		*Familienname*
detail ['diːteɪl]		Detail, Einzelheit
to **try** [traɪ]	*Try* table tennis. It's fun!	versuchen, (aus)probieren
table tennis ['teɪbl ˌtenɪs]		Tischtennis
°**fan** [fæn]		Fan
at lunchtime [ət 'lʌntʃtaɪm]	*At lunchtime* we can do a lot of things.	in der Mittagspause
to **join** [dʒɔɪn]		beitreten, Mitglied werden
player ['pleɪə]		Spieler
sports centre ['spɔːts ˌsentə]		Sportzentrum
°**Singh** [sɪŋ]		*Familienname*
⟨3⟩ poem ['pəʊɪm]		Gedicht
over ['əʊvə]		vorbei
to end [end]		enden, beenden

Step D **Simon's new friend**

Barry ['bærɪ]		*männl. Vorname*
Jenkins ['dʒeŋkɪnz]		*Familienname*
Mike [maɪk]		*männl. Vorname*
bully ['bʊlɪ]		Rabauke, Rüpel, Tyrann
worried about ['wʌrɪd]		besorgt wegen
probably ['prɒbəblɪ]		wahrscheinlich
over ['əʊvə]		vorbei, zu Ende
corridor ['kɒrɪdɔː]		Korridor, Gang
at once [ət 'wʌns]	*at once* = right away	sofort
to **turn round** [ˌtɜːn 'raʊnd]		sich umdrehen
Off you go! ['ɒf jʊ ˌgəʊ]		Fort mit dir/euch!
full of ['fʊl‿əv]	Look, the playground is *full of* children.	voll (von)
suddenly ['sʌdnlɪ]		plötzlich
outside ['aʊtsaɪd]	*outside* ⟷ *inside*	(draußen) vor
newsagent's ['njuːzˌeɪdʒnts]	*At the newsagent's* ist eine Kurzform und bedeutet eigentlich: *At the newsagent's shop*.	*Laden für Zeitungen, Zeitschriften, Tabakwaren, Süßigkeiten usw.*

Vocabulary

quick [kwɪk]		schnell
to **hide** [haɪd]	Let's *hide*. They mustn't see us.	(sich) verstecken
purse [pɜːs]		Portmonee, Geldbeutel
out of ['aʊt‿əv]		aus
towards [tə'wɔːdz]		auf … zu
Stop it! ['stɒp‿ɪt]		Hör/Hört auf!
to **stop** [stɒp]	*to stop* ⟷ to begin	aufhören, anhalten

Step E **Let's check**

⟨4⟩ to bully ['bʊlɪ]		schikanieren, tyrannisieren

Unit 2 Adventures in Nottingham

Vokabeltraining – kleine Tricks mit großer Wirkung

1. Plane fürs Vokabellernen mindestens dreimal 5–10 Minuten Zeit ein.
2. Lege vorher alles bereit, was du zum Lernen brauchst.
3. Arbeite zu Hause an einem Platz, an dem dich niemand stört und störe dich auch selbst nicht beim Wörterlernen, indem du z.B. nur noch die Hausaufgabe für ein anderes Fach heraussuchen oder Bleistifte spitzen musst. Arbeite konzentriert 5–10 Minuten an den Vokabeln. Du kannst dir auch einen Wecker stellen, der nach 10 Minuten läutet.
4. Wenn der Wecker klingelt, hast du (und dein Gehirn) eine kleine Pause verdient. Jetzt kannst du dir beispielsweise etwas zu trinken holen oder Bleistifte spitzen oder …
5. Als nächste Lernaufgabe solltest du danach etwas ganz anderes als Englisch machen. Aber vergiss nicht dir die englischen Wörter später nochmals vorzunehmen.

Step A **The adventure centre**

adventure [əd'ventʃə]		Abenteuer
°**tale** [teɪl]	A *tale* is a story.	Geschichte, Sage
weekend [ˌwiːk'end]	 Have a nice *weekend*.	Wochenende
film [fɪlm]		Film
leaflet ['liːflɪt]		Prospekt, Informationsblatt
just [dʒʌst]		genau, gerade
°**outlaw** ['aʊtlɔː]	 Robin Hood is an *outlaw*.	Gesetzlose/r, Vogelfreie/r, Bandit/in
Sherwood Forest [ˌʃɜːwʊd 'fɒrɪst]		*Wald nördlich von Nottingham*
forest ['fɒrɪst]		Wald
to **shoot** [ʃuːt]		schießen
°**bow** [bəʊ]		Bogen
°**arrow** ['ærəʊ]		Pfeil
°**sheriff** ['ʃerɪf]		Sheriff
enemy ['enəmɪ]	Sometimes cats and dogs are *enemies*.	Feind/in

to **catch** [kætʃ]	The sheriff can't *catch* Robin Hood.	fangen
to **take prisoner** [ˌteɪk ˈprɪznə]		gefangen nehmen
news (*no pl*) [nju:z]	That's good *news*!	Nachricht/en, Neuigkeit/en

Step B **Robin Hood**

we **were** [wɜ:]		wir waren
yesterday [ˈjestədeɪ]	*yesterday* ← today → tomorrow	gestern
it **was** [wɒz]		es war
we **had** [hæd]		wir hatten
he **lived** [lɪvd]	Robin Hood *lived* in Sherwood Forest.	er lebte
to help, **helped** [helpt]		half
to try, **tried** [traɪd]	Hängst du eine Endung an, wird „y“ zu „i“ – doch bei Vokal + „y“ gilt diese Regel nie!	versuchte
to **stop, stopped** [stɒpt]		verhindern, stoppen, verhinderte, stoppte
trick [trɪk]		Streich, Trick
Robin **played tricks on** him. [ˌpleɪd ˈtrɪks]		Robin spielte ihm Streiche.

Step B **The weekend**

Did you have …? [ˈdɪd ju: ˌhæv]		Hattest du …?
to do, **did** [dɪd]		tat, machte
to **be scared of** [bɪ ˈskeəd‿əv]	Are you *scared of* snakes?	Angst haben vor
at first [ət ˈfɜ:st]	*at first* → then → after that	zuerst
when [wen]	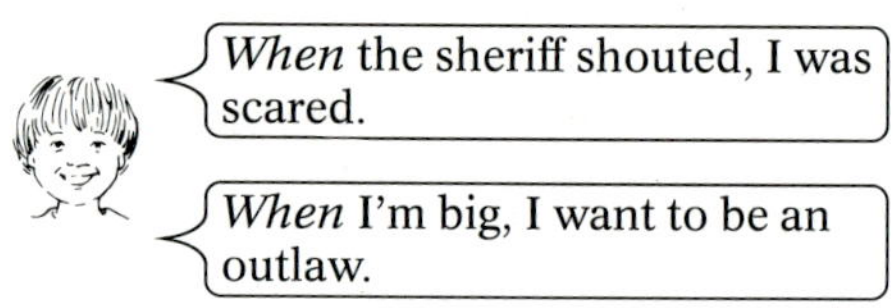	wenn; als

Step B **A strange dream**

strange [streɪndʒ]		seltsam, merkwürdig
dream [dri:m]	Do you often have *dreams*?	Traum
to say, **said** [sed]		sagte
to go, **went** [went]		ging
to get, **got** [gɒt]		holte
could, couldn't [kʊd, ˈkʊdnt]		konnte, konnte nicht
to run, **ran** [ræn]		lief, rannte
to hear, **heard** [hɜ:d]		hörte
to see, **saw** [sɔ:]		sah
to come, **came** [keɪm]		kam
up [ʌp]	*up* ←→ down	nach oben, herauf
to give, **gave** [geɪv]		gab
to sit, **sat** (down) [sæt]		saß, setzte sich hin
shock [ʃɒk]		Schock
to **wake up, woke up** [ˌweɪk‿ˈʌp, ˌwəʊk‿ˈʌp]	Yesterday I *woke up* with a shock: I had a terrible dream.	aufwachen, aufwecken, wachte auf, weckte auf
irregular [ɪˈregjʊlə]		unregelmäßig

Looking at the UK: In and around Nottingham

around [ə'raʊnd]	Are there many trees *around* your house?	um
fair [feə]	The Oktoberfest is a famous German *fair.*	Volksfest, Jahrmarkt
Goose Fair [ˌguːs 'feə]		*Name eines Jahrmarkts*
to **go on for** [gəʊ‿'ɒn fə]		(an)dauern
to sell, **sold** [səʊld]		verkaufte
°**goose**, geese (*pl*) [guːs, giːs]		Gans, Gänse
to **be called** [bɪ 'kɔːld]		heißen
°**the Major Oak** [ðə ˌmeɪdʒər‿'əʊk]		*Name einer alten Eiche im Sherwood Forest*
°**oak** [əʊk]	*Oaks* are often very, very old.	Eiche
°**cave** [keɪv]	There are a lot of *caves* under Nottingham Castle.	Höhle

Step C In the History lesson

°**the Middle Ages** [ðə ˌmɪdl 'eɪdʒɪz]	the time between 1000 and 1400	das Mittelalter
middle ['mɪdl]		Mitte
in those days [ɪn 'ðəʊz ˌdeɪz]		damals
°**Lee** [liː]		*Familienname*
to **catch, caught** [kætʃ, kɔːt]		fangen, fing
potato, potatoes (*pl*) [pə'teɪtəʊ, pə'teɪtəʊz]	You can make chips and crisps from *potatoes.*	Kartoffel, Kartoffeln
meat [miːt]		Fleisch
to eat, **ate** [eɪt]		aß
rich [rɪtʃ]	*rich* ⟷ poor	reich
life [laɪf]	In Robin Hood's time *life* wasn't easy.	Leben
before [bɪ'fɔː]	*before* ⟷ after	bevor
to **wash** [wɒʃ]	Today people usually *wash* in their bathrooms.	(sich) waschen
river ['rɪvə]	In Robin Hood's time people got water from the *river.*	Fluss
most [məʊst]		die meiste(n)
work [wɜːk]	In those days children started *work* before they were eight.	Arbeit
as soon as [əz 'suːn‿əz]		sobald
age [eɪdʒ]	What's your *age*? = How old are you?	Alter

Step D Robin Hood and the Sheriff

°**Will Scarlet** [ˌwɪl 'skɑːlət]		*Personenname*
to take, **took** [tʊk]	Yesterday we *took* Tabby to the vet's.	nahm, brachte
°**gallows** ['gæləʊz]		Galgen
to **happen** ['hæpən]		passieren, geschehen
prisoner ['prɪznə]		Gefangene/r
°**hangman** ['hæŋmən]		Henker
°**Friar Tuck** [ˌfraɪə 'tʌk]		*Personenname* („Bruder Tuck")
to wear, **wore** [wɔː]		trug (Kleidung)
coat [kəʊt]		Mantel
to meet, **met** [met]		traf (auf)
°**hood** [hʊd]		Kapuze

Vocabulary

	°**rope** [rəʊp]		Seil, Strick
	to stand, **stood** [stʊd]		stand
	to drink, **drank** [dræŋk]		trank
	wine [waɪn]		Wein
	up to [ˈʌp tə]	A man came *up to* me and asked the way.	auf … zu
	to **throw, threw** [θrəʊ, θruː]	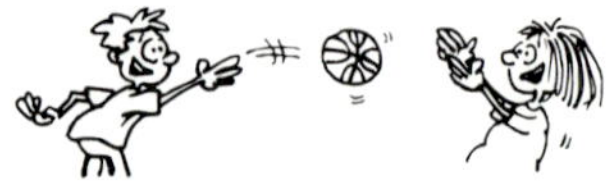 The boy *throws* the ball and the girl catches.	werfen, warf
	idiot [ˈɪdɪət]		Idiot
	off [ɒf]		ab, weg
	to **take off, took off** [ˌteɪk‿ˈɒf, ˌtʊk‿ˈɒf]		ausziehen, zog … aus
	crowd [kraʊd]	A lot of people are called a *crowd*. There was a big *crowd* at the football match.	Menschenmenge
	to **shoot, shot** [ʃuːt, ʃɒt]		schießen, schoss
	straight [streɪt]		direkt, gerade(wegs)
	hat [hæt]		Hut
	to feel, **felt** [felt]		fühlte sich
	gone [gɒn]		weg, verschwunden
2	**beginning** [bɪˈgɪnɪŋ]	*beginning* ⟷ end; ending	Anfang
3	°**signal** [ˈsɪgnl]		Signal, Hinweis
	simple past [ˌsɪmpl ˈpɑːst]		Vergangenheitsform
	simple [ˈsɪmpl]		einfach
	exercise book [ˈeksəsaɪz ˌbʊk]		(Übungs)Heft
6	**part** [pɑːt]		Teil
9	**each** [iːtʃ]		jede/r/s (einzelne)
	person [ˈpɜːsn]		Person

Unit 3 Nottingham Goose Fair

Vokabellernen mit Musik?

Viele Schülerinnen und Schüler brauchen zum Wörterlernen völlige Ruhe. Einige jedoch können sich besser konzentrieren, wenn im Hintergrund Musik läuft. Dies funktioniert aber nur, wenn die Musik einen ruhigen Rhythmus hat und nicht zu laut ist. Probiere aus, was für dich besser ist. Eines aber geht **nicht** zusammen: Wörterlernen und Fernsehen. Dein Auge und dein Ohr sind dabei zu sehr abgelenkt.

Vokabellernen mit dem Kassettenrekorder?

Du kannst Wörter aber auch mit einem Kassettenrekorder üben:

- Nimm dir deine Lernportion von etwa 10–12 Wörtern vor und sprich die deutsche Bedeutung jedes Wortes auf die Kassette, lass eine nicht zu kurze Sprechpause und sprich dann die englische Bedeutung des Wortes darauf.
- Beim Abhören sprichst du dann die englische Bedeutung in die Sprechpause.
- So kannst du nach und nach ein Lernpäckchen nach dem anderen aufnehmen. Ein „Walkman" ist dabei auch ganz praktisch. Du kannst damit die Wörter üben, wo du auch bist.

Step A **It's here again!**

important [ɪmˈpɔːtnt]		wichtig
famous [ˈfeɪməs]		berühmt
popular [ˈpɒpjʊlə]	Nottingham Goose Fair is very *popular with* the Nottingham children.	beliebt

	young [jʌŋ]	 *young* ⟷ old 	jung
	to **visit** [ˈvɪzɪt]		besuchen
	cheap [tʃiːp]		billig
	ride [raɪd]		Fahrt
	to **have a ride on** [ˌhæv‿əˈraɪd‿ɒn]		fahren auf
	ghost [ɡəʊst]		Geist, Gespenst
	°**ghost train** [ˈɡəʊst ˌtreɪn]		Geisterbahn
	°the **dodgems** [ˈdɒdʒəmz]		Autoskooter
	expensive [ɪkˈspensɪv]	*expensive* ⟷ cheap	teuer
	hot dog [ˌhɒt ˈdɒg]		Hot Dog
	popcorn [ˈpɒpkɔːn]		Popcorn
	to win, **won** [wʌn]		gewann
	teddy [ˈtedɪ]		Teddybär
1a)	**cassette** [kəˈset]		Kassette
	American [əˈmerɪkən]		amerikanisch, Amerikaner/in
2	**adjective** [ˈædʒɪktɪv]		Adjektiv

Step B **Thanks, Dad!**

	old, **older** [ˈəʊldə]	David is *older than* Mark.	älter
	than [ðæn, ðən]		als
	lucky, **luckier** [ˈlʌkɪə]	*I'm happy.* – Ich bin glücklich.	(mehr) Glück haben
	anyway [ˈenɪweɪ]	*I'm lucky.* – Ich habe Glück.	jedenfalls, sowieso
	as … **as** [æz … əz]	Sarah is *as old as* David but she isn't *as old as* Robert.	so … wie
	cheaper, (the) cheapest [ðə ˈtʃiːpɪst]		billiger, am billigsten
	world [wɜːld]	*in the world* – auf der Welt	Welt
	bad, **worse, (the) worst** [wɜːs, ðə ˈwɜːst]		schlechter, am schlechtesten
2	to **compare** [kəmˈpeə]		vergleichen

Step B **In the park**

more important [mɔː]		wichtiger
most exciting [məʊst]		am aufregendsten
interesting [ˈɪntrəstɪŋ]		interessant
difficult [ˈdɪfɪkəlt]	*difficult* ⟷ easy	schwierig

Step C **All the fun of the fair**

1	to **have a go** [ˌhæv‿əˈɡəʊ]		etwas versuchen
	a go [ə ˈɡəʊ]	The dodgems are £1 *a go.*	pro Fahrt, pro Versuch
	°**knuckle** [ˈnʌkl]		Fingerknöchel
	°**white knuckle ride** [ˌwaɪt nʌkl ˈraɪd]		wilde Fahrt auf Achterbahn und Ähnlichem
	°**coconut shy** [ˈkəʊkənʌt ˌʃaɪ]		Wurfbude
	°**Big Wheel** [ˌbɪɡ‿ˈwiːl]		Riesenrad
	wheel [wiːl]		Rad

Vocabulary

	°**roundabout** ['raʊndəbaʊt]		Karussell
	°**coconut** ['kəʊkənʌt]		Kokosnuss
5	what you were **like** [laɪk]		wie du warst
6	to **describe** [dɪ'skraɪb]	Can you *describe* a coconut shy?	beschreiben
⟨7⟩	lovely bunch [ˌlʌvlɪ 'bʌntʃ]		eine schöne Menge
	Barney ['bɑːnɪ]		*männl. Vorname*
	showman ['ʃəʊmən]		Schausteller
	underneath [ˌʌndə'niːθ]		unter
	flare [fleə]		Leuchtsignal
	row [rəw]		Reihe
	Give'em a twist, a flick of the wrist [ˌgɪvəm‿ə'twɪst ə ˌflɪk‿əv ðə 'rɪst]		*etwa:* Hau sie runter!
	wife [waɪf]		Ehefrau
	idol ['aɪdl]		Idol
	to roll [rəʊl]		rollen
	to bowl [bəʊl]		werfen
	penny ['penɪ]		Penny (*alte Münze*)
	a pitch [pɪtʃ]		pro Wurf

Step D **Two and one make three**

	to **go wrong** [ˌgəʊ 'rɒŋ]		schief gehen
	to **jump** [dʒʌmp]		springen
	to drive, **drove** [drəʊv]		fuhr
	Crash! [kræʃ]		Krach!
	to **hit, hit** [hɪt]		schlagen, schlug
	from behind [ˌfrɒm bɪ'haɪnd]		von hinten
	stall [stɔːl]		Stand
	throw [θrəʊ]		Wurf
	to **laugh at** ['lɑːf‿ˌæt]	Mark says funny things, so everyone *laughs at* him.	sich lustig machen über
	nervous about ['nɜːvəs‿əˌbaʊt]		nervös, aufgeregt wegen
	to **run off, ran off** [ˌrʌn‿'ɒf, ˌræn‿'ɒf]		weglaufen, lief weg
	miserable ['mɪzrəbl]	 Achte auf die Aussprache!	unglücklich, elend
	to **leave, left** [liːv, left]		(ver)lassen, (ver)ließ
	leave me alone ['liːv mɪ‿ə'ləʊn]		lass mich in Ruhe
	alone [ə'ləʊn]		allein
	friendly ['frendlɪ]		freundlich, freundschaftlich
	sorry about ['sɒrɪ ˌəbaʊt]	I'm *sorry about* last night. I wasn't very *friendly*.	tut mir Leid wegen
2	**summary** ['sʌmərɪ]		Zusammenfassung
	simple present [ˌsɪmpl 'preznt]		Präsens
4	°**progressive** (form) [prəʊ'gresɪv]		Verlaufsform

Step E **Let's check**

4	to think, **thought** [θɔːt]		dachte

Unit 4 The junior play

„Da steckt doch ein schon gelerntes Wort drin!"

Wörter behältst du besser, wenn du sie nicht einzeln lernst, sondern in möglichst vielen Zusammenhängen. Eine Möglichkeit dazu ist das Einhängen eines neu gelernten Wortes in seine Wortfamilie. Im Vokabular findest du dazu oft Hilfen (z.B. in dieser Unit *to laugh* → *laugh*). Bei einem neuen Wort solltest du dir immer die Frage stellen: Welches Wort kenne ich aus dieser Wortfamilie noch?

Beispiele:

- In Unit 1 hast du das Verb *to meet* gelernt. Mit welchem Substantiv ist dieses Verb „verwandt"?
- Wie heißt das Adjektiv zum Verb *to open* oder das Substantiv zu *surprised*?
- Man kann auch ein neues Wort in Verbindung mit seinem Gegenteil (z.B. *to stop* ⟷ *to begin*), mit einer oder mehreren Zusammensetzungen (z.B. *house – housework – housekeeper*) oder mit einem Wort mit gleicher Bedeutung (z.B. *at once* = *right away*) lernen.

Step A **Costumes for the play**

°**costume** ['kɒstju:m]		Verkleidung, Kostüm
Christmas ['krɪsməs]	Achte auf die Aussprache: Das 't' wird nicht gesprochen.	Weihnachten
part [pɑ:t]		Rolle, Teil
°**prompter** ['prɒmptə]	The *prompter* helps you in the play when you don't know your words.	Souffleur/Souffleuse
Shabina [ʃæ'bi:nə]		*weibl. Vorname*
°**Ismaili** [ˌɪz'meɪlɪ]		*Familienname*
cupboard ['kʌbəd]		Schrank
skirt [skɜ:t]	At English schools girls usually wear *skirts*.	Rock
pretty ['prɪtɪ]		hübsch
ago [ə'gəʊ]	Achte auf die Wortstellung: three years *ago* – *vor* drei Jahren	vor
a hundred years ago [ə ˌhʌndrəd 'jɪəz‿əˌgəʊ]		vor hundert Jahren
dress [dres]		Kleid
lovely ['lʌvlɪ]	Ooh! What *lovely* cakes! Can I have one?	schön, herrlich
short [ʃɔ:t]	*short* ⟷ long	kurz
jacket ['dʒækɪt]		Jacke
useful ['ju:sfʊl]	A bike is an exciting present. A pen is a *useful* present.	nützlich
tights (*pl*) [taɪts]		Strumpfhose
shirt [ʃɜ:t]		Hemd
clean [kli:n]	*clean* ⟷ dirty	sauber
beard [bɪəd]		Bart
to **try on** [ˌtraɪ‿'ɒn]		ausprobieren, anprobieren
frightening ['fraɪtnɪŋ]	A strange noise in the night can be *frightening*.	Furcht erregend, erschreckend
2 °**alphabetical** [ælfə'betɪkl]		alphabetisch

Step B **Robert the ghost**

	will [wɪl]		werden, wird
	stage [steɪdʒ]		Bühne
	to **forget, forgot** [fə'get, fə'gɒt]	The prompter will help you when you *forget* your words on the stage.	vergessen, vergaß
	you'll be **fine** [faɪn]		es wird schon gut gehen
	as [æz]		*hier:* in der Rolle von, als
	voice [vɔɪs]		Stimme
	laugh [lɑːf]	to laugh → *laugh*	Lachen
1	°**Mason** ['meɪsn]		*Familienname*

Step B **Who knows?**

	if [ɪf]	*If* it's sunny tomorrow, we'll go swimming.	wenn

Step B **The Canterville Ghost**

	Otis ['əʊtɪs]		*Familienname*
	Canterville Chase [ˌkæntəvɪl 'tʃeɪs]		*Ort in England*
	°**Underwood** ['ʌndəwʊd]		*Familienname*
	Virginia [və'dʒɪnjə]		*weibl. Vorname*
	daughter ['dɔːtə]	Achte auf die Aussprache: Das 'gh' wird nicht gesprochen.	Tochter
	Washington ['wɒʃɪŋtən]		*männl. Vorname*
	son [sʌn]	Simon is the Burtons' *son* and Becky is their daughter.	Sohn
	°**Blackwell** ['blækwel]		*Familienname*
8	°**preposition** [ˌprepə'zɪʃn]	'On', 'under', 'between' are *prepositions*.	Präposition, Verhältniswort

Looking at the UK: Theatre groups

theatre ['θɪətə]		Theater
°**puppet** ['pʌpɪt]		Marionette
°**professional** [prə'feʃənl]		professionell

Step C **Don't worry, Jenny!**

	ill [ɪl]	If you are *ill*, you must see the doctor.	krank
	by heart [baɪ 'hɑːt]	What English song can you sing *by heart*?	auswendig
	°**heart** [hɑːt]		Herz
2	**information** (*pl*) [ɪnfə'meɪʃn]	Can you give me more *information* about ghosts, please?	Information(en), Auskunft
⟨3⟩	mile [maɪl]		Meile
	to miss [mɪs]		verpassen
	whistle ['wɪsl]		Pfeife
	to blow [bləʊ]		blasen, *hier:* pfeifen
	Lord [lɔːd]		Herr
	this-a-way ['ðɪsəweɪ]		auf diese Weise, so

Step D **On the stage**

	that [ðæt/ðət]		dass
	to **clap** [klæp]	Come on! *Clap* your hands everyone!	klatschen, Beifall geben
	behind the scenes [bɪˌhaɪnd ðə ˈsiːnz]		hinter den Kulissen
	°**sound effects** [ˈsaʊnd‿ɪˌfekts]		Toneffekte
	scene [siːn]		Szene
	°**Umney** [ˈʌmniː]		*Familienname*
	°**housekeeper** [ˈhaʊsˌkiːpə]		Haushälter/in
	thunder [ˈθʌndə]		Donner
	lightning [ˈlaɪtnɪŋ]	After *lightning* you can hear thunder.	Blitz
	loud [laʊd]	*loud* ⟷ quiet	laut
	side [saɪd]		Seite
	on [ɒn]		auf, *hier:* auf der Bühne
	°**pillow** [ˈpɪləʊ]		Kopfkissen
	all right [ˌɔːl ˈraɪt]	*all right* = OK	in Ordnung
	face [feɪs]	He's got a funny *face*.	Gesicht
	to **come off** [kʌm‿ˈɒf]		runterfallen
	even more [ˌiːvn ˈmɔː]		noch mehr
	row [rəʊ]	In a theatre there are a lot of *rows* of seats.	Reihe
1	**title** [ˈtaɪtl]	The *title* of this book is Green Line New 2.	Titel
	line [laɪn]		Linie, Zeile
2	°**Jeff** [dʒef]		*männl. Vorname*
	°**Dickens** [ˈdɪkɪnz]		*Familienname*
4	**future** [ˈfjuːtʃə]		Zukunft

Unit 5 In town

Wörterlernen im Zusammenhang

Auch mit Wörternetzen kannst du neue Wörter besser behalten und wiederholen. Ein Wörternetz enthält für ein Wort wie z. B. *DRAMA* (siehe Seite 33) viele andere Wörter, die mit dem Ausgangswort etwas zu tun haben. Das fertige Wörternetz kannst du dann in deinem *English folder* aufbewahren. Ähnliches kann man auch mit Wörtern machen, die in verschiedenen Zusammenhängen benutzt werden.

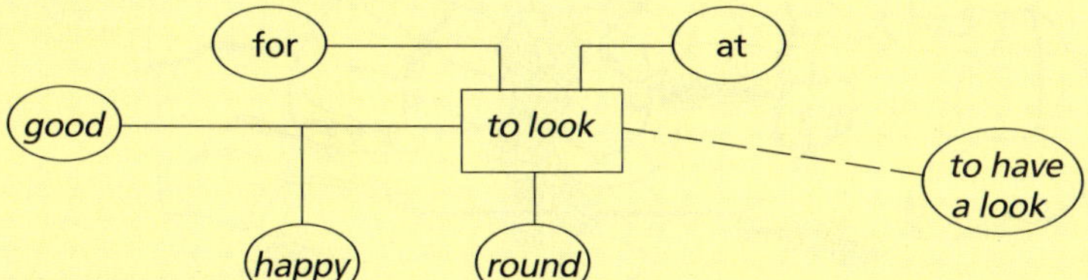

Du behältst Wörter gut, wenn du sie in Sätzen oder Wendungen lernst. Im Vokabular findest du viele Beispiele in der Mittelspalte.

department store → *A department store sells nearly everything.*
→ *The tea shop is next to the department store.*

morning → *In the morning …*

I'd … → *I'd like some sweets, please.*

Let's play with words

1 Family words

① Alan Penrose — ② Rose Penrose

③ Pat (Miller) — ④ Colin Penrose — ⑤ Helen (Penrose) — ⑥ Michael Leinert

⑦ David Penrose — ⑧ Mark Penrose — ⑨ Jenny Leinert

Do you know the family words?

Example: ⑥ → ⑨ *What is Mr Leinert to Jenny? He's her father.*
Now try:
⑦ → ⑧ ⑤ → ④ ⑨ → ⑦ ⑤ → ⑧ ④ → ⑨ ② → ⑧ ① → ⑦ ⑧ → ④ ⑨ → ⑤

2 What a mess!

Becky and Simon's bag is a real mess! Write a list of thirteen things for your folder. The letters for ten things are here. Can you find three more things in the bag?

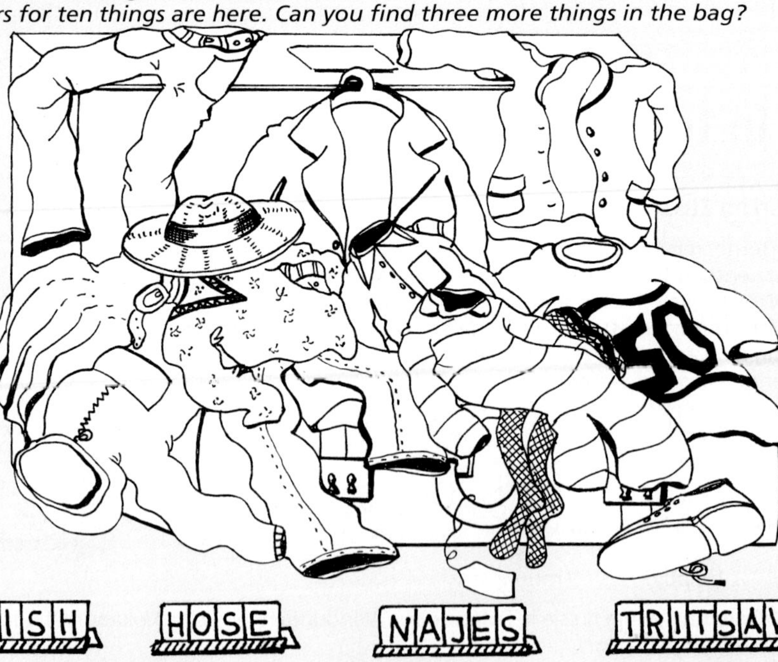

TRISH HOSE NAJES TRITSAWESH

TECKAJ SERDS KORANA

VULELPOR SORTURES TOCA

Step A **In the shopping centre**

shopping centre [ˈʃɒpɪŋ ˌsentə]		Einkaufszentrum
escalator [ˈeskəleɪtə]		Rolltreppe
lift [lɪft]		Aufzug, Fahrstuhl
clock [klɒk]		Uhr
car park [ˈkɑː pɑːk]		Parkhaus, Parkplatz
restaurant [ˈrestərɔːŋ]		Restaurant
°**Jessop** [ˈdʒesəp]		*Familienname*
department store [dɪˈpɑːtmənt stɔː]		Kaufhaus
upper [ˈʌpə]	 This is the *upper floor* of the house.	obere/r/s
floor [flɔː]		Stockwerk
above [əˈbʌv]	 Achte auf die Aussprache!	über
°**Food Court** [ˈfuːd ˌkɔːt]		*Imbissbereich im Einkaufszentrum*
next to [ˈnekst tə]	 A is *next to* B.	neben
lower [ˈləʊə]	*lower* ⟷ upper	untere/r/s
°**pizza** [ˈpiːtsə]		Pizza
in the middle of [ɪn ðə ˈmɪdl‿əv]		in der Mitte von, mitten in
sock [sɒk]		Socke
°**coffee shop** [ˈkɒfɪː ˌʃɒp]		Café
°**Teens** [tiːnz]		*Name eines Bekleidungsgeschäftes*
2 **opposite** [ˈɒpəzɪt]		gegenüber
3 °**Sue** [suː]		*weibl. Vorname*
°**tea shop** [ˈtiː ˌʃɒp]		Café, Teestube
°**Broadwood** [ˈbrɔːdwʊd]		*Familienname*
°**Taj Mahal** [ˌtɑːdʒməˈhɑːl]		*Name eines indischen Palastes*
to **find out** [ˌfaɪnd‿ˈaʊt]		entdecken, herausfinden

Step B **Just looking**

fantastic [fænˈtæstɪk]		fantastisch, toll
trainers (*pl*) [ˈtreɪnəz]		Turnschuhe
corner [ˈkɔːnə]		Ecke
to **pay, paid** [peɪ, peɪd]	I'll *pay for* Mum's birthday present.	(be)zahlen, (be)zahlte
1 **customer** [ˈkʌstəmə]	*customer* ⟷ shop assistant	Kunde
3 **busy** [ˈbɪzɪ]		beschäftigt

Step B **Something silly**

nearly [ˈnɪəlɪ]	Jenny is still twelve, but she's *nearly* thirteen.	fast, beinahe
top [tɒp]		oberste/r/s
to **look round** [ˌlʊk ˈraʊnd]		sich umsehen
anywhere [ˈenɪweə]		(n)irgendwo

Vocabulary

	somewhere ['sʌmweə]		irgendwo
	somebody ['sʌmbədɪ]		jemand
	anybody ['enɪbɒdɪ]		(irgend) jemand
4a)	°**compound** ['kɒmpaʊnd]	'timetable', 'sheepdog', 'skateboard', 'supermarket', 'football' – all these words are *compounds*, too	zusammengesetztes Wort
6	°**Ken** [ken]		*männl. Vorname*

Step B **Sarah's favourite**

	°**Ripple** ['rɪpl]		*Familienname*
	so what? [ˌsəʊ 'wɒt]		na und?
	°**autograph** ['ɔːtəgrɑːf]	My sister collects *autographs*.	Autogramm
9	to **plan** [plæn]		planen
	to **complete** [kəm'pliːt]		fertig stellen, beenden

Looking at the UK: Things to do

	°**Twycross Zoo** ['twaɪkrɒs zuː]		Zoo bei Twycross (*Ort in England*)
	zoo [zuː]		Zoo
	skate [skeɪt]	 These are *skates*.	Schlittschuh, Rollschuh
	°to **hire** ['haɪə]		mieten
	ice rink ['aɪsrɪŋk]		Eisstadion
	swimming pool ['swɪmɪŋpuːl]	Our town has got two *swimming pools* but it hasn't got an *ice rink*.	Schwimmbad
	adult ['ædʌlt]	*adult* ⟷ child	Erwachsener
	°to **smoke** [sməʊk]		rauchen
	°**Lace Museum** [ˌleɪs mjuː'zɪəm]		*Museum in Nottingham*
	museum [mjuː'zɪəm]		Museum
	°**lace** [leɪs]		Spitze (*Gewebeart*)
	°**non-swimmer** [ˌnɒn 'swɪmə]		Nichtschwimmer
	sign [saɪn]		Schild
	it doesn't matter [ɪt 'dʌznt 'mætə]	I can't swim – *It doesn't matter.* I'll show you.	es macht nichts
1	to **mean** [miːn]	 What does this *sign mean*? – No idea!	bedeuten

Step C **Something different**

1	**I'd like = I would like** [aɪd 'laɪk]		ich möchte, ich hätte gern
	Could you …? [kʊd‿juː]		Könntest du …?, Könnten Sie …?
	Would you like …? ['wʊd juː ˌlaɪk]	*Would you like* some cake? – Yes, please.	Möchtest du …?, Möchten Sie …?
	polite [pə'laɪt]	It's *polite* to say 'please' when you ask for something.	höflich

2 °**clap'n rap** ['klæpn ˌræp]		klatschen und „rappen“
°**rhythm** ['rɪðəm]		Rhythmus

Step D **A present from Robert**

°**haircut** ['heəkʌt]	I need a *haircut.* 	Haarschnitt, Frisur
hair (*sg/pl*) [heə]	one *hair*  a lot of *hair*	Haar/e
to **add** [æd]		hinzufügen
°**great uncle** [greɪt‿'ʌŋkl]		Großonkel
°**Arthur** ['ɑːθə]		*männl. Vorname*
anyone ['enɪwʌn]		jemand
everywhere ['evrɪweə]		überall
half an hour [ˌhɑːf‿ən‿'aʊə]		eine halbe Stunde
hour ['aʊə]		Stunde
wonderful ['wʌndəfʊl]		wunderbar
time [taɪm]		Mal
pink [pɪŋk]		rosa, pink
°**wig** [wɪg]		Perücke
actor ['æktə]	*actor* → to act	Schauspieler
What on earth ...? [ˌwɒt‿ɒn‿'ɜːθ]	 *What on earth* are you doing here?	Was in aller Welt ...?
earth [ɜːθ]		Erde
to **smile** [smaɪl]		lächeln
°**mirror** ['mɪrə]		Spiegel
to **use** [juːz]	 Achte auf die Aussprache!	benutzen
°**tea-cosy** ['tiːkəʊzɪ]		Teewärmer, Kaffeemütze
1 **and so on** [ənd 'səʊ ɒn]		und so weiter
3 **piece** [piːs]	A *piece* of pizza, a *piece* of cake.	Stück
paper ['peɪpə]		Papier
4 °**Harry** ['hærɪ]		*männl. Vorname*
to feed, **fed** [fed]		fütterte

no – any – some – every

no books	**any** chairs	**some** bottles	**every** house
no food	**any** wine	**some** milk	**every** pupil
no one	**anyone**	**someone**	**everyone**
nobody	**anybody**	**somebody**	**everybody**
nothing	**anything**	**something**	**everything**
nowhere	**anywhere**	**somewhere**	**everywhere**

Nobody heard the burglar because **everybody** was asleep.

Did you see anybody near the house? – Well, I didn't see **anybody** yesterday, but I saw **somebody** in the garden earlier today.

Unit 6 Food, food, food

Lernen mit Eselsbrücken

Manches, was sich nur schwer behalten lässt, kann man sich – auch im Englischen – mit einer Eselsbrücke besser merken. Eselsbrücken helfen dir am besten, wenn du sie dir selbst ausdenkst. Du kannst sie aber dann auch mit Freunden austauschen.
Hier ein paar Beispiele:

- Wenn man die deutschen Bedeutungen von *to lie* und *to lay* immer verwechselt, kann man sie sich so merken: ***To lie*** heißt „**liegen**", es fängt ja auch genauso an.
- Wenn man nie so genau weiß, ob man *to choose* mit einem oder mit zwei „O" schreibt, sollte man daran denken, dass *to choose* „auswählen" heißt. Und beim Auswählen muss man sich ja auch zwischen zwei Sachen entscheiden, deshalb zwei „O".
- Man verwechselt die Fragewörter *where* and *who* nicht, wenn man daran denkt, dass in **where** die Antwort **here** schon drinsteckt.

Step A **Letters to a magazine**

to tell, **told** [təʊld]		sagte, erzählte
°**Chinese** [ˌtʃaɪˈniːz]		chinesisch
someone [ˈsʌmwʌn]		jemand
recipe [ˈresɪpɪ]	Look! Here's a book with Chinese *recipes*.	(Koch)Rezept
to **cook** [kʊk]		kochen
meal [miːl]	Great, let's cook a Chinese *meal*.	Mahlzeit, Essen
°**Tim** [tɪm]		*männl. Vorname*
°**Price** [praɪs]		*Familienname*
°**Belfast** [ˌbelˈfɑːst]		*Stadt in Nordirland*
to **kill** [kɪl]		töten
fruit (sg/*pl*) [fruːt]	*fruit* = apples, bananas …	Obst, Frucht, Früchte
vegetable [ˈvedʒtəbl]		Gemüse
°**Emma** [ˈemə]		*weibl. Vorname*
°**Martin** [ˈmɑːtɪn]		*Familienname*
°**Leeds** [liːdz]		*Stadt in England*
°**roast beef** [rəʊst ˈbiːf]		Rinderbraten
°**beef** [biːf]		Rindfleisch
°**roast potatoes** [ˌrəʊst pəˈteɪtəʊz]		im Ofen gebratene Kartoffeln
I can't stand … [aɪ ˈkɑːnt‿ˈstænd]		ich kann … nicht leiden/… ausstehen
cabbage [ˈkæbɪdʒ]	I can't stand *cabbage*! It's terrible.	Kohl
°**Lee** [liː]		*männl. Vorname*
°**Brown** [braʊn]		*Familienname*
°**Truro** [ˈtrʊərəʊ]		*Ort in Cornwall*
to **grow, grew** [grəʊ, gruː]	I *grow* vegetables and flowers in my garden.	wachsen, (an)pflanzen
carrot [ˈkærət]	Achte auf die Schreibung!	Karotte, Möhre
bean [biːn]		Bohne
to **taste** [teɪst]	Carrot cake *tastes* great!	schmecken, probieren
2 to **bring, brought** [brɪŋ, brɔːt]		bringen, brachte

Step B **Sunday morning**

	to **cut, cut** [kʌt]		schneiden
	finished ['finiʃt]		fertiggestellt
	almost ['ɔːlməʊst]	It's 5.58. It's *almost* 6 o'clock.	fast
	helped [helpt]		geholfen
	made [meɪd]		gemacht
	been [biːn]		gewesen
	had [hæd]		gehabt
1	to **invite** [ɪn'vaɪt]	Grandma has *invited* us to lunch.	einladen
3	°**infinitive** [ɪn'fɪnətɪv]		Infinitiv, Grundform
4	°**past participle** [ˌpɑːst 'pɑːtɪsɪpl]		Partizip Perfekt
6	**sauerkraut** ['saʊəkraʊt]		Sauerkraut

Step B **A guest from Karlsruhe**

	yet [jet]		schon
	bookshop ['bʊkʃɒp]		Buchhandlung
	dictionary ['dɪkʃənrɪ]	If you don't know a word, you can look in a *dictionary.*	Wörterbuch, Lexikon
10	to **practise** ['præktɪs]		üben
	°**present perfect** [ˌpreznt 'pɜːfɪkt]		*englische Vergangenheitsform*
〈12〉	soup [suːp]		Suppe

Step C **Something to drink**

1	**thirsty** ['θɜːstɪ]	If you are *thirsty* you need something to drink.	durstig
	cup [kʌp]	A *cup* of tea, a *cup* of hot chocolate.	Tasse
	coffee ['kɒfɪ]		Kaffee
	glass [glɑːs]	A *glass* of water, a *glass* of wine, a *glass* of milk.	Glas
	to understand, understood, **understood** [ˌʌndə'stʊd]		verstanden

Looking at the UK: Nottingham 'takeaways'

	°**takeaway** ['teɪkəˌweɪ]	You buy meals at a *takeaway* and eat them at home.	*Imbissstube, Schnellgaststätte mit Straßenverkauf*
	kind [kaɪnd]		Art
	Indian ['ɪndjən]		indisch, Inder/in
	to **choose, chose, chosen** [tʃuːz, tʃəʊz, 'tʃəʊzn]	Achte auf die Aussprache und Schreibung!	wählen, aussuchen

Step D **Saturday lunch**

to **pick up** [pɪk‿'ʌp]		aufheben, abholen
fork [fɔːk]		Gabel
plate [pleɪt]		Teller
mince [mɪns]		Hackfleisch
shopping list ['ʃɒpɪŋ ˌlɪst]		Einkaufsliste
curry ['kʌrɪ]		Curry (*indisches Gericht*)
to **ring, rang, rung** [rɪŋ, ræŋ, rʌŋ]		klingeln
cream [kriːm]	Would you like *cream* on your cake?	Sahne
to **clean** [kliːn]		putzen, sauber machen
in time [ˌɪn 'taɪm]	Am I late? – No, you're just *in time*!	rechtzeitig
to **drop** [drɒp]		fallen(lassen)
while [waɪl]	Achte auf die Schreibung!	während
hard [hɑːd]		hart, schwer
to be **proud of** ['praʊd‿ˌəv]		stolz sein auf
2 to **explain** [ɪk'spleɪn]		erklären

to be

David **is** very hungry.
Are you sure?
I'm excited/nervous/happy.
Don't be afraid!
Be quiet!
Jenny **isn't** scared of ghosts.
This **is** a nice colour.
The radio **is** on.
You're lucky.
It's my birthday today.

to have

Mark **has** a bath every evening.
We **had** a lot of fun at Goose Fair last week.
Have you **had** lunch yet?
I **had** a ride/a go on the roundabout.
Simon **has** new shoes on today.
Have a look at this picture.
Let's **have** a party!

Unit 7 A week in Scotland

Looking at the UK: Beautiful Britain

beautiful ['bjuːtəfʊl]		schön
Britain ['brɪtn]	*Britain* = (short form for) Great Britain	Großbritannien
north [nɔːθ]		Norden, Nord-, nördlich
west [west]		Westen, West-, westlich
south [saʊθ]		Süden, Süd-, südlich
east [iːst]		Osten, Ost-, östlich
°**The Isle of Wight** [ˌaɪl‿əv'waɪt]		*Insel vor der Südküste Englands*
to **travel** ['trævl]		reisen
island ['aɪlənd]	*island* bezeichnet eine Insel im Allgemeinen, *isle* wird meist nur in Namen verwendet	Insel
Wales [weɪlz]		Wales (*Teil Großbritanniens*)

	horse [hɔːs]		Pferd
	to **enjoy** [ɪnˈdʒɔɪ]		genießen, gern tun
	to **ride** [raɪd]	You can ride a horse or a bike.	reiten, fahren (Fahrrad, Motorrad)
1	**brochure** [ˈbrəʊʃə]		Broschüre, Prospekt
2	I **wouldn't** like [ˈwʊdnt]	*I wouldn't like* to go to school on Sunday.	ich möchte nicht, ich würde ungern

Step A **At the travel agent's**

travel agent's [ˈtrævl‿ˌeɪdʒənts]		Reisebüro
Easter [ˈiːstə]	*Easter* is in spring. Christmas is in winter.	Ostern
coach [kəʊtʃ]	You can go on holiday by *coach* and to school by bus.	Reisebus
°**bed and breakfast place** [ˌbed‿ənd ˈbrekfəst pleɪs]		Frühstückspension
address [əˈdres]	Achte auf die Schreibung!	Adresse, Anschrift

Step B **From Jenny's travel diary**

	°**diary** [ˈdaɪərɪ]		Tagebuch, Terminkalender
	on [ɒn]		*hier:* an
	°**Loch Lomond** [ˌlɒk ˈləʊmənd]		*See in Schottland*
	°**loch** [lɒk]		(schottischer) See
	°**M6** [ˌem ˈsɪks]		*Autobahn in England*
	to **go wrong** [ˌgəʊ ˈrɒŋ]		*hier:* sich verfahren
	twice [twaɪs]	That's a great film. I've seen it *twice*!	zweimal
	in the end [ˌɪn ðɪ‿ˈend]		schließlich, zum Schluss
	°**MacTavish** [məkˈtævɪʃ]		*Familienname*
	°to **row** [rəʊ]		rudern
3	**thunderstorm** [ˈθʌndəstɔːm]	 thunder + lightning = *thunderstorm*	Gewitter
	dangerous [ˈdeɪndʒərəs]		gefährlich

Let's play with words

1 Food!

Can you make 25 (or more) things to eat from these letters?

Example: CHEESE

Make a list for your folder.

2 Word map

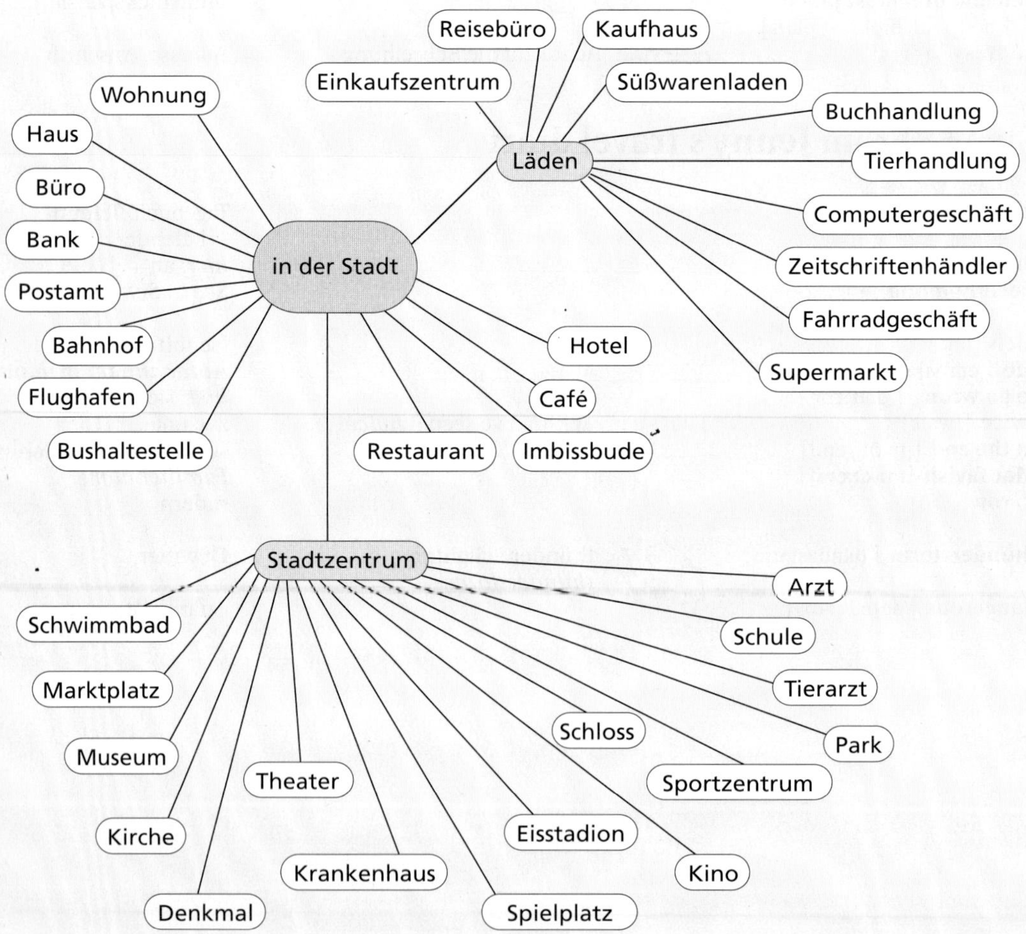

Make this word map for the English words and put it in your folder.

Vocabulary

Step B **Have you ever ...?**

ever ['evə]	Have you *ever* been to Spain? – No, I haven't.	je, jemals
°**porridge** ['pɒrɪdʒ]		Haferbrei
°**kilt** [kɪlt]		Schottenrock
the day before yesterday [ðə 'deɪ bɪˌfɔː 'jestədeɪ]	 *the day before yesterday* yesterday today	vorgestern
°**bagpipes** ['bægpaɪps]	 kilt bagpipes	Dudelsack
live [laɪv]		live, direkt
°**student** ['stjuːdnt]		Student
a long time ago [ə ˌlɒŋ taɪm‿ə'gəʊ]		lange her

Step C **At Fort William**

°**Fort William** [ˌfɔːt‿'wɪljəm]		*Ort in Schottland*
°**Campbell** ['kæmbl]		*Familienname*
°**Ben Nevis** [ˌben 'nevɪs]		*(höchster) Berg in Schottland*
high [haɪ]		hoch
°**Loch Ness** [ˌlɒk 'nes]		*See in Schottland*
the day after tomorrow [ðə 'deɪ‿ˌɑːftə tə'mɒrəʊ]	*the day after tomorrow* ⟷ the day before yesterday	übermorgen
weather forecast ['weðə ˌfɔːkɑːst]	The *weather forecast* tells you about tomorrow's weather.	Wetterbericht
deep [diːp]		tief
2 **tourist** ['tʊərɪst]		Tourist/in
3⟩ rolling ['rəʊlɪŋ]		rollend
border ['bɔːdə]		Grenze, *hier: Grenzgebiet in Schottland*
to bury ['berɪ]		begraben, vergraben
low [ləʊ]		tief
bonny ['bɒnɪ]		schön, hübsch
Tweed [twiːd]		*Fluss in Schottland*
to flow [fləʊ]		fließen
sweet [swiːt]		süß, schön
wide [waɪd]		weit
Hudson ['hʌdsən]		*Fluss in Nordamerika*
Clyde [klaɪd]		*Fluss in Schottland*
to court [kɔːt]		um eine Frau werben
to love dearly ['dɪəlɪ]		sehr lieben
chorus ['kɔːrəs]		Refrain
certain ['sɜːtn]		gewisse/r/s
peace of mind [ˌpiːs‿ɒv 'maɪnd]		innere Ruhe
lassies (*pl*) ['læsɪz]		Mädchen
hard [hɑːd]		hart
but yet [ˌbʌt 'jet]		aber doch
kind [kaɪnd]		nett, freundlich
among [ə'mʌŋ]		zwischen

Vocabulary

Step D **On Ben Nevis**

to **warn** [wɔ:n]		warnen
to **change** [tʃeɪndʒ]		(sich) ändern, verändern, wechseln
the Alps (*pl*) [ælps]		die Alpen
path [pɑ:θ]		Pfad, Weg
slippery ['slɪpərɪ]	 a *steep* and *slippery* path	rutschig, glatt
°**steep** [sti:p]		steil
to **have on** [ˌhæv 'ɒn]	*to have on* = to wear	anhaben (Kleidung)
after a time [ˌɑ:ftər‿ə 'taɪm]	*after a time* = some time later	nach einer Weile
although [ɔ:l'ðəʊ]		obwohl
only ['əʊnlɪ]	 the *only* answer – die einzige Antwort; *only* five minutes – nur fünf Minuten	einzige/r/s
to **turn back** [ˌtɜ:n 'bæk]		zurückgehen
to **be right** [bɪ 'raɪt]	*to be right* ⟷ to be wrong	Recht haben
°**Judy** ['dʒu:dɪ]		*weibl. Vorname*
to **hurt** [hɜ:t]	I *hurt* my arm last week. – Does it still *hurt* now?	verletzen, weh tun
°**mountain rescue** ['maʊntɪn 'reskju:]		Bergwacht
to **hurry** ['hʌrɪ]		sich beeilen
that way ['ðæt‿weɪ]		in die Richtung
short cut [ˌʃɔ:t 'kʌt]		Abkürzung
until [ən'tɪl]		bis
to **rescue** ['reskju:]	*to rescue* = to save	retten, bergen
to **put the telephone down** [pʊt ðə 'telɪfəʊn ˌdaʊn]		den Hörer auflegen
to **send, sent, sent** [send, sent, sent]		schicken
2 **rule** [ru:l]	Every game has *rules*.	Regel
4a) **van** [væn]		Kleinlastwagen
°**fruit cake** ['fru:t keɪk]		*engl. Kuchen*
5b) °**conjunction** [kən'dʒʌŋkʃn]		Konjunktion, Bindewort

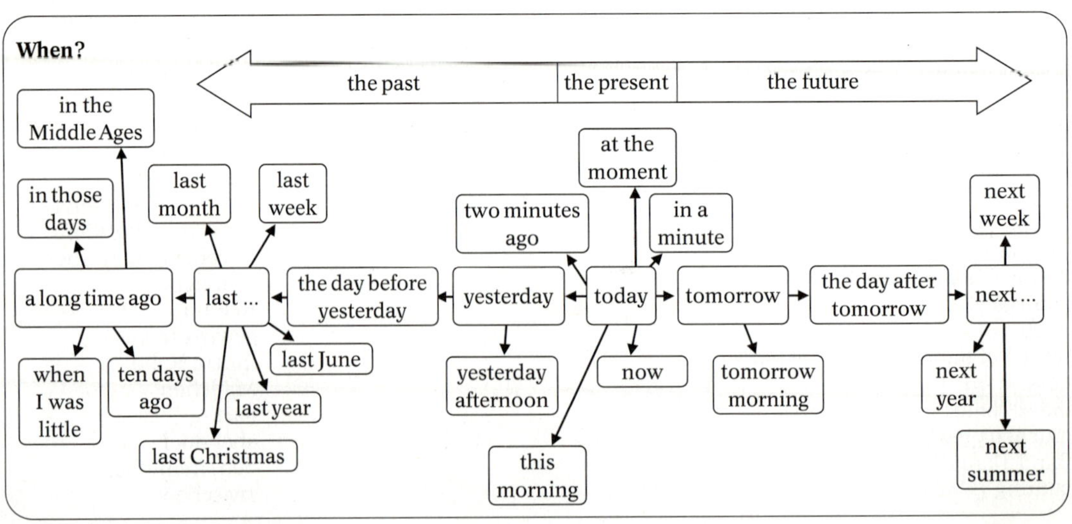

Unit 8 Help

Vocabulary

Step A The champion skater

champion ['tʃæmpjən]		Champion-, Meister-
skater ['skeɪtə]		Skateboardfahrer/in, Rollschuhläufer/in, Schlittschuhläufer/in
to **let, let, let** [let]	David doesn't *let* Mark use his new pens.	lassen, ließ, gelassen
°**helmet** ['helmɪt]		Helm
to **lie down** [ˌlaɪ 'daʊn]	You must *lie down* when you're really ill.	sich hinlegen
go away! [ˌgəʊ‿ə'weɪ]		geh weg!, weg mit dir!
1 to **break, broke, broken** [breɪk, brəʊk, 'brəʊkən]		brechen, kaputtmachen
2 to **cut out** [ˌkʌt‿'aʊt]		ausschneiden
nose [nəʊz]		Nase
ear [ɪə]		Ohr
finger ['fɪŋgə]	Achte auf die Aussprache: das 'g' nicht vergessen!	Finger
knee [niː]	Achte auf die Aussprache: das 'k' wird nicht gesprochen. Bei welchen anderen Wörtern ist das auch so?	Knie
shoulder ['ʃəʊldə]		Schulter

Step B The next morning

to **feel well** [ˌfiːl 'wel]	I don't *feel well* – I've eaten too much cake!	sich wohl fühlen
to **have to** ['hæv ˌtuː]	I *have to* do my homework before I can go swimming.	müssen
headache ['hedeɪk]	Mrs Croft has got **a** terrible *headache*.	Kopfweh

Step B The doctor's visit

visit ['vɪzɪt]	After the doctor's *visit* Mrs Croft had to go to hospital.	Besuch
Dr ['dɒktə]		*Anrede für Arzt*, Herr/Frau Doktor
°**Patel** [pə'tel]		*Familienname*
patient ['peɪʃnt]	teacher ⟷ pupil doctor ⟷ *patient*	Patient/in, Kranke(r)
to **sit up** [ˌsɪt‿'ʌp]		sich aufsetzen
to **be able to** [bɪ‿'eɪbl tə]	Sometimes patients are so ill that they *aren't able to* sit up.	können
test [test]		Test, Probe, Prüfung

Vocabulary

Step B **Mrs Croft in hospital**

ⓐ	to **be allowed to** [bɪ‿ə'laʊd tə]	Children *are not allowed to* drive cars.	dürfen
	to **rest** [rest]		sich ausruhen
7	**nurse** [nɜ:s]	*Nurses* work in hospitals. They help patients.	Krankenschwester, Krankenpfleger
ⓑ	**mine** [maɪn]	Is that my pen? – No, it's *mine*.	meine/r/s
	yours [jɔ:z]	*Yours* is over there.	deine/r/s, eure/r/s, Ihre/r/s
	ours ['aʊəz]		unsere/r/s
	his [hɪz]		seine/r/s
	hers [hɜ:z]		ihr/e
	its [ɪts]		seine/r/s, ihr/e
	theirs [ðeəz]		ihr/e

Step C **At the doctor's**

	at the doctor's [ət ðə 'dɒktəz]	Wenn du bei einer Person bist, verwendest du den s-Genitiv, um den Ort anzugeben: *at the doctor's*, at Becky's, at the newsagent's ABER: at the supermarket, at home, at school	beim Arzt
	Suvina [su:'vi:nə]		*weibl. Vorname*
	What's wrong? [ˌwɒts 'rɒŋ]	What's wrong, Becky?	Was ist los?
	sore throat [ˌsɔ: 'θrəʊt]	– I've got **a** *sore throat*.	Halsweh
	throat [θrəʊt]		Hals, Rachen
	Matthew ['mæθju:]		*Familienname*
°	**prescription** [prɪ'skrɪpʃn]	Ein deutsches Wort: zwei Bedeutungen! (Arzt-)Rezept = *prescription* (Koch-)Rezept = recipe	(Arzt-)Rezept
	chemist's ['kemɪsts]		Apotheke
	Ouch [aʊtʃ]		*Ausruf:* Aua!
	stomach-ache ['stʌməkeɪk]		Bauchweh, Magenschmerzen
	nasty ['nɑ:stɪ]	The weather is *nasty*. It's cold and wet.	schrecklich, scheußlich
	medicine ['medsɪn]	You can buy *medicine* at the chemist's.	Medizin
	temperature ['temprətʃə]	Has Suvina got **a** *temperature*? – Yes, she has.	Fieber

Step D **Happy Helpers**

	helper ['helpə]		Helfer
	Haywood Herald ['heɪwʊd 'herəld]		*Schülerzeitung der Haywood Schule*
	at least [ət 'li:st]	Verwechslungsgefahr! The holidays have come **at last**. I've got *at least* twenty sweets here.	wenigstens, mindestens
	lady ['leɪdɪ]		Dame
	operation [ˌɒpə'reɪʃn]		Operation
	a little [ə 'lɪtl]	*a little* = a bit	ein bisschen
°	**ward** [wɔ:d]		Krankensaal
	sweet [swi:t]	Chocolate is *sweet*. Pets or children can be *sweet*, too.	süß, niedlich
°	**appendix** [ə'pendɪks]		Blinddarm
1	**report** [rɪ'pɔ:t]		(Zeitungs-)Reportage

5a) **Davis** ['deɪvɪs]		*Familienname*
°**Sniffy** ['snɪfɪ]		*Name*
by [baɪ]		von
°**the Beatles** [ðə 'bi:tlz]		die Beatles *(Popgruppe)*
⟨6⟩ in any way [ɪn‿'enɪ ˌweɪ]		auf irgendeine Weise
self-assured [ˌselfə'ʃɔ:d]		selbstbewusst
mind [maɪnd]		*hier:* Meinung
down [daʊn]		schlecht, deprimiert
to appreciate [ə'pri:ʃɪəɪt]		etwas schätzen, mögen
you being round [ju: ˌbi:ɪŋ 'raʊnd]		dass du da bist
feet *(pl)* [fi:t]		Füße
ground [graʊnd]		Boden, Erde

to do

Have you **done** your homework yet?
Can you **do** this exercise?
What did you **do** on holiday last year?
What are you **doing** here?
Have you **done** the washing up?

to make

Mrs Croft has **made** a cake.
Mini is **making** a mess in the living room.
Can I **make** a request? – Please play 'Help'.
Please don't **make** a noise here!

to take

Robert is **taking** a photo of Sarah.
Please listen and **take** notes.
The sheriff **took** the man prisoner.
Please **take** off your shoes.
Who has **taken** my pencil?

to get

Get well soon!
Last week I **got** lost in Sherwood Forest.
Tabby **got** stuck in a tree yesterday.
What time do you **get** up on Sundays?
Before I go to school I **get** my books ready.
Don't forget to **get** off the bus at Larwood Grove!

Unit 9 Animal world

Step A **Pets**

°**Snowy** ['snəʊɪ]		*Name*
rabbit ['ræbɪt]		Kaninchen
mouse, mice *(pl)* [maʊs, maɪs]		Maus, Mäuse
°**Tom** [tɒm]		*männl. Vorname*
cage [keɪdʒ]		Käfig
twice a week ['twaɪs‿ə 'wi:k]	*twice a week* = two times a week	zweimal die Woche
hamster ['hæmstə]		Hamster
°**Bloggs** ['blɒgz]		*Name*
at night [ət 'naɪt]	Beachte: in the morning / in the afternoon / in the evening / ABER: *at night*	nachts
°**Yasmin** [jæz'mi:n]		*weibl. Vorname*

Vocabulary

	fish tank ['fɪʃ ˌtæŋk]	Ann has got fourteen **fish** in her *fish tank*.	Aquarium
	budgie ['bʌdʒɪ]		Wellensittich
	°**Jackie** ['dʒækɪ]		*Name*
	to **fly, flew, flown** [flaɪ, fluː, fləʊn]	Last time I went to England, I *flew* to Heathrow Airport.	fliegen, flog, geflogen
	to **keep, kept, kept** [kiːp, kept, kept]	You must *keep* medicine away from children.	(be)halten, (be)hielt, (be)halten
	closed [kləʊzd]	*closed* ⟷ open	zu, geschlossen
	°**Nina** ['niːnə]		*weibl. Vorname*
	riding school ['raɪdɪŋ ˌskuːl]	At a *riding school* you can learn to ride. And what can you learn at a driving school?	Reitschule
	pony ['pəʊnɪ]	Achte auf den Plural: *ponies*	Pony
	°**Belle** [bel]		*Name*
	°**Susan** ['suːzn]		*weibl. Vorname*
1	to **swim, swam, swum** [swɪm, swæm, swʌm]		schwimmen, schwamm, geschwommen

Step B **Sarah's video diary**

	hobby ['hɒbɪ]	What are your *hobbies*? – I play football and I collect autographs.	Hobby
	camcorder ['kæmˌkɔːdə]		Videokamera
	to **film** [fɪlm]		filmen
	to **put down** [ˌpʊt 'daʊn]		abstellen, weglegen
	to **have breakfast** [ˌhæv 'brekfəst]		frühstücken
	°**Gosh!** [gɒʃ]		*Ausruf des Erstaunens*
	milkman ['mɪlkmən]	In Britain the *milkman* comes every day.	Milchmann
	to **fall over** [ˌfɔːl‿'əʊvə]		hinfallen, umfallen
	°**action** ['ækʃn]	Achte auf die Aussprache! Sie ist anders als im Deutschen.	Handlung, Geschehen
3	°**memory** ['memərɪ]		Gedächtnis, Erinnerung
	°**past progressive** [ˌpɑːst prəʊ'gresɪv]		*Verlaufsform der Vergangenheit*

Step B **Hard work**

	loudly ['laʊdlɪ]		laut *(Adverb-Form)*
	quietly ['kwaɪətlɪ]		leise, ruhig
	fast [fɑːst]	She's got a *fast* car and she usually drives *fast*, too.	schnell, rasch
	slow [sləʊ]		langsam *(Adjektiv-Form)*
	slowly ['sləʊlɪ]		langsam *(Adverb-Form)*
	to **try hard** [ˌtraɪ 'hɑːd]		(sich) anstrengen
	well [wel]	*well* ⟷ badly	gut
8a)	°**adverb** ['ædvɜːb]		Adverb
8b)	**correct** [kə'rekt]		richtig, korrekt
9b)	**meaning** ['miːnɪŋ]		Bedeutung

Looking at the UK: Animals in the zoo

lion ['laɪən]		Löwe
monkey ['mʌŋkɪ]		Affe
tiger ['taɪgə]		Tiger
seal [si:l]		Robbe
bear [beə]		Bär
elephant ['elɪfənt]	*Elephants* are scared of mice.	Elefant
2 **Europe** ['jʊərəp]		Europa
North America [ˌnɔ:θ‿ə'merɪkə]		Nordamerika
South America [ˌsaʊθ‿ə'merɪkə]		Südamerika
Africa ['æfrɪkə]		Afrika
Asia ['eɪʃə]	A lot of people live in Africa and *Asia.*	Asien
Australia [ɒ'streɪljə]	When it's summer in *Australia,* it's winter in Europe.	Australien
Antarctica [æn'tɑ:ktɪkə]	There aren't many people in *Antarctica*!	Antarktis

Step C **Escape!**

escape [ɪ'skeɪp]		Flucht, Ausbruch
to **escape** [ɪ'skeɪp]	I've just heard the news. The prisoners *have escaped*!	fliehen, entkommen
⟨5⟩ policeman [pə'li:smən]		Polizist
⟨6⟩ Momma ['mɒmə]		Mama, Mutti
how about ...? ['haʊ‿ə'baʊt]		wie wär's mit ...?
trunk [trʌŋk]		Rüssel
to swing [swɪŋ]		*hier:* pendeln
great big ['greɪt ˌbɪg]		riesengroß
to sniff up [ˌsnɪf‿'ʌp]		aufschnuppern
peanut ['pi:nʌt]		Erdnuss
to scratch [skrætʃ]		kratzen
to hang [hæŋ]		hängen
tail [teɪl]		Schwanz
to womp [wɒmp]		*etwa:* schnaufen
heavy ['hevɪ]		schwer
don't get too near [dəʊnt get tu: 'nɪə]		geh nicht zu nahe ran
to honk [hɒŋk]		hupen, tuten
sleepy ['sli:pɪ]		schläfrig
Daddy ['dædɪ]		Papa, Vati

Vocabulary

Step D **Rabbits for sale**

for sale [fə 'seɪl]	Do you want to buy my car? It's *for sale.*	zu verkaufen
°to **bend down, bent, bent** [ˌbend 'daʊn, bent, bent]		sich bücken
to **seem** [siːm]		scheinen
to **think of** ['θɪŋk‿əv]		denken an
to **take for a walk** [ˌteɪk fər‿ə 'wɔːk]	*to take* the dogs *for a walk* = to go for a walk with the dogs	(Hund) ausführen, spazieren führen
as [æz]		während
to **hold, held, held** [həʊld, held, held]		halten
to **look down** [ˌlʊk 'daʊn]	*to look down* ⟷ to look up	nach unten sehen
quickly ['kwɪklɪ]	*quickly* = fast	schnell, rasch
excitedly [ɪk'saɪtɪdlɪ]		aufgeregt
to **pull** [pʊl]	You *pull* a **pullover** *over* your head.	ziehen
°to **drown** [draʊn]		ertrinken, ertränken
miserably ['mɪzrəblɪ]		traurig
pet shop ['pet ʃɒp]		Tierhandlung
°**summer fete** [ˌsʌmə 'feɪt]		Sommerbazar, Sommerfest
to **look after** [ˌlʊk‿'ɑːftə]	Can you *look after* the dogs on Saturday? We're going to a fete. – Yes, fine.	aufpassen, hüten
to **mind** [maɪnd]	Mum, Sarah's coming to tea. Do you *mind*?	jdm. etw. ausmachen
2 °**babysitting** ['beɪbɪˌsɪtɪŋ]		Babysitten

Jobs

actor	Schauspieler	**clerk**	Büroangestellte/r
ambulance driver	Krankenwagenfahrer/in	**doctor**	Arzt/Ärztin
		fireman	Feuerwehrmann
bank clerk	Bankangestellte/r	**housekeeper**	Haushälter/in
bus driver	Busfahrer/in	**mechanic**	Mechaniker/in
chemist	Apotheker/in	**milkman**	Milchmann
newsagent	Zeitschriftenhändler	**teacher**	Lehrer/in
nurse	Krankenschwester/pfleger	**travel agent**	Reiseverkehrskaufmann/frau
police officer	Polizist/in	**vet**	Tierarzt/ärztin
shop assistant	Verkäufer/in	**vet's assistant**	Tierarzthelfer/in

Let's play with words

1 Animal words

Can you find four animals in this word wheel?

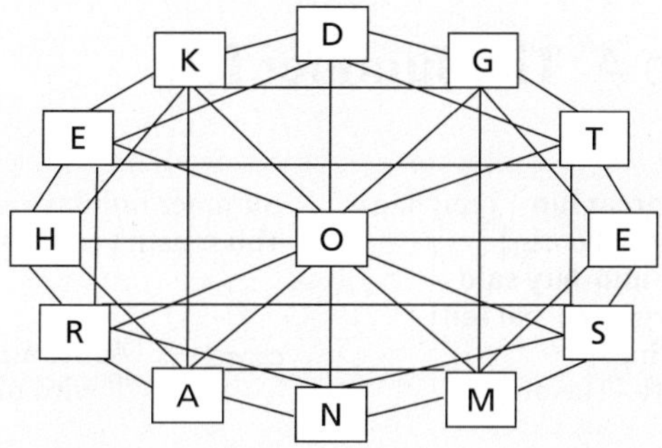

2 Funny pictures

Look at these funny pictures. Can you understand them? Write the sentences in your English folder.

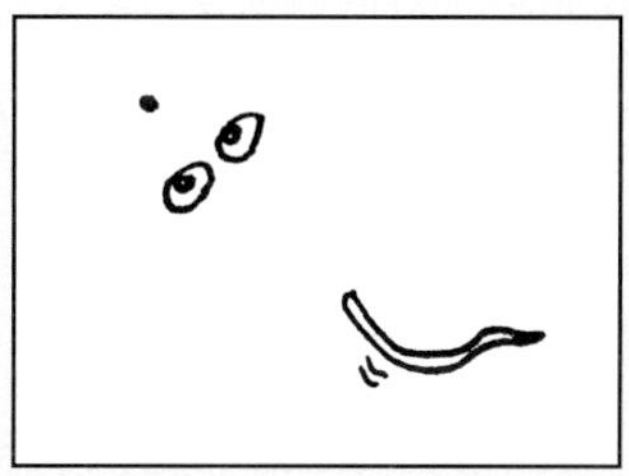

A white OSEMU is running home through the snow.

A BRAC is saying hello to a SHIF.

A NILO has left its cage.

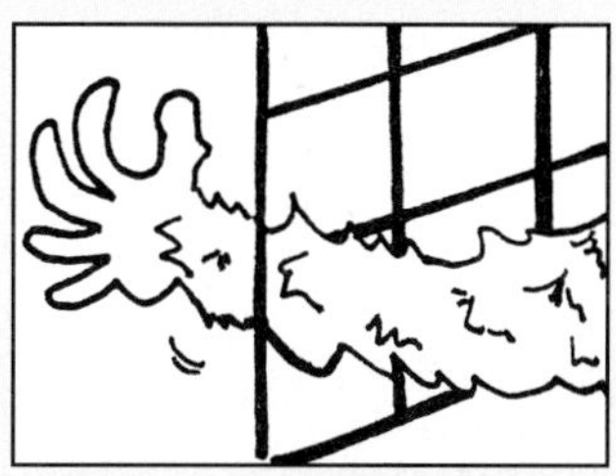

A NEKYMO is asking for a banana.

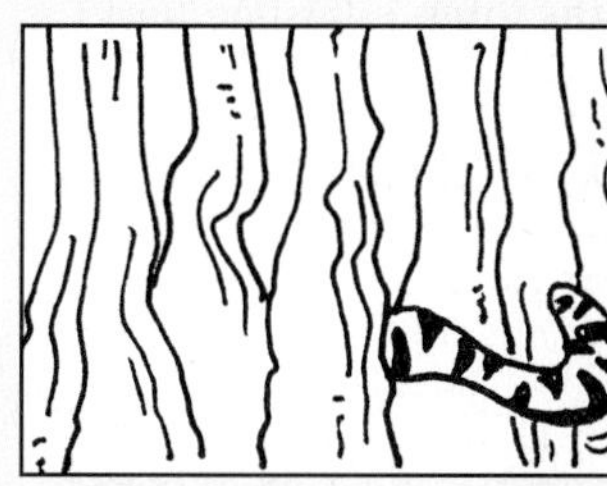

A RIGET is going through the forest.

A BRIBAT doesn't like its carrot.

A black ERAB is talking to his friend, a black HEPESGOD, at night.

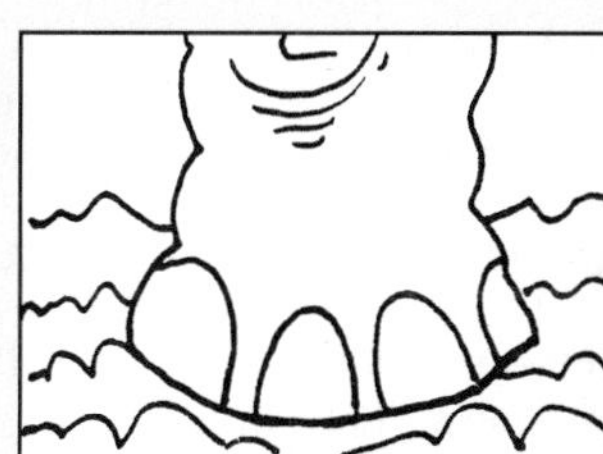

An APHELENT is standing in a pond.

Can you make funny pictures for your friends? Put them in your folder, too.

Unit 10 The end of the school year

Step A **The summer fete**

	to be **great fun** [ˌgreɪt ˈfʌn]	Summer holidays are *great fun*.	viel Spaß machen
	during [ˈdjʊərɪŋ]	You mustn't eat *during* lessons!	während
	°**bring-and-buy sale** [ˌbrɪŋ‿ænd ˈbaɪ seɪl]		Flohmarkt
	half [hɑːf]	Achte auf die Aussprache: Das 'l' wird nicht gesprochen.	die Hälfte
	charity [ˈtʃærətɪ]		Wohltätigkeitsverein
	member [ˈmembə]	Are you a *member* of a sports club?	Mitglied
	°**brass band** [ˌbrɑːs ˈbænd]		Blasorchester
	band [bænd]		(Musik-)Gruppe
	concert [ˈkɒnsət]	Have you ever been to a pop *concert*?	Konzert
2	to **give away** [ˌgɪv‿əˈweɪ]		*hier:* weggeben, verschenken

Step B **Before the fete**

	just the thing [ˌdʒʌst ðə ˈθɪŋ]		genau das Richtige
	toy [tɔɪ]		Spielzeug
	trumpet [ˈtrʌmpɪt]		Trompete
1a)	**singer** [ˈsɪŋə]		Sänger/in

Looking at the UK: Charities

country [ˈkʌntrɪ]	A lot of people spend their holidays in another *country*.	Land
to **make money** [ˌmeɪk ˈmʌnɪ]	Some pop singers *make* a lot of *money*.	Geld verdienen
in different ways [ɪn ˌdɪfrənt‿ˈweɪz]	You can learn your vocabulary *in different ways*.	auf verschiedene Weise
a long way [ə ˌlɒŋ‿ˈweɪ]	It's *a long way* from London to Berlin.	eine weite Entfernung
youth group [ˈjuːθ ˌgruːp]		Jugendgruppe
to **organize** [ˈɔːgənaɪz]		organisieren
°**disco** [ˈdɪskəʊ]		Diskothek, Disco
car wash [ˈkɑː wɒʃ]		Autowaschanlage
°**programme** [ˈprəʊgræm]		Programm
even [ˈiːvn]	We organized a disco last week. *Even* the teachers enjoyed it!	sogar
a few [ə ˈfjuː]	I've forgotten my money. Can you lend me *a few* pounds?	ein paar

Step C **Let's have fun**

to **sound** [saʊnd]	Holidays in America? That *sounds* good.	klingen, sich anhören
should [ʃʊd]	You *should* eat more fruit – it's good for you.	sollte(n)
2 °to **match** [mætʃ]		das Dazupassende finden
situation [ˌsɪtjʊ'eɪʃn]		Lage, Situation
⟨5⟩ to heed [hiːd]		Aufmerksamkeit schenken
certain ['sɜːtn]		gewisse/r/s
call [kɔːl]		Ruf
to lend a hand [ˌlend‿ə'hænd]		helfen
life [laɪf]		Leben
greatest gift ['greɪtɪst ˌgɪft]		größtes Geschenk
to pretend [prɪ'tend]		so tun als ob
day by day ['deɪ baɪ 'deɪ]		tagein, tagaus, jeden Tag
change [tʃeɪndʒ]		Veränderung
God [gɒd]		Gott
truth [truːθ]		Wahrheit
bright [braɪt]		hell
choice [tʃɔɪs]		Wahl
own [əʊn]		eigene/r/s
true [truː]		wahr
to care [keə]		mitfühlen
strong [strɒŋ]		stark
to turn [tɜːn]		*hier:* verwandeln
down and out [ˌdaʊn‿ən‿'aʊt]		*hier:* hoffnungslos, in Schwierigkeiten
to believe [bɪ'liːv]		glauben
whoa [wəʊ]		*Ausruf*
to realize ['rɪəlaɪz]		einsehen

Step D **Lucky weather**

dry [draɪ]	*dry* ⟷ wet	trocken
just then [ˌdʒʌst 'ðen]		in diesem Moment
Stuart ['stjʊət]		*Familienname*
to **bother s.o.** ['bɒðə]	Mark, *don't bother me* with your broken kite now. I have to do my homework.	jemanden stören
and with that [ˌænd‿wɪð 'ðæt]		und damit
to **get out of bed on the wrong side** [get‿aʊt‿əv ˌbed‿ɒn ðə rɒŋ 'saɪd]		mit dem falschen Fuß aufstehen
grumpy ['grʌmpɪ]	This man looks grumpy. 	mürrisch
or so [ˌɔː 'səʊ]		oder ungefähr
you shouldn't ['ʃʊdnt]	You *shouldn't* ride your bike without a helmet.	du sollst nicht, sie sollen nicht, ihr sollt nicht
out of the way [ˌaʊt‿əv ðə 'weɪ]		aus dem Weg

	°**front seat** [ˌfrʌnt ˈsiːt]		Vordersitz
	sunroof [ˈsʌnruːf]		Schiebedach
	cloud [klaʊd]		Wolke
	to **carry** [ˈkærɪ]	 You *carry* things like books or bottles, but you **wear** clothes.	tragen
	°**drop** [drɒp]		Tropfen
	°**Assembly Hall** [əˈsemblɪ ˌhɔːl]		Versammlungssaal, Aula
	rain [reɪn]	to rain → *rain*	Regen
2	°**mistake** [miˈsteɪk]		Fehler
3	°**noun** [naʊn]	'Cloud', 'trumpet' and 'rain' are *nouns*.	Substantiv
3a)	**smile** [smaɪl]		Lächeln
	stay [steɪ]	The Germans enjoyed their *stay* in Nottingham.	Aufenthalt
	wash [wɒʃ]	 This car needs a *wash*!	Wäsche, Waschen
3b)	**jump** [dʒʌmp]		Sprung
	to **bully** [ˈbʊlɪ]		schikanieren, tyrannisieren

in	on	at
in February	**on** holiday	**at** the weekend
in the evening	**on** the radio/on TV	**at** once
in front of the house	**on** the left/right	**at** lunchtime
in hospital	**on** 6th of June	**at** the bottom of the hill
	on the telephone	**at** the door
	on Monday	**at** 6 o'clock
		at school
		at the Burtons' house
		at night

Let's play with words

1 Packets of crisps

In each packet there is one 'wrong' crisp. Find them and draw the fourth packet of crisps in your exercise book. Now think of two more words for crisps to finish the packet.

2 Word games

This is a word game with the title 'ill'. Now play this game in your exercise book for the title 'summer holidays'. How many words can you find?

```
h
e
l
p r e s c r i p t i o n
                      u
                      r
                      s
                      e x a m i n e
                                  a
                                  r e s t
                                        e
                                        s
                                        t e m p e r a t u r e
```

3 Word stars

This is a word star for 'a book'. Draw these word stars in your book and finish them. Can you make another word star for your friends?

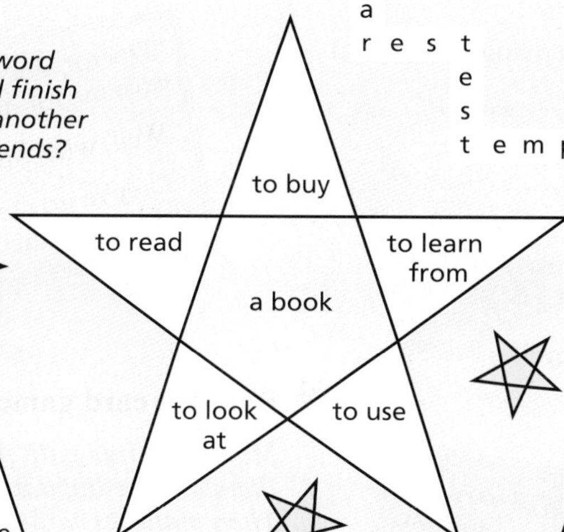

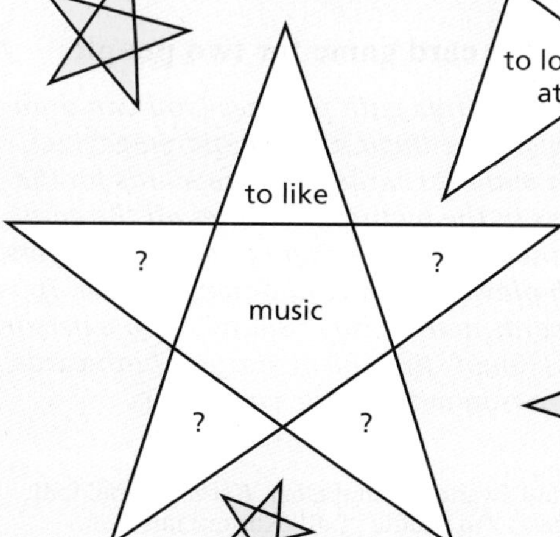

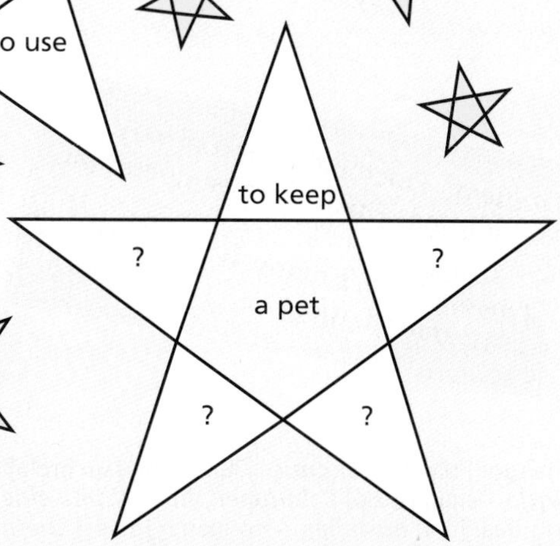

⟨Just for fun⟩

The teapot[1] game

Think of a thing. That's your "teapot". Your partner asks you questions. He or she must find out what your "teapot" is.

Your partner: Is your "teapot" big?
You: No, it isn't.
Your partner: Has your "teapot" got legs?
You: Yes, it has.
Your partner: Can your "teapot" walk?
You: No, it can't.
Your partner: Is your teapot a …? *Go on.*

"Waiter[3], waiter, can I have a cup of coffee without cream, please?"

"Sorry, we haven't got any cream. Would you like it without milk?"

Sign in a hospital canteen:

Our spoons are not medicine. Don't take them after meals.

A man fell down a very deep hole. His friend was very worried and called down the hole, "Are you OK? Have you broken anything?"
"Oh no," answered the man. "Don't worry. There isn't anything to break down here!"

"Doctor, doctor, – those pills[4] you gave me for my stomach … ."
"Well, what about them?"
"They're no good. They fall off my stomach in the night."

Patient: Doctor, doctor, I'm very worried. This is my first operation.

Doctor: That's funny. It's my first operation, too.

Snap[5]: a card game for two people

Make 20 cards with pictures (you can draw them or take them from an old magazine). Then make 20 cards with the words for the things in the pictures. Shuffle[6] all the cards together, then deal[7] them to the two players. Both players put a card down together. If the cards match[8], say "Snap!". If one person says "Snap!" first, he or she gets both cards. The person with all the cards wins.

[1]teapot ['ti:pɒt] *Teekanne* – [2]umbrella [ʌm'brelə] Regenschirm – [3]waiter ['weɪtə] *Ober, Kellner* – [4]pill [pɪl] *Pille* –[5]snap [snæp] *Schnippen; hier: Name eines Kartenspiels* – [6]to shuffle ['ʃʌfl] (Karten) mischen – [7]to deal [di:l] *austeilen* – [8]to match [mætʃ] *zueinander passen*

Alphabetical word list

In dieser alphabetischen Liste ist das gesamte Vokabular von *Green Line New 1* und *2* enthalten. Namen werden in einer gesonderten Liste nach dem Vokabular aufgeführt.

Die mit einem ° gekennzeichneten Wörter zeichnen den rezeptiven Wortschatz aus. In Bundesländern, in denen nicht ausdrücklich rezeptiver Wortschatz verlangt wird, werden diese Wörter genauso behandelt wie der übrige Wortschatz. Die rezeptiv gekennzeichneten Wörter können innerhalb der Unit, in der sie erstmalig vorkommen, eigenständig von den Schülerinnen und Schülern angewandt werden. Falls sie in späteren Units auftauchen, werden sie nur mit Hilfe von Vorgaben verlangt.

Der Wortschatz aus Übungen und Texten, die in Spitzklammern ⟨ ⟩ stehen, ist wahlfrei.
Das Zeichen * nach einem Verb bedeutet: unregelmäßiges Verb.
Die Zahlen verweisen auf das erstmalige Vorkommen der Wörter, z. B.
about [ə'baʊt] über **I** = Green Line New Band 1
above [ə'bʌv] über **II 5**, 42 = Green Line New Band 2, Unit 5, Seite 42

A

a [ə] ein/eine **I**
to be **able to** [bɪ‿'eɪbl tə] können **II 8**, 73
about [ə'baʊt] über **I**
to talk about ['tɔ:k‿əˌbaʊt] reden über, sprechen über **I**
to write about ['raɪt‿əˌbaʊt] schreiben über **I**
What about…? ['wɒt‿əˌbaʊt] Was ist mit…?, Wie wär's mit…? **I**
above [ə'bʌv] über **II 5**, 42
accident ['æksɪdənt] Unfall **I**
to **act** [ækt] spielen, nachspielen **I**
°**action** ['ækʃn] Handlung, Geschehen **II 9**, 81
activity [æk'tɪvətɪ] Tätigkeit, Unternehmung **I**
actor ['æktə] Schauspieler **II 5**, 49
to **add** [æd] hinzufügen **II 5**, 49
address [ə'dres] Adresse, Anschrift **II 7**, 63
adjective ['ædʒɪktɪv] Adjektiv **II 3**, 25
adult ['ædʌlt] Erwachsener **II 5**, 47
adventure [əd'ventʃə] Abenteuer **II 2**, 15
°**adverb** ['ædvɜ:b] Adverb **II 9**, 83
after ['ɑ:ftə] nach **I**
after a time [ˌɑ:ftər‿ə 'taɪm] nach einer Weile **II 7**, 67
afternoon [ˌɑ:ftə'nu:n] Nachmittag **I**
in the afternoon [ɪn ðɪ‿ˌɑ:ftə'nu:n] am Nachmittag, nachmittags **I**
this afternoon [ðɪs‿ˌɑ:ftə'nu:n] heute Nachmittag **I**
again [ə'gen] noch einmal, wieder **I**
age [eɪdʒ] Alter **II 2**, 20
°the Middle Ages [ðə ˌmɪdl 'eɪdʒɪz] das Mittelalter **II 2**, 20
travel **agent's** ['trævl‿ˌeɪdʒənts] Reisebüro **II 7**, 63
ago [ə'gəʊ] vor **II 4**, 33
a hundred years ago [ə ˌhʌndrəd 'jɪəz‿əˌgəʊ] vor hundert Jahren **II 4**, 33
a long time ago [ə ˌlɒŋ taɪm‿ə'gəʊ] lange her **II 7**, 65
airport ['eəpɔ:t] Flughafen **I**
all [ɔ:l] ganz, völlig **I**
all over ['ɔ:l‿ˌəʊvə] überall (auf) **I**
all right [ˌɔ:l 'raɪt] in Ordnung **II 4**, 39
all [ɔ:l] alle/alles **I**
to be **allowed to** [bɪ‿ə'laʊd tə] dürfen **II 8**, 74
almost ['ɔ:lməʊst] fast **II 6**, 53
alone [ə'ləʊn] allein **II 3**, 31
leave me alone ['li:v mɪ‿ə'ləʊn] lass mich in Ruhe **II 3**, 31
alphabet ['ælfəbet] Alphabet **I**
°**alphabetical** [ælfə'betɪkl] alphabetisch **II 4**, 33
already [ɔ:l'redɪ] schon, bereits **I**
although [ɔ:l'ðəʊ] obwohl **II 7**, 67
always ['ɔ:lweɪz] immer **I**
ambulance ['æmbjʊləns] Krankenwagen **I**
American [ə'merɪkən] amerikanisch, Amerikaner/in **II 3**, 25
⟨among⟩ [ə'mʌŋ] zwischen **II 7**, 66
an [ən] ein/eine **I**
and [ænd/ənd] und **I**
and so on [ənd 'səʊ ɒn] und so weiter **II 5**, 50
angry ['æŋgrɪ] böse, verärgert **I**
animal ['ænɪml] Tier **I**
anorak ['ænəræk] Anorak **I**
another [ə'nʌðə] ein anderer/eine andere/ein anderes; noch ein/eine **I**
answer ['ɑ:nsə] Antwort **I**
to **answer** ['ɑ:nsə] antworten, beantworten **I**
any ['enɪ] etwas, einige, irgend- **I**
anybody ['enɪbɒdɪ] (irgend)jemand **II 5**, 45
anyone ['enɪwʌn] (irgend)jemand **II 5**, 49
anything ['enɪθɪŋ] (irgend)etwas **I**
anyway ['enɪweɪ] jedenfalls, sowieso **II 3**, 26
anywhere ['enɪweə] irgendwo **II 5**, 45
°**appendix** [ə'pendɪks] Blinddarm **II 8**, 76
apple ['æpl] Apfel **I**
⟨to appreciate⟩ [ə'pri:ʃɪəɪt] etwas schätzen **II 8**, 78
April ['eɪprəl] April **I**
arm [ɑ:m] Arm **I**
around [ə'raʊnd] um **II 2**, 19
to **arrive** [ə'raɪv] ankommen **I**
°**arrow** ['ærəʊ] Pfeil **II 2**, 15
Art [ɑ:t] Kunst **II 1**, 8
as [æz] in der Rolle von, als **II 4**, 34
as [æz] während **II 9**, 87
as … as [əz … əz] so … wie **II 3**, 26
as soon as [əz 'su:n‿əz] sobald **II 2**, 20
to **ask** [ɑ:sk] fragen **I**
to ask for ['ɑ:sk fə] bitten um **I**
°**assembly** [ə'semblɪ] Versammlung **I**
°Assembly Hall [ə'semblɪ ˌhɔ:l] Versammlungssaal, Aula **II 10**, 95
assistant [ə'sɪstənt] Helfer/in, Assistent/in **I**
shop assistant ['ʃɒp‿əˌsɪstənt] Verkäufer/in **I**
vet's assistant ['vets‿əˌsɪstənt] Tierarzthelfer/in **I**
at [æt/ət] an; um *(bei Zeitangaben)* **I**
at first [ət 'fɜ:st] zuerst **II 2**, 17
at home [ət 'həʊm] zu Hause **I**
at last [ət 'lɑ:st] schließlich, zuletzt **I**
at least [ət 'li:st] wenigstens **II 8**, 76

at lunchtime [ət 'lʌntʃtaɪm] in der Mittagspause **II 1**, 11
at night [ət 'naɪt] nachts **II 9**, 80
at once [ət 'wʌns] sofort **II 1**, 12
at the bottom of [ət ðə 'bɒtəm_əv] ganz unten, hinten **I**
at the doctor's [ət ðə 'dɒktəz] beim Arzt **II 8**, 75
at the door [ət ðə 'dɔ:] an der Tür **I**
at the top of... [ət ðə 'tɒp_əv] ganz oben **I**
August ['ɔ:gəst] August **I**
aunt [ɑ:nt] Tante **I**
aunty ['ɑ:ntɪ] *Anrede für eine Tante* **I**
° **autograph** ['ɔ:təgra:f] Autogramm **II 5**, 46
autumn ['ɔ:təm] Herbst **I**
away [ə'weɪ] weg, fort **I**
to give away [ˌgɪv_ə'weɪ] weggeben, verschenken **II 10**, 90
go away! [ˌgəʊ_ə'weɪ] geh weg!, weg mit dir! **II 8**, 71

B

baby ['beɪbɪ] Baby **I**
° **babysitting** ['beɪbɪˌsɪtɪŋ] Babysitten **II 9**, 88
back [bæk] zurück **I**
back door [ˌbæk 'dɔ:] Hintertür **I**
bad [bæd] schlecht, schlimm **I**
badminton ['bædmɪntən] Federballspiel **I**
bag [bæg] Tasche **I**
° **bagpipes** ['bægpaɪps] Dudelsack **II 7**, 65
ball [bɔ:l] Ball **I**
banana [bə'na:nə] Banane **I**
band [bænd] (Musik-)Gruppe **II 10**, 90
° brass band [ˌbrɑ:s 'bænd] Blasorchester **II 10**, 90
bank [bæŋk] Bank **I**
bank clerk ['bæŋk ˌklɑ:k] Bankangestellte/r **I**
bar [bɑ:] Tafel, Stück **I**
° to **bark** [bɑ:k] bellen **I**
bath [bɑ:θ] Bad, Badewanne **I**
° bubble bath ['bʌbl ˌbɑ:θ] Schaumbad **I**
to have a bath [ˌhæv_ə 'bɑ:θ] baden, ein Bad nehmen **I**
bathroom ['bɑ:θrʊm] Badezimmer **I**
to **be*** [bɪ] sein **I**
to be able to [bɪ_'eɪbl tə] können **II 8**, 73
to be allowed to [bɪ_ə'laʊd tə] dürfen **II 8**, 74
to be called [bɪ 'kɔ:ld] heißen **II 2**, 19
to be careful [bɪ 'keəfʊl] vorsichtig sein, Acht geben **I**
to be excited [bɪ_ɪk'saɪtɪd] aufgeregt sein **I**
to be finished [bɪ 'fɪnɪʃt] fertig sein **I**
to be fun [bɪ 'fʌn] Spaß machen **I**
to be going to [bɪ 'gəʊɪŋ tə] werden **I**
to be good at... [bɪ 'gʊd_ət] gut sein in ... **I**
to be lucky [bɪ 'lʌkɪ] Glück haben **I**
to be on [bɪ_'ɒn] eingeschaltet sein **I**
to be quiet [bɪ 'kwaɪət] ruhig sein, still sein **I**
to be right [bɪ 'raɪt] Recht haben **II 7**, 67
to be scared of [bɪ 'skeəd_əv] Angst haben vor **II 2**, 17
to be sure [bɪ 'ʃɔ:] sicher sein **I**
to be surprised [bɪ sə'praɪzd] überrascht sein **I**
beach [bi:tʃ] Strand **I**
bean [bi:n] Bohne **II 6**, 52
bear [beə] Bär **II 9**, 84
beard [bɪəd] Bart **II 4**, 33
beautiful ['bju:təfʊl] schön **II 7**, 62
because [bɪ'kɒz] weil **I**
bed [bed] Bett **I**
° bed and breakfast place [ˌbed_ənd 'brekfəst pleɪs] Frühstückspension **II 7**, 63
to get out of bed on the wrong side [get_aʊt_əv ˌbed_ɒn ðə rɒŋ 'saɪd] mit dem falschen Fuß aufstehen **II 10**, 95
bedroom ['bedrʊm] Schlafzimmer **I**
° **beef** [bi:f] Rindfleisch **II 6**, 52
° roast beef [ˌrəʊst 'bi:f] Rinderbraten **II 6**, 52
° **beetle** ['bi:tl] Käfer **I**
before [bɪ'fɔ:] bevor **II 2**, 20; vor *(zeitlich)* **I**
to **begin*** [bɪ'gɪn] beginnen, anfangen **II 1**, 7
beginning [bɪ'gɪnɪŋ] Anfang **II 2**, 22
behind [bɪ'haɪnd] hinter **I**
from behind [ˌfrɒm bɪ'haɪnd] von hinten **II 3**, 30
⟨to believe⟩ [bɪ'li:v] glauben **II 10**, 94
° to **bend down*** [ˌbend 'daʊn] sich bücken **II 9**, 87
best [best] beste/bester/bestes **I**
best of all ['best_əv_ɔ:l] am allerbesten **I**
better ['betə] besser **I**
between [bɪ'twi:n] zwischen **I**
big [bɪg] groß **I**
⟨great big⟩ ['greɪt ˌbɪg] riesengroß **II 9**, 86
° **Big Wheel** [ˌbɪg_'wi:l] Riesenrad **II 3**, 28
bike [baɪk] Fahrrad **I**
bird [bɜ:d] Vogel **II 1**, 11
° bird watcher ['bɜ:d ˌwɒtʃə] Vogelbeobachter/in **II 1**, 11
biro ['baɪrəʊ] Kugelschreiber, Kuli **I**
birthday ['bɜ:θdeɪ] Geburtstag **I**
biscuit ['bɪskɪt] Keks **I**
dog biscuit ['dɒg ˌbɪskɪt] Hundekuchen **I**
a **bit** [ə_'bɪt] etwas, ein bisschen **I**
black [blæk] schwarz **I**
⟨to blow⟩ [bləʊ] blasen, *hier:* pfeifen **II 4**, 38
blue [blu:] blau **I**
notice **board** ['nəʊtɪs bɔ:d] Schwarzes Brett **II 1**, 9
boat [bəʊt] Boot **I**
boating lake ['bəʊtɪŋ leɪk] Bootsteich **I**
body ['bɒdɪ] Körper **I**
⟨bonny⟩ ['bɒnɪ] schön, hübsch **II 7**, 66
book [bʊk] Buch **I**
exercise book ['eksəsaɪz ˌbʊk] (Übungs-)Heft **II 2**, 22
bookshop ['bʊkʃɒp] Buchhandlung **II 6**, 55
⟨border⟩ ['bɔ:də] Grenze, *hier: Grenzgebiet in Schottland* **II 7**, 66
boring ['bɔ:rɪŋ] langweilig **I**
both [bəʊθ] beide **II 1**, 8
to **bother s.o.** ['bɒðə] jdn. stören **II 10**, 95
bottle ['bɒtl] Flasche **I**
at the **bottom of** [ət ðə 'bɒtəm_əv] ganz unten, hinten **I**
° **bow** [bəʊ] Bogen **II 2**, 15
⟨to bowl⟩ [bəʊl] werfen **II 3**, 28
box [bɒks] Schachtel, Kiste, Dose **I**
lunch box ['lʌntʃ ˌbɒks] *Dose für belegte Brote zum Mittagessen* **I**
boy [bɔɪ] Junge **I**
° **brass band** [ˌbrɑ:s 'bænd] Blasorchester **II 10**, 90
bread [bred] Brot **I**
break [breɪk] Pause **II 1**, 8
to **break*** [breɪk] brechen, kaputtmachen **II 8**, 71
breakfast ['brekfəst] Frühstück **I**
to have breakfast [ˌhæv 'brekfəst] frühstücken **II 9**, 81
fire **brigade** ['faɪə brɪˌgeɪd] Feuerwehr **I**
⟨bright⟩ [braɪt] hell **II 10**, 94
to **bring*** [brɪŋ] bringen **II 6**, 52
to bring here [brɪŋ 'hɪə] herbringen **I**
° **bring-and-buy sale** [ˌbrɪŋ_nd 'baɪ seɪl] Flohmarkt **II 10**, 90
British ['brɪtɪʃ] britisch, Britisch **I**
brochure ['brəʊʃə] Broschüre, Prospekt **II 7**, 62

broken ['brəʊkn] zerbrochen, kaputt **I**
brother ['brʌðə] Bruder **I**
brown [braʊn] braun **I**
°**bubble bath** ['bʌbl ˌbɑ:θ] Schaumbad **I**
bucket ['bʌkɪt] Eimer **I**
budgie ['bʌdʒɪ] Wellensittich **II 9**, 80
bully ['bʊlɪ] Rabauke, Rüpel, Tyrann **II 1**, 12
to **bully** ['bʊlɪ] schikanieren, tyrannisieren **II 10**, 96
⟨lovely bunch⟩ [ˌlʌvlɪ 'bʌntʃ] eine schöne Menge **II 3**, 28
°**burglar** ['bɜ:glə] Einbrecher/in **I**
⟨to bury⟩ ['berɪ] begraben, vergraben **II 7**, 66
bus [bʌs] Bus **I**
bus stop ['bʌs‿stɒp] Bushaltestelle **I**
busy ['bɪzɪ] beschäftigt **II 5**, 44
but [bʌt] aber **I**
⟨but yet⟩ [ˌbʌt 'jet] aber doch **II 7**, 66
butter ['bʌtə] Butter **I**
to **buy*** [baɪ] kaufen **I**
by [baɪ] mit **I**; von **II 8**,78
by heart [baɪ 'hɑ:t] auswendig **II 4**, 38

C

cabbage ['kæbɪdʒ] Kohl **II 6**, 52
cage [keɪdʒ] Käfig **II 9**, 80
cake [keɪk] Kuchen, Torte **I**
°fruit cake ['fru:t keɪk] *engl. Kuchen* **II 7**, 69
calf, calves *(pl)* [kɑ:f] Kalb, Kälber **I**
⟨call⟩ [kɔ:l] Ruf **II 10**, 95
to **call** [kɔ:l] rufen, anrufen **I**
to be called [bɪ 'kɔ:ld] heißen **II 2**, 19
camcorder ['kæmˌkɔ:də] Videokamera **II 9**, 81
camera ['kæmərə] Fotoapparat, Kamera **I**
°to go **camping** [ˌgəʊ 'kæmpɪŋ] zelten gehen **I**
can* [kæn] können **I**
°**candle** ['kændl] Kerze **I**
°**canteen** [kæn'ti:n] Kantine, Cafeteria **I**
car [kɑ:] Auto **I**
car park ['kɑ: pɑ:k] Parkhaus, Parkplatz **II 5**, 42
car wash ['kɑ: wɒʃ] Autowaschanlage **II 10**, 92
°**caravan** ['kærəvæn] Wohnwagen **I**
card [kɑ:d] Karte **I**
⟨to care⟩ [keə] mitfühlen **II 10**, 94
to be **careful** [bɪ 'keəfʊl] vorsichtig sein, Acht geben **I**
carefully ['keəflɪ] vorsichtig, sorgfältig **II 9**, 83
carrot ['kærət] Karotte, Möhre **II 6**, 52
to **carry** ['kærɪ] tragen **II 10**, 95
pencil **case** ['pensl keɪs] Federmäppchen **I**
cassette [kə'set] Kassette **II 3**, 25
castle ['kɑ:sl] Burg **I**
cat [kæt] Katze **I**
to **catch*** [kætʃ] fangen **II 2**, 15
°**cave** [keɪv] Höhle **II 2**, 19
CD [si:'di:] CD **I**
CD player [si:'di: pleɪə] CD-Spieler **I**
centre ['sentə] Zentrum, Mitte **I**
city centre [ˌsɪtɪ 'sentə] Stadtzentrum **I**
shopping centre ['ʃɒpɪŋ ˌsentə] Einkaufszentrum **II 5**, 42
sports centre ['spɔ:ts ˌsentə] Sportzentrum **II 1**, 11
⟨certain⟩ ['sɜ:tn] gewisse/r/s **II 7**, 66
chair [tʃeə] Stuhl **I**
champion ['tʃæmpjən] Champion-, Meister- **II 8**, 71
⟨change⟩ [tʃeɪndʒ] Veränderung **II 10**, 94
to **change** [tʃeɪndʒ] (sich) ändern, verändern, wechseln **II 7**, 67
character ['kærəktə] Person, Charakter **I**
charity ['tʃærətɪ] Wohltätigkeitsverein **II 10**, 90
cheap [tʃi:p] billig **II 3**, 25
to **check** [tʃek] überprüfen, kontrollieren **I**
cheese [tʃi:z] Käse **I**
chemist's ['kemɪsts] Apotheke **II 8**, 75
chicken ['tʃɪkn] Huhn **I**
child, children [tʃaɪld] Kind, Kinder **I**
Chinese [ˌtʃaɪ'ni:z] chinesisch, Chinesisch, Chinese/Chinesin **II 6**, 52
chips [tʃɪps] Pommes frites **I**
chocolate ['tʃɒklət] Schokolade **I**
⟨choice⟩ [tʃɔɪs] Wahl **II 10**, 94
to **choose*** [tʃu:z, tʃəʊz, 'tʃəʊzn] wählen, aussuchen **II 6**, 58
⟨chorus⟩ ['kɔ:rəs] Refrain **II 7**,66
Christmas ['krɪsməs] Weihnachten **II 4**, 33
°**church** [tʃɜ:tʃ] Kirche **I**
cinema ['sɪnəmə] Kino **I**
city ['sɪtɪ] Stadt **I**
city centre [ˌsɪtɪ 'sentə] Stadtzentrum **I**
City Information Centre [ˌsɪtɪ‿ɪnfə'meɪʃn ˌsentə] Touristeninformation **I**
to **clap** [klæp] klatschen, Beifall geben **II 4**, 39
class [klɑ:s] Klasse (*in einer deutschen Schule*) **I**
classroom ['klɑ:srʊm] Klassenzimmer **I**
clean [kli:n] sauber **II 4**, 33
to **clean** [kli:n] putzen, sauber machen **II 6**, 59
clerk [klɑ:k] Büroangestellte/r **I**
bank clerk ['bæŋk ˌklɑ:k] Bankangestellte/r **I**
clever ['klevə] intelligent, klug **I**
to **climb up** [ˌklaɪm‿'ʌp] heraufklettern **I**
climbing ['klaɪmɪŋ] Bergsteigen, Klettern **II 1**, 11
clock [klɒk] Uhr **II 5**, 42
to **close** [kləʊz] (sich) schließen **I**
closed [kləʊzd] zu, geschlossen **II 9**, 80
clothes [kləʊðz] Kleidung **I**
cloud [klaʊd] Wolke **II 10**, 95
club [klʌb] Klub, Verein **II 1**, 11
coach [kəʊtʃ] Reisebus **II 7**, 63
coat [kəʊt] Mantel **II 2**, 21
°**coconut** ['kəʊkənʌt] Kokosnuss **II 3**, 28
°coconut shy ['kəʊkənʌt ˌʃaɪ] Wurfbude **II 3**, 28
coffee ['kɒfɪ] Kaffee **II 6**, 57
°coffee shop ['kɒfɪ ˌʃɒp] Café **II 5**, 43
cold [kəʊld] kalt **I**
to **collect** [kə'lekt] abholen; sammeln, einsammeln **I**
colour ['kʌlə] Farbe **I**
to **colour in** [ˌkʌlər‿'ɪn] anmalen **I**
to **come*** [kʌm] kommen **I**
Come on. [kʌm‿'ɒn] Komm/t schon. **I**
to come in [kʌm‿'ɪn] hereinkommen **I**
to come off [kʌm‿'ɒf] runterfallen **II 4**, 39
comic ['kɒmɪk] Comic **I**
to **compare** [kəm'peə] vergleichen **II 3**, 26
competition [ˌkɒmpə'tɪʃn] Wettbewerb, Preisausschreiben **I**
to **complete** [kəm'pli:t] fertig stellen, beenden **II 5**, 46
°**compound** ['kɒmpaʊnd] zusammengesetztes Wort **II 5**, 45
computer [kəm'pju:tə] Computer **I**
concert ['kɒnsət] Konzert **II 10**, 90
°**conjunction** [kən'dʒʌŋkʃn] Konjunktion, Bindewort **II 7**, 69
to **cook** [kʊk] kochen **II 6**, 52
corner ['kɔ:nə] Ecke **II 5**, 44
cornflakes ['kɔ:nfleɪks] Cornflakes **I**
to **correct** [kə'rekt] berichtigen, verbessern **I**
correct [kə'rekt] richtig, korrekt **II 9**, 83

corridor ['kɒrɪdɔ:] Korridor, Gang **II 1**, 12
to **cost*** [kɒst] kosten **I**
° **costume** ['kɒstju:m] Verkleidung, Kostüm **II 4**, 33
° **cottage** ['kɒtɪdʒ] Häuschen **I**
could [kʊd] konnten/könntest **II 5**, 48; konnte **II 2**, 18
to **count** [kaʊnt] zählen **I**
° **counter** ['kaʊntə] Schalter, Theke **I**
country ['kʌntrɪ] Land **II 10**, 92
of **course** [əv‿'kɔ:s] natürlich, selbstverständlich **I**
⟨to court⟩ [kɔ:t] um eine Frau werben **II 7**, 66
cousin ['kʌzn] Cousin/e **I**
cow [kaʊ] Kuh **I**
° **crab** [kræb] Krebs **I**
° **Crash!** [kræʃ] Krach! **II 3**, 30
crayon ['kreɪən] Buntstift **I**
crazy ['kreɪzɪ] verrückt **I**
cream [kri:m] Sahne **II 6**, 59
cricket ['krɪkɪt] Kricket (*englischer Rasensport*) **I**
crisps (*pl*) [krɪsps] Kartoffelchips **I**
° **Croak!** [krəʊk] Quak! **I**
crowd [kraʊd] Menschenmenge **II 2**, 22
cup [kʌp] Tasse **II 6**, 57
cupboard ['kʌbəd] Schrank **II 4**, 33
curry ['kʌrɪ] Curry (*indisches Gericht*) **II 6**, 59
customer ['kʌstəmə] Kunde/Kundin **II 5**, 44
to **cut*** [kʌt] schneiden **II 6**, 53
to cut out [ˌkʌt‿'aʊt] ausschneiden **II 8**, 71

D

dad [dæd] Vati, Papi **I**
⟨Daddy⟩ ['dædɪ] Papa, Vati **II 9**, 86
dangerous ['deɪndʒərəs] gefährlich **II 7**, 65
date [deɪt] Datum, Termin **II 1**, 11
daughter ['dɔ:tə] Tochter **II 4**, 36
day [deɪ] Tag **I**
⟨day by day⟩ ['deɪ baɪ 'deɪ] tagein, tagaus, jeden Tag **II 10**, 94
in those days [ɪn 'ðəʊz ˌdeɪz] damals **II 2**, 20
the day after tomorrow [ðə 'deɪ‿ˌɑ:ftə tə'mɒrəʊ] übermorgen **II 7**, 66
the day before yesterday [ðə 'deɪ bɪˌfɔ: 'jestədeɪ] vorgestern **II 7**, 65
° **Day Rider Ticket** ['deɪ‿raɪdə ˌtɪkɪt] Tagesticket **I**
° **dead** [ded] tot **I**
dear [dɪə] liebe/lieber/liebes **I**
Oh dear! [əʊ 'dɪə] Oje!, Meine Güte! **I**
⟨to love dearly⟩ ['dɪəlɪ] sehr lieben **II 7**, 66
December [dɪ'sembə] Dezember **I**
deep [di:p] tief **II 7**, 66
department store [dɪ'pɑ:tmənt stɔ:] Kaufhaus **II 5**, 42
to **describe** [dɪ'skraɪb] beschreiben **II 3**, 29
desk [desk] Schreibtisch, Pult **I**
detail ['di:teɪl] Detail, Einzelheit **II 1**, 11
dialogue ['daɪəlɒg] Dialog, Gespräch **I**
° **diary** ['daɪərɪ] Tagebuch, Terminkalender **II 7**, 64
dice [daɪs] Würfel **I**
dictionary ['dɪkʃənrɪ] Wörterbuch, Lexikon **II 6**, 55
to **die** [daɪ] sterben **I**
different ['dɪfrənt] anders, verschieden, unterschiedlich **I**
in different ways [ɪn ˌdɪfrənt‿'weɪz] auf verschiedene Weise **II 10**, 92
difficult ['dɪfɪkəlt] schwierig **II 3**, 27
dining-room ['daɪnɪŋrʊm] Esszimmer **I**
dirty ['dɜ:tɪ] schmutzig, dreckig **I**
° **disco** ['dɪskəʊ] Diskothek **II 10**, 92
to **do*** [du:] tun, machen **I**
to do the washing-up ['du: ðə ˌwɒʃɪŋ‿'ʌp] den Abwasch machen, spülen **I**
doctor ['dɒktə] Ärztin/Arzt **I**
at the doctor's [ət ðə 'dɒktəz] beim Arzt **II 8**, 75
° the **dodgems** ['dɒdʒəmz] Autoskooter **II 3**, 25
dog [dɒg] Hund **I**
dog biscuit ['dɒg ˌbɪskɪt] Hundekuchen **I**
° dog-free ['dɒgfri:] hundefrei **I**
door [dɔ:] Tür **I**
at the door [ət ðə 'dɔ:] an der Tür **I**
back door [ˌbæk 'dɔ:] Hintertür **I**
front door [ˌfrʌnt 'dɔ:] Haustür **I**
double ['dʌbl] zweimal, Doppel- **I**
down [daʊn] herunter, hinunter **I**
⟨down⟩ [daʊn] schlecht, deprimiert **II 8**, 78
⟨down and out⟩ [ˌdaʊn‿ən‿'aʊt] hoffnungslos, in Schwierigkeiten **II 10**, 94
downstairs [ˌdaʊn'steəz] unten (in Gebäuden) **I**
Dr ['dɒktə] *Anrede für Arzt/Ärztin*, Herr/Frau Doktor **II 8**, 73
drama ['drɑ:mə] Schauspiel **I**
to **draw*** [drɔ:] zeichnen **I**
dream [dri:m] Traum **II 2**, 18
dress [dres] Kleid **II 4**, 33
to **drink*** [drɪŋk] trinken **I**
to **drive*** [draɪv] fahren **I**
° **driver** ['draɪvə] Fahrer/in **I**
° **drop** [drɒp] Tropfen **II 10**, 95
to **drop** [drɒp] fallen(lassen) **II 6**, 59
° to **drown** [draʊn] ertrinken, ertränken **II 9**, 87
dry [draɪ] trocken **II 10**, 95
duck [dʌk] Ente **I**
during ['djʊərɪŋ] während **II 10**, 90

E

each [i:tʃ] jede/jeder/jedes (einzelne) **II 2**, 23
ear [ɪə] Ohr **II 8**, 71
early ['3:lɪ] früh **I**
earth [3:θ] Erde **II 5**, 49
What on earth ...? [ˌwɒt‿ɒn‿'3:θ] Was in aller Welt ...? **II 5**, 49
east [i:st] Osten, Ost-, östlich **II 7**, 62
Easter ['i:stə] Ostern **II 7**, 63
easy ['i:zɪ] leicht, einfach **I**
to **eat*** [i:t] essen **I**
egg [eg] Ei **I**
elephant ['elɪfənt] Elefant **II 9**, 84
else [els] sonst (noch) **I**
empty ['emptɪ] leer **I**
end [end] Ende, Schluss **I**
in the end [ˌɪn ðɪ‿'end] schließlich, zum Schluss **II 7**, 64
⟨to end⟩ [end] enden, beenden **II 1**, 11
ending ['endɪŋ] Ende, Schluss (*bei Geschichten*) **I**
enemy ['enəmɪ] Feind/in **II 2**, 15
English ['ɪŋglɪʃ] englisch, Englisch **I**
in English [ɪn‿ɪnglɪʃ] auf Englisch **I**
to **enjoy** [ɪn'dʒɔɪ] genießen, gern tun **II 7**, 62
enough [ɪ'nʌf] genug **I**
° **er** [3:] äh **I**
escalator ['eskəleɪtə] Rolltreppe **II 5**, 42
escape [ɪ'skeɪp] Flucht, Ausbruch **II 9**, 85
to **escape** [ɪ'skeɪp] fliehen, entkommen **II 9**, 85
even ['i:vn] sogar **II 10**, 92
even more [ˌi:vn 'mɔ:] noch mehr **II 4**, 39

evening ['i:vnɪŋ] Abend **I**
in the evening [ɪn ðɪ‿'i:vnɪŋ] am Abend, abends **I**
ever ['evə] je, jemals **II 7**, 65
every ['evrɪ] jede/jeder/jedes **I**
everyone ['evrɪwʌn] jede/jeder, alle **I**
everything ['evrɪθɪŋ] alles **I**
everywhere ['evrɪweə] überall **II 5**, 49
to **examine** [ɪg'zæmɪn] untersuchen **I**
example [ɪg'zɑ:mpl] Beispiel **I**
for example [fər‿ɪg'zɑ:mpl] zum Beispiel **I**
to be **excited** [bɪ‿ɪk'saɪtɪd] aufgeregt sein **I**
excitedly [ɪk'saɪtɪdlɪ] aufgeregt **II 9**, 87
exciting [ɪk'saɪtɪŋ] aufregend, spannend **I**
to **excuse** [ɪks'kju:z] (sich) entschuldigen **I**
Excuse me. [ɪks'kju:z mɪ] Entschuldigung., Entschuldigen Sie bitte. **I**
exercise ['eksəsaɪz] Übung, Aufgabe **I**
exercise book ['eksəsaɪz ˌbʊk] (Übungs-)Heft **II 2**, 22
expensive [ɪk'spensɪv] teuer **II 3**, 25
to **explain** [ɪk'spleɪn] erklären **II 6**, 60
°**extra** ['ekstrə] zusätzlich, Zusatz-, Sonder- **I**
eye [aɪ] Auge **I**

F

face [feɪs] Gesicht **II 4**, 39
fair [feə] Volksfest, Jahrmarkt **II 2**, 19
to **fall*** [fɔ:l] fallen **I**
to fall over [ˌfɔ:l‿'əʊvə] hinfallen, umfallen **II 9**, 81
family ['fæməlɪ] Familie **I**
famous ['feɪməs] berühmt **II 3**, 25
°**fan** [fæn] Fan **II 1**, 11
fantastic [fæn'tæstɪk] fantastisch, toll **II 5**, 44
far [fɑ:] weit **I**
farm [fɑ:m] Bauernhof **I**
fast [fɑ:st] schnell, rasch **II 9**, 83
fat [fæt] dick, fett **I**
father ['fɑ:ðə] Vater **I**
favourite ['feɪvərɪt] Lieblings- **I**
February ['febrʊərɪ] Februar **I**
to **feed*** [fi:d] füttern **I**
to **feel*** [fi:l] fühlen, sich fühlen **I**
to feel well [ˌfi:l 'wel] sich wohl fühlen **II 8**, 72
°**feeler** ['fi:lə] Fühler **I**
⟨feet (pl)⟩ [fi:t] Füße **II 8**, 78
°**ferry** ['ferɪ] Fähre **I**
°**fete** [feɪt] Bazar, Fest **II 9**, 88
a **few** [ə 'fju:] ein paar **II 10**, 92
film [fɪlm] Film **II 2**, 15
to **film** [fɪlm] filmen **II 9**, 81
to **find*** [faɪnd] finden **I**
to find out [ˌfaɪnd‿'aʊt] entdecken, herausfinden **II 5**, 43
you'll be **fine** [faɪn] es wird schon gut gehen **II 4**, 34
finger ['fɪŋgə] Finger **II 8**, 71
fish finger [ˌfɪʃ 'fɪŋgə] Fischstäbchen **I**
to **finish** ['fɪnɪʃ] beenden, aufhören **I**
to be finished [ˌbɪ 'fɪnɪʃt] fertig sein **I**
fire brigade ['faɪə brɪˌgeɪd] Feuerwehr **I**
°**fireman** ['faɪəmən] Feuerwehrmann **I**
firm [fɜ:m] Firma **I**
first [fɜ:st] erste/erster/erstes; zuerst **I**
fish [fɪʃ] Fisch **I**
fish finger [ˌfɪʃ 'fɪŋgə] Fischstäbchen **I**
fish tank ['fɪʃ ˌtæŋk] Aquarium **II 9**, 80
⟨flare⟩ [fleə] Leuchtsignal **II 3**, 28
flat [flæt] Wohnung **I**
floor [flɔ:] Boden, Fußboden **I**; Stockwerk **II 5**, 42
⟨to flow⟩ [fləʊ] fließen **II 7**, 66
°**flowerpot** ['flaʊəpɒt] Blumentopf **I**
to **fly*** [flaɪ] fliegen **II 9**, 80
folder ['fəʊldə] Hefter, Mappe **I**
food [fu:d] Essen, Futter **I**
°Food Court ['fu:d ˌkɔ:t] *Imbissbereich im Einkaufszentrum* **II 5**, 42
foot [fʊt] Fuß **I**
to go on foot [ˌgəʊ‿ɒn 'fʊt] zu Fuß gehen **I**
football ['fʊtbɔ:l] Fußball **I**
for [fɔ:/fə] für **I**
for sale [fə 'seɪl] zu verkaufen **II 9**, 87
for example [fər‿ɪg'zɑ:mpl] zum Beispiel **I**
weather **forecast** ['weðə ˌfɔ:kɑ:st] Wetterbericht **II 7**, 66
forest ['fɒrɪst] Wald **II 2**, 15
to **forget*** [fə'get] vergessen **II 4**, 34
fork [fɔ:k] Gabel **II 6**, 59
form [fɔ:m] Form **I**
free [fri:] frei **I**
free time [ˌfri:‿'taɪm] Freizeit **I**
°**French** [frentʃ] französisch, Französisch **I**
Friday ['fraɪdeɪ] Freitag **I**
friend [frend] Freund/in **I**
friendly ['frendlɪ] freundlich, freundschaftlich **II 3**, 31
frightening ['fraɪtnɪŋ] Furcht erregend, erschreckend **II 4**, 33
frog [frɒg] Frosch **I**
from [frɒm/frəm] aus, von **I**
from behind [ˌfrɒm bɪ'haɪnd] von hinten **II 3**, 30
from ... to [frəm ... tə] von ... bis; von ... nach **I**
front
front door [ˌfrʌnt 'dɔ:] Haustür **I**
°front seat [ˌfrʌnt 'si:t] Vordersitz **II 10**, 95
in front of [ɪn 'frʌnt‿əv] vor **I**
fruit [fru:t] Obst, Frucht, Früchte **II 6**, 52
°fruit cake ['fru:t keɪk] *engl. Kuchen* **II 7**, 69
full of ['fʊl‿əv] voll (von) **II 1**, 12
fun [fʌn] Spaß **I**
great fun [ˌgreɪt 'fʌn] viel Spaß **II 10**, 90
to be fun [bɪ 'fʌn] Spaß machen **I**
to have fun [hæv 'fʌn] Spaß haben **I**
funny ['fʌnɪ] lustig, ulkig, komisch **I**
future ['fju:tʃə] Zukunft **II 4**, 40

G

°**gallows** ['gæləʊz] Galgen **II 2**, 21
game [geɪm] Spiel **I**
garage ['gærɑ:dʒ] Garage **I**
garden ['gɑ:dn] Garten **I**
Geography [dʒɪ'ɒgrəfɪ] Erdkunde, Geografie **II 1**, 8
German ['dʒɜ:mən] deutsch, Deutsch, Deutsche/r **I**
to **get*** [get] bekommen; fangen, auffangen; holen, erwischen **I**
⟨don't get too near⟩ [dəʊnt get tu: 'nɪə] geh nicht zu nahe ran **II 9**, 86
Get out! [get‿'aʊt] Hinaus mit dir/euch! **I**
Get well. [get 'wel] Gute Besserung. **I**
to get lost [get 'lɒst] sich verirren, verloren gehen **I**
to get off [get‿'ɒf] aussteigen **I**
to get on [get‿'ɒn] einsteigen **I**
to get out of bed on the wrong side [get‿aʊt‿əv ˌbed‿ɒn ðə rɒŋ 'saɪd] mit dem falschen Fuß aufstehen **II 10**, 95
to get ... ready [get 'redɪ] (sich) vorbereiten, zubereiten **I**
°to get stuck [get 'stʌk] stecken bleiben **I**

to get there ['get ðeə] hinkommen **I**
to get up [get‿'ʌp] aufstehen **I**
ghost [gəʊst] Geist, Gespenst **II 3**, 25
°ghost train ['gəʊst ˌtreɪn] Geisterbahn **II 3**, 25
⟨greatest gift⟩ ['greɪtɪst ˌgɪft] größtes Geschenk **II 10**, 94
girl [gɜ:l] Mädchen **I**
to **give*** [gɪv] geben **I**
⟨Give'em a twist, a flick of the wrist⟩ [ˌgɪvəm‿ə'twɪst ə ˌflɪk‿əv ðə 'rɪst] *etwa:* Hau sie runter! **II 3**, 28
to give away [ˌgɪv‿ə'weɪ] weggeben, verschenken **II 10**, 90
glad [glæd] froh **I**
glass [glɑ:s] Glas **II 6**, 57
go [gəʊ] Fahrt, Versuch **II 3**, 28
a go [ə 'gəʊ] pro Fahrt, pro Versuch **II 3**, 28
to have a go [ˌhæv‿ə'gəʊ] etwas versuchen **II 3**, 28
to **go*** [gəʊ] gehen, fahren **I**
go away! [ˌgəʊ‿ə'weɪ] geh weg!, weg mit dir! **II 8**, 71
°to go camping [ˌgəʊ 'kæmpɪŋ] zelten gehen **I**
to go for a walk [ˌgəʊ fər‿ə 'wɔ:k] spazieren gehen **I**
to go home [gəʊ 'həʊm] nach Hause gehen **I**
to go on [gəʊ 'ɒn] weitermachen **I**
to go on foot [ˌgəʊ‿ɒn 'fʊt] zu Fuß gehen **I**
to go on for [gəʊ‿'ɒn fə] (an)dauern **II 2**, 19
to go swimming [gəʊ 'swɪmɪŋ] schwimmen gehen **I**
to go to ['gəʊ tə] gehen nach/zu **I**
to go to the shops [ˌgəʊ tə‿ðə 'ʃɒps] einkaufen gehen **I**
to go wrong [ˌgəʊ 'rɒŋ] schief gehen **II 3**, 30; sich verfahren **II 7**, 64
°**goal** [gəʊl] Tor *(beim Sport)* **I**
⟨God⟩ [gɒd] Gott **II 10**, 94
to be **going to** [bɪ 'gəʊɪŋ tə] werden **I**
gone [gɒn] weg, verschwunden **II 2**, 22
good [gʊd] gut **I**
Good morning. [ˌgʊd 'mɔ:nɪŋ] Guten Morgen. **I**
to be good at ... [bɪ 'gʊd‿ət] gut sein in ... **I**
Goodbye. [ˌgʊd'baɪ] Auf Wiedersehen., Tschüs. **I**
°**goose,** geese *(pl)* [gu:s, gi:s] Gans, Gänse **II 2**, 19
°**Gosh!** [gɒʃ] *Ausruf des Erstaunens* **II 9**, 81
have **got** [ˌhæv 'gɒt] haben, besitzen **I**
grandma ['grænmɑ:] Oma **I**
grandpa ['grænpɑ:] Opa **I**
great [greɪt] toll, großartig **I**
great big ['greɪt ˌbɪg] riesengroß **II 9**, 86
great fun [ˌgreɪt 'fʌn] viel Spaß **II 10**, 90
°**great uncle** [greɪt‿'ʌŋkl] Großonkel **II 5**, 49
°**Greek** [gri:k] griechisch, Griechisch **I**
green [gri:n] grün **I**
⟨ground⟩ [graʊnd] Boden, Erde **II 8**, 78
group [gru:p] Gruppe **I**
youth group ['ju:θ ˌgru:p] Jugendgruppe **II 10**, 92
to **grow*** [grəʊ] wachsen, (an)pflanzen **II 6**, 52
grumpy ['grʌmpɪ] mürrisch **II 10**, 95
guest [gest] Gast **I**
°guest house ['gest‿haʊs] Pension, Gästehaus **I**
guitar [gɪ'tɑ:] Gitarre **I**

H

hair [heə] Haar/e **II 5**, 49
°**haircut** ['heəkʌt] Haarschnitt, Frisur **II 5**, 49
half [hɑ:f] die Hälfte **II 10**, 90
half an hour [ˌhɑ:f‿ən‿'aʊə] eine halbe Stunde **II 5**, 49
half past *(eleven)* ['hɑ:f pɑ:st] halb (zwölf) **I**
hall [hɔ:l] Diele, Flur **I**
ham [hæm] gekochter Schinken **I**
hamster ['hæmstə] Hamster **II 9**, 80
hand [hænd] Hand **I**
⟨to hang⟩ [hæŋ] hängen **II 9**, 86
°**hangman** ['hæŋmən] Henker **II 2**, 21
to **happen** ['hæpən] passieren, geschehen **II 2**, 21
happy ['hæpɪ] glücklich, fröhlich **I**
hard [hɑ:d] hart, schwer **II 6**, 59
⟨hard⟩ [hɑ:d] hart **II 7**, 66
hat [hæt] Hut **II 2**, 22
to **have*** [hæv] haben **I**
have got [ˌhæv' gɒt] haben, besitzen **I**
to have a bath [ˌhæv‿ə 'bɑ:θ] baden, ein Bad nehmen **I**
to have a look [hæv‿ə 'lʊk] sich etw. ansehen **I**
to have a ride on [ˌhæv‿ə'raɪd‿ɒn] fahren auf **II 3**, 25
to have breakfast [ˌhæv 'brekfəst] frühstücken **II 9**, 81
to have fun [hæv 'fʌn] Spaß haben **I**
to have lunch [hæv 'lʌntʃ] zu Mittag essen **I**
to have on [ˌhæv 'ɒn] anhaben (Kleidung) **II 7**, 67
to have to ['hæv ˌtu:] müssen **II 8**, 72
he [hi:] er **I**
head [hed] Kopf **I**
headache ['hedeɪk] Kopfweh **II 8**, 72
°**headteacher** [ˌhed'ti:tʃə] Schuldirektor/in **I**
healthy ['helθɪ] gesund **I**
healthy living [ˌhelθɪ 'lɪvɪŋ] gesunde Lebensweise **I**
to **hear*** [hɪə] hören **I**
°**heart** [hɑ:t] Herz **II 4**, 38
by heart [baɪ 'hɑ:t] auswendig **II 4**, 38
⟨heavy⟩ ['hevɪ] schwer **II 9**, 86
⟨to heed⟩ [hi:d] Aufmerksamkeit schenken **II 10**, 94
hello [hə'ləʊ] Hallo., Guten Tag. **I**
to say **hello to** [ˌseɪ hə'ləʊ‿tə] grüßen **I**
°**helmet** ['helmɪt] Helm **II 8**, 71
help [help] Hilfe **I**
to **help** [help] helfen **I**
helper ['helpə] Helfer/in **II 8**, 76
her [hɜ:] ihr/ihre; ihr/sie **I**
here [hɪə] hier **I**
Here you are. [ˌhɪə ju:‿'ɑ:] Hier, bitte schön. **I**
hers [hɜ:z] ihr/ihre **II 8**, 74
Hey! [heɪ] He!, Oh! **I**
Hi! [haɪ] Hallo! **I**
to **hide*** [haɪd] (sich) verstecken **II 1**, 12
high [haɪ] hoch **II 7**, 66
hill [hɪl] Hügel **I**
him [hɪm] ihm/ihn **I**
°to **hire** ['haɪə] mieten **II 5**, 47
his [hɪz] sein/seine **I**; seine/r/s **II 8**, 74
History ['hɪstrɪ] Geschichte **II 1**, 8
to **hit*** [hɪt] schlagen **II 3**, 30
hobby ['hɒbɪ] Hobby **II 9**, 81
hockey ['hɒkɪ] Hockey **I**
to **hold*** [həʊld] halten **II 9**, 87
hole [həʊl] Loch **I**
holidays *(pl)* ['hɒlɪdeɪz] Ferien **I**
on holiday [ɒn 'hɒlɪdeɪ] im Urlaub **I**
home [həʊm] Zuhause, Heim **I**
at home [ət 'həʊm] zu Hause **I**
home [həʊm] nach Hause **I**
to go home [gəʊ 'həʊm] nach Hause gehen **I**
homework ['həʊmwɜ:k] Hausaufgabe, Hausaufgaben **I**
⟨to honk⟩ [hɒŋk] hupen, tuten **II 9**, 86
°**hood** [hʊd] Kapuze **II 2**, 21
to **hope** [həʊp] hoffen **I**
horse [hɔ:s] Pferd **II 7**, 62

hospital ['hɒspɪtl] Krankenhaus **I**
hot [hɒt] heiß **I**
hot dog [ˌhɒt 'dɒg] Hot Dog **II 3**, 25
hotel [həʊ'tel] Hotel **I**
hour ['aʊə] Stunde **II 5**, 49
half an hour [ˌhɑːf‿ən‿'aʊə] eine halbe Stunde **II 5**, 49
house [haʊs] Haus **I**
° **housekeeper** ['haʊsˌkiːpə] Haushälter/in **II 4**, 39
housework ['haʊswɜːk] Hausarbeit **I**
° **hovercraft** ['hɒvəkrɑːft] Luftkissenboot **I**
how [haʊ] wie **I**
⟨how about ...?⟩ ['haʊ‿ə'baʊt] wie wär's mit ...? **II 9**, 86
How are you? [ˌhaʊ‿'ɑː juː] Wie geht es dir/euch/Ihnen? **I**
how many [haʊ 'menɪ] wie viele **I**
how much [haʊ 'mʌtʃ] wie viel **I**
° **Humanities** *(pl)* [hjuː'mænətɪz] *(in der Schule)* Geschichte und Erdkunde **II 1**, 8
hungry ['hʌŋgrɪ] hungrig **I**
to **hurry** ['hʌrɪ] sich beeilen **II 7**, 68
to **hurt*** [hɜːt] weh tun, schmerzen **I**; verletzen **II**

I

I [aɪ] ich **I**
I'd like (= *I would like*) [aɪd] ich möchte **II 5**, 48
I'll (= *I will*) [aɪl] ich werde **II 4**, 34
I'm (= *I am*) [aɪm] ich bin **I**
ice cream [ˌaɪs‿'kriːm] Eiskrem **I**
ice rink ['aɪsrɪŋk] Eisstadion **II 5**, 47
idea [aɪ'dɪə] Idee **I**
idiot ['ɪdɪət] Idiot/in **II 2**, 22
⟨idol⟩ ['aɪdl] Idol **II 3**, 28
if [ɪf] wenn **II 4**, 35
ill [ɪl] krank **II 4**, 38
important [ɪm'pɔːtnt] wichtig **II 3**, 25
in [ɪn] in **I**
in different ways [ɪn ˌdɪfrənt‿'weɪz] auf verschiedene Weise **II 10**, 92
in front of [ɪn 'frʌnt‿əv] vor **I**
in the end [ˌɪn ðɪ‿'end] schließlich, zum Schluss **II 7**, 64
in the evening [ɪn ðɪ‿'iːvnɪŋ] am Abend, abends **I**
in the middle of [ɪn ðə 'mɪdl‿əv] in der Mitte von, mitten in **II 5**, 42
in those days [ɪn 'ðəʊz ˌdeɪz] damals **II 2**, 20
in time [ˌɪn 'taɪm] rechtzeitig **II 6**, 59
° **Indian** ['ɪndjən] indisch, Inder/in **II 6**, 58
° **infinitive** [ɪn'fɪnətɪv] Infinitiv, Grundform **II 6**, 54
information [ɪnfə'meɪʃn] Information(en), Auskunft/Auskünfte **II 4**, 38
inside [ɪn'saɪd] drinnen **I**
interesting ['ɪntrəstɪŋ] interessant **II 3**, 27
into ['ɪntʊ] in, hinein **I**
invitation [ɪnvɪ'teɪʃn] Einladung **I**
to **invite** [ɪn'vaɪt] einladen **II 6**, 53
irregular [ɪ'regjʊlə] unregelmäßig **I**
is [ɪz] ist **I**
there is [ðeər‿'ɪz] es gibt, es ist **I**
island ['aɪlənd] Insel **II 7**, 62
it [ɪt] es/er/sie; es/ihn/sie/ihm/ihr **I**
° **Italian** [ɪ'tæljən] italienisch, Italienisch, Italiener/in **I**
its [ɪts] sein/seine, ihr/ihre **I**; seine/r/s, ihr/e **II 8**, 74

J

jacket ['dʒækɪt] Jacke **II 4**, 33
January ['dʒænjʊərɪ] Januar **I**
jeans [dʒiːnz] Jeans **I**
job [dʒɒb] Beruf, Arbeit, Arbeitsplatz **I**
to **join** [dʒɔɪn] beitreten, Mitglied werden **II 1**, 11
joke [dʒəʊk] Witz, Scherz **I**
July [dʒuː'laɪ] Juli **I**
jump [dʒʌmp] Sprung **II 10**, 96
to **jump** [dʒʌmp] springen **II 3**, 30
June [dʒuːn] Juni **I**
° **junior** ['dʒuːnjə] Unterstufen- **II 1**, 9
just [dʒʌst] genau, gerade **II 2**, 15; eben, nur **I**
just the thing [ˌdʒʌst ðə 'θɪŋ] genau das Richtige **II 10**, 91
just then [ˌdʒʌst 'ðen] in diesem Moment **II 10**, 95

K

to **keep*** [kiːp] (be)halten **II 9**, 80
to **kick** [kɪk] treten, mit dem Fuß stoßen, kicken **I**
to **kill** [kɪl] töten **II 6**, 52
° **kilt** [kɪlt] Schottenrock **II 7**, 65
kind [kaɪnd] Art **II 6**, 58
⟨kind⟩ [kaɪnd] nett, freundlich **II 7**, 66
kitchen ['kɪtʃən] Küche **I**
kite [kaɪt] Drachen **I**
knee [niː] Knie **II 8**, 71
knife [naɪf] Messer **I**
to **know*** [nəʊ] wissen, kennen **I**
° **knuckle** ['nʌkl] Fingerknöchel **II 3**, 28
° white knuckle ride [ˌwaɪt nʌkl 'raɪd] wilde Fahrt auf Achterbahn und Ähnlichem **II 3**, 28

L

° **lace** [leɪs] Spitze *(Gewebeart)* **II 5**, 47
° **ladder** ['lædə] Leiter **I**
lady ['leɪdɪ] Dame **II 8**, 76
lake [leɪk] See, Teich **I**
lamb [læm] Lamm **I**
⟨lassies (pl)⟩ ['læsɪz] Mädchen **II 7**, 66
last [lɑːst] letzte/letzter/letztes **I**
at last [ət 'lɑːst] schließlich, zuletzt **I**
late [leɪt] spät, zu spät **I**
to work late [ˌwɜːk 'leɪt] länger arbeiten **I**
laugh [lɑːf] Lachen **II 4**, 34
to **laugh** [lɑːf] lachen **I**
to laugh at ['lɑːf‿æt] sich lustig machen über **II 3**, 30
° to **lay*** [leɪ] legen **I**
leaflet ['liːflɪt] Prospekt, Informationsblatt **II 2**, 15
to **learn*** [lɜːn] lernen **I**
to **leave*** [liːv] abfahren, verlassen, zurücklassen **I**
leave me alone ['liːv mɪ‿ə'ləʊn] lass mich in Ruhe **II 3**, 31
left [left] links **I**
on the left [ɒn ðə 'left] links sein, links liegen **I**
leg [leg] Bein **I**
lemonade [ˌlemə'neɪd] Limonade **I**
to **lend*** [lend] leihen, verleihen **I**
⟨to lend a hand⟩ [ˌlend‿ə'hænd] helfen **II 10**, 94
lesson ['lesn] Unterrichtsstunde **I**
to **let*** [let] lassen **II 8**, 71
let's [lets] lass uns/lasst uns **I**
letter ['letə] Brief; Buchstabe **I**

letterbox ['letəbɒks] Briefkasten **I**
to **lie*** [laɪ] liegen **I**
to lie down [ˌlaɪ 'daʊn] sich hinlegen **II 8**, 71
life [laɪf] Leben **II 2**, 20
lift [lɪft] Aufzug, Fahrstuhl **II 5**, 42
lightning ['laɪtnɪŋ] Blitz **II 4**, 39
to **like** [laɪk] mögen, gern haben **I**
I'd like [aɪd 'laɪk] ich möchte, ich hätte gern **II 5**, 48
like [laɪk] (so) wie **I**
like this [ˌlaɪk 'ðɪs] so **I**
what you were like [laɪk] wie du warst **II 3**, 28
line [laɪn] Linie, Zeile **II 4**, 40
lion ['laɪən] Löwe **II 9**, 84
list [lɪst] Liste **I**
shopping list ['ʃɒpɪŋ ˌlɪst] Einkaufsliste **II 6**, 59
to **listen** ['lɪsn] zuhören **I**
°**listening practice** ['lɪsnɪŋ ˌpræktɪs] Hörverstehensübung **I**
little ['lɪtl] klein **I**
a **little** [ə 'lɪtl] ein bisschen **II 8**, 76
to **live** [lɪv] leben, wohnen **I**
live [laɪv] live, direkt **II 7**, 65
living-room ['lɪvɪŋrʊm] Wohnzimmer **I**
°**loch** [lɒk] (schottischer) See **II 7**, 64
°**locked** [lɒkt] abgeschlossen **I**
long [lɒŋ] lang **I**
a long time ago [ə ˌlɒŋ taɪm‿ə'gəʊ] lange her **II 7**, 65
a long way [ə ˌlɒŋ‿'weɪ] eine weite Entfernung **II 10**, 92
to have a **look** [hæv‿ə 'lʊk] sich etw. ansehen **I**
to **look** [lʊk] aussehen; sehen, ansehen **I**
to look after [ˌlʊk‿'ɑːftə] aufpassen, hüten **II 9**, 88
to look at ['lʊk‿ət] anschauen **I**
to look down [ˌlʊk 'daʊn] nach unten sehen **II 9**, 87
to look for ['lʊk fə] suchen **I**
to look round [ˌlʊk 'raʊnd] sich umsehen **II 5**, 45
⟨Lord⟩ [lɔːd] Herr **II 4**, 38
to get **lost** [get 'lɒst] sich verirren, verloren gehen **I**
a **lot of** [ə 'lɒt‿əv] viel/viele **I**
loud [laʊd] laut **II 4**, 39
love [lʌv] alles Liebe, herzliche Grüße *(als Briefschluss)*; Liebe **I**
to **love** [lʌv] lieben **I**
lovely ['lʌvlɪ] schön, herrlich **II 4**, 33
⟨low⟩ [ləʊ] tief **II 7**, 66
lower ['ləʊə] untere/unterer/unteres **II 5**, 42
lucky ['lʌkɪ] glücklich, Glücks- **I**
to be lucky [bɪ 'lʌkɪ] Glück haben **I**
lunch [lʌntʃ] Mittagessen **I**
lunch box ['lʌntʃ ˌbɒks] *Dose für belegte Brote zum Mittagessen* **I**
to have lunch [hæv 'lʌntʃ] zu Mittag essen **I**

M

magazine [ˌmægə'ziːn] Zeitschrift **I**
to **make*** [meɪk] machen **I**
to make a request [ˌmeɪk‿ə rɪ'kwest] eine Bitte äußern, einen Wunsch äußern **I**
to make money [ˌmeɪk 'mʌnɪ] Geld verdienen **II 10**, 92
man [mæn] Mann **I**
many ['menɪ] viele **I**
how many [haʊ 'menɪ] wie viele **I**
map [mæp] Landkarte **I**
March [mɑːtʃ] März **I**
market square [ˌmɑːkɪt 'skweə] Marktplatz **I**
°**mascot** ['mæskət] Maskottchen **I**
°to **match** [mætʃ] das Dazupassende finden **II 10**, 93
Maths [mæθs] Mathematikunterricht, Mathe **II 1**, 8
it doesn't **matter** [ɪt 'dʌznt 'mætə] es macht nichts **II 5**, 47
May [meɪ] Mai **I**
may [meɪ] dürfen, könnte/könnten **I**
maybe ['meɪbiː] vielleicht **I**
me [miː] mir/mich **I**
meal [miːl] Mahlzeit, Essen **II 6**, 52
to **mean*** [miːn] bedeuten **II 5**, 47
meaning ['miːnɪŋ] Bedeutung **II 9**, 83
meat [miːt] Fleisch **II 2**, 20
°**mechanic** [mɪ'kænɪk] Mechaniker/in **I**
medicine ['medsɪn] Medizin **II 8**, 75
to **meet*** [miːt] (sich) treffen **I**
meeting ['miːtɪŋ] Treffen, Besprechung **II 1**, 9
member ['membə] Mitglied **II 10**, 90
°**memory** ['memərɪ] Gedächtnis, Erinnerung **II 9**, 81
mess [mes] Unordnung **I**
middle ['mɪdl] Mitte **II 2**, 20
°the Middle Ages [ðə ˌmɪdl 'eɪdʒɪz] das Mittelalter **II 2**, 20
in the middle of [ɪn ðə 'mɪdl‿əv] in der Mitte von, mitten in **II 5**, 42
⟨mile⟩ [maɪl] Meile **II 4**, 38
milk [mɪlk] Milch **I**
milkman ['mɪlkmən] Milchmann **II 9**, 81
mince [mɪns] Hackfleisch **II 6**, 59
⟨mind⟩ [maɪnd] *hier:* Meinung **II 8**, 78
to **mind** [maɪnd] jdm. etw. ausmachen **II 9**, 88
never mind ['nevə 'maɪnd] mach dir nichts daraus, macht nichts **I**
mine [maɪn] meine/meiner/meines **II 8**, 74
minute ['mɪnɪt] Minute **I**
°**mirror** ['mɪrə] Spiegel **II 5**, 50
miserable ['mɪzrəbl] unglücklich, elend **II 3**, 30
⟨to miss⟩ [mɪs] verpassen **II 4**, 38
°**mistake** [mɪ'steɪk] Fehler **II 10**, 96
moment ['məʊmənt] Moment, Augenblick **I**
⟨Momma⟩ ['mɒmə] Mama, Mutti **II 9**, 86
Monday ['mʌndeɪ] Montag **I**
money ['mʌnɪ] Geld **I**
pocket money ['pɒkɪt ˌmʌnɪ] Taschengeld **I**
to make money [ˌmeɪk 'mʌnɪ] Geld verdienen **II 10**, 92
monkey ['mʌŋkɪ] Affe **II 9**, 84
monster ['mɒnstə] Monster, Ungeheuer **I**
month [mʌnθ] Monat **I**
more [mɔː] mehr **I**
one more [ˌwʌn 'mɔː] noch ein/eine **I**
morning ['mɔːnɪŋ] Morgen **I**
Good morning. [ˌgʊd 'mɔːnɪŋ] Guten Morgen. **I**
most [məʊst] die meiste(n) **II 2**, 20
mother ['mʌðə] Mutter **I**
mountain ['maʊntɪn] Berg **I**
°mountain rescue ['maʊntɪn 'reskjuː] Bergwacht **II 7**, 67
mouse, mice *(pl)* [maʊs, maɪs] Maus, Mäuse **II 9**, 80
mouth [maʊθ] Mund **I**
Mr ['mɪstə] Herr *(Anrede für Männer)* **I**
Mrs ['mɪsɪz] Frau *(Anrede für verheiratete Frauen)* **I**
much [mʌtʃ] viel **I**
how much [haʊ 'mʌtʃ] wie viel **I**
very much [ˌverɪ 'mʌtʃ] sehr **I**
°**muddle** ['mʌdl] Durcheinander **I**
mum [mʌm] Mama, Mutti **I**
museum [mjuː'zɪəm] Museum **II 5**, 47

music ['mju:zɪk] Musik **I**
pop music ['pɒp‿mju:zɪk] Popmusik **I**
must [mʌst] müssen **I**
mustn't ['mʌsnt] nicht dürfen **I**
my [maɪ] mein/meine **I**

N

name [neɪm] Name **I**
nasty ['nɑ:stɪ] schrecklich, scheußlich **II 8**, 75
°**nationality** [ˌnæʃə'nælɪtɪ] Nationalität **I**
near ['nɪə] nahe, in der Nähe von **I**
nearly ['nɪəlɪ] fast, beinahe **II 5**, 45
to **need** [ni:d] brauchen, benötigen **I**
needn't ['ni:dnt] nicht müssen, nicht brauchen **I**
neighbour ['neɪbə] Nachbar/in **I**
neighbourhood ['neɪbəhʊd] Nachbarschaft, Wohnviertel **I**
nervous about ['nɜ:vəs‿əˌbaʊt] nervös, aufgeregt wegen **II 3**, 30
never ['nevə] niemals, nie **I**
°never mind ['nevə 'maɪnd] mach dir nichts daraus, macht nichts **I**
new [nju:] neu **I**
news [nju:z] Nachricht/en, Neuigkeit/en **II 2**, 15
newsagent's ['nju:zˌeɪdʒnts] *Laden für Zeitungen, Zeitschriften, Tabakwaren, Süßigkeiten usw.* **II 1**, 12
next [nekst] nächste/r/s **I**
next time ['nekst‿ˌtaɪm] nächstes Mal **I**
next to ['neks tə] neben **II 5**, 42
nice [naɪs] nett, schön **I**
night [naɪt] Nacht **I**
at night [ət 'naɪt] nachts **II 9**, 80
no [nəʊ] kein/keine; nein **I**
No, thank you. [nəʊ 'θæŋk‿ju:] Nein, danke. **I**
nobody ['nəʊbədɪ] niemand, keiner **I**
noise [nɔɪz] Lärm, Krach, Geräusch **I**
°**non-swimmer** [ˌnɒn 'swɪmə] Nichtschwimmer/in **II 5**, 47
north [nɔ:θ] Norden, Nord-, nördlich **II 7**, 62
nose [nəʊz] Nase **II 8**, 71
not [nɒt] nicht **I**
not ... yet [nɒt 'jet] noch nicht **I**
note [nəʊt] Notiz **I**
nothing ['nʌθɪŋ] nichts **I**
notice ['nəʊtɪs] Aushang, Schild **II 1**, 9
notice board ['nəʊtɪs bɔ:d] Schwarzes Brett **II 1**, 9
°**noun** [naʊn] Substantiv **II 10**, 96
November [nəʊ'vembə] November **I**
now [naʊ] jetzt, nun **I**
number ['nʌmbə] Zahl, Nummer **I**
nurse [nɜ:s] Krankenschwester, Krankenpfleger **II 8**, 74
nursery school ['nɜ:srɪ ˌsku:l] Kindergarten **I**

O

o [əʊ] Null **I**
°**oak** [əʊk] Eiche **II 2**, 19
at ... **o'clock** [ə'klɒk] um ... Uhr **I**
October [ɒk'təʊbə] Oktober **I**
of [ɒv/əv] von **I**
of course [əv‿'kɔ:s] natürlich, selbstverständlich **I**
off [ɒf] ab, weg **II 2**, 22
Off you go! ['ɒf jʊ ˌgəʊ] Fort mit dir/euch! **II 1**, 12
office ['ɒfɪs] Büro, Amt **I**
°police **officer** [pə'li:s‿ˌɒfɪsə] Polizist/in **I**
often ['ɒfn] oft **I**
oh [əʊ] oh **I**
OK [ˌəʊ'keɪ] OK, in Ordnung **I**
old [əʊld] alt **I**
on [ɒn] an **II 7**,64; auf **I**; auf der Bühne **II 4**, 39
on holiday [ɒn 'hɒlɪdeɪ] im Urlaub **I**
on (*Radio Nottingham*) [ɒn (ˌreɪdɪəʊ 'nɒtɪŋəm)] im (Radio Nottingham) **I**
on the left [ɒn ðə 'left] links sein, links liegen **I**
on the right [ɒn ðə 'raɪt] rechts sein, rechts liegen **I**
on the seventh of [ɒn ðə 'sevnθ‿əv] am siebten **I**
on the telephone [ɒn ðə 'telɪfəʊn] am Telefon **I**
to be on [bɪ‿'ɒn] eingeschaltet sein **I**
to go on [gəʊ 'ɒn] weitermachen **I**
to have on [ˌhæv 'ɒn] anhaben (Kleidung) **II 7**, 67
one [wʌn] eins **I**
one more [ˌwʌn 'mɔ:] noch ein/eine **I**
only ['əʊnlɪ] einzige/einziger/einziges **II 7**, 67; nur, erst **I**
to **open** ['əʊpn] öffnen, aufmachen **I**
open ['əʊpn] offen, geöffnet **I**
operation [ˌɒpə'reɪʃn] Operation **II 8**, 76
opposite ['ɒpəzɪt] Gegenteil **I**
opposite ['ɒpəzɪt] gegenüber **II 5**, 42
or [ɔ:] oder **I**
or so [ˌɔ: 'səʊ] oder ungefähr **II 10**, 95
order ['ɔ:də] Reihenfolge, Ordnung **I**
to **organize** ['ɔ:gənaɪz] organisieren **II 10**, 92
other ['ʌðə] andere/anderer/anderes **I**
Ouch [aʊtʃ] *Ausruf:* Aua! **II 8**, 75
our ['aʊə] unser/unsere **I**
ours ['aʊəz] unsere/unserer/unseres **II 8**, 74
out [aʊt] heraus, draußen **I**
out of ['aʊt‿əv] aus **II 1**, 12
out of the way [ˌaʊt‿əv ðə 'weɪ] aus dem Weg **II 10**, 95
°**outlaw** ['aʊtlɔ:] Gesetzlose/r, Vogelfreie/r, Bandit/in **II 2**, 15
outside [aʊt'saɪd] draußen **I**; (draußen) vor **II 1**, 12
over ['əʊvə] über **I**
over ['əʊvə] vorbei, zu Ende **II 1**, 12
over there [ˌəʊvə 'ðeə] da drüben, dort **I**
⟨own⟩ [əʊn] eigene/r/s **II 10**, 94

P

packet ['pækɪt] Päckchen **I**
page [peɪdʒ] Seite **I**
pair [peə] Paar **I**
paper ['peɪpə] Papier **II 5**, 50
parents (*pl*) ['peərənts] Eltern **I**
park [pɑ:k] Park **I**
car park ['kɑ: pɑ:k] Parkhaus, Parkplatz **II 5**, 42
part [pɑ:t] Rolle **II 4**, 33; Teil **II 2**, 22
°past **participle** [ˌpɑ:st 'pɑ:tɪsɪpl] Partizip Perfekt **II 6**, 54
partner ['pɑ:tnə] Partner/in **I**
party ['pɑ:tɪ] Party, Feier **I**
to **pass** [pɑ:s] reichen, weitergeben **I**
past [pɑ:st] nach (*bei Uhrzeiten*) **I**
half past *(eleven)* ['hɑ:f pɑ:st] halb (zwölf) **I**
quarter past *(eleven)* ['kwɔ:tə pɑ:st] Viertel nach (elf) **I**
°**past participle** [ˌpɑ:st 'pɑ:tɪsɪpl] Partizip Perfekt **II 6**, 54
°**past progressive** [ˌpɑ:st prəʊ'gresɪv] *Verlaufsform der Vergangenheit* **II 9**, 82
simple **past** [ˌsɪmpl 'pɑ:st] Vergangenheitsform **II 2**, 22

path [pɑ:θ] Pfad, Weg **II 7**, 67
patient ['peɪʃnt] Patient/in, Kranke(r) **II 8**, 73
to **pay*** [peɪ] (be)zahlen **II 5**, 44
° **PE** (= **Physical Education**) [ˌpi: 'i: = 'fɪzɪkl ˌedju:'keɪʃn] Sportunterricht **II 1**, 8
⟨peace of mind⟩ [ˌpi:s‿əv 'maɪnd] innere Ruhe **II 7**, 66
⟨peanut⟩ ['pi:nʌt] Erdnuss **II 9**, 86
pen [pen] Füller **I**
pence (= **p**) [pens] *britische Geldeinheit* **I**
pencil ['pensl] Bleistift **I**
pencil case ['pensl keɪs] Federmäppchen **I**
⟨penny⟩ ['penɪ] Penny (*alte Münze*) **II 3**, 28
people *(pl)* ['pi:pl] Leute **I**
° present **perfect** [ˌpreznt 'pɜ:fɪkt] *englische Vergangenheitsform* **II 6**, 56
person ['pɜ:sn] Person **II 2**, 22
pet [pet] Haustier **I**
pet shop ['pet ʃɒp] Tierhandlung **II 9**, 87
to **phone** [fəʊn] anrufen **I**
photo ['fəʊtəʊ] Foto **I**
to take a photo of [ˌteɪk‿ə 'fəʊtəʊ‿əv] ein Foto machen von **I**
piano [pɪ'ænəʊ] Klavier **II 1**, 11
to **pick up** [pɪk‿'ʌp] aufheben, abholen **II 6**, 59
picture ['pɪktʃə] Bild **I**
in the picture [ɪn ðə 'pɪktʃə] auf dem Bild **I**
piece [pi:s] Stück **II 5**, 50
pig [pɪg] Schwein **I**
° **pillow** ['pɪləʊ] Kopfkissen **II 4**, 39
pink [pɪŋk] rosa, pink **II 5**, 49
pint [paɪnt] *britische Mengenangabe* (*etwa 1/2 Liter*) **I**
⟨a pitch⟩ [pɪtʃ] pro Wurf **II 3**, 28
° **pizza** ['pi:tsə] Pizza **II 5**, 42
place [pleɪs] Ort, Platz **I**
plan [plæn] Plan **I**
to **plan** [plæn] planen **II 5**, 46
plane [pleɪn] Flugzeug **I**
plate [pleɪt] Teller **II 6**, 59
play [pleɪ] Theaterstück **II 1**, 9
role play ['rəʊl pleɪ] Rollenspiel **I**
to **play** [pleɪ] spielen **I**
Robin **played tricks on** him. [ˌpleɪd 'trɪks] Robin spielte ihm Streiche. **II 2**, 16
player ['pleɪə] Spieler/in **II 1**, 11
playground ['pleɪgraʊnd] Schulhof, Spielplatz **I**
in the playground [ɪn ðə 'pleɪgraʊnd] auf dem Schulhof, auf dem Spielplatz **I**
please [pli:z] bitte **I**
pocket ['pɒkɪt] Tasche (*bei Kleidung*) **I**
pocket money ['pɒkɪt ˌmʌnɪ] Taschengeld **I**
⟨poem⟩ ['pəʊɪm] Gedicht **II 1**, 11
police [pə'li:s] Polizei **I**
° police officer [pə'li:s‿ˌɒfɪsə] Polizist/in **I**
⟨policeman⟩ [pə'li:smən] Polizist **II 9**, 86
polite [pə'laɪt] höflich **II 5**, 48
pond [pɒnd] Teich **I**
pony ['pəʊnɪ] Pony **II 9**, 80
pool [pu:l] Schwimmbad **II 5**, 47
poor [pɔ:] arm **I**
pop music ['pɒp‿mju:zɪk] Popmusik **I**
popcorn ['pɒpkɔ:n] Popcorn **II 3**, 25
popular ['pɒpjʊlə] beliebt **II 3**, 25
° **porridge** ['pɒrɪdʒ] Haferbrei **II 7**, 65
post office ['pəʊst‿ˌɒfɪs] Post, Postamt **I**
postcard ['pəʊstkɑ:d] Postkarte **I**
poster ['pəʊstə] Poster, Plakat **I**
potato [pə'teɪtəʊ] Kartoffel **II 2**, 20
° roast potatoes [ˌrəʊst pə'teɪtəʊz] im Ofen gebratene Kartoffeln **II 6**, 52
pound (= **£**) [paʊnd] Pfund (*britische Währung*) **I**
pound (= **lb**) [paʊnd] *britische Gewichtseinheit* (*etwa ein Pfund*) **I**
° word **power** ['wɜ:d ˌpaʊə] die Kraft der Wörter **I**
practice ['præktɪs] Übung, Training **I**
° listening practice ['lɪsnɪŋ ˌpræktɪs] Hörverstehensübung **I**
° sound practice ['saʊnd ˌpræktɪs] Ausspracheübung **I**
to **practise** ['præktɪs] üben **II 6**, 56
° **preposition** [ˌprepə'zɪʃn] Präposition, Verhältniswort **II 4**, 36
° **prescription** [prɪ'skrɪpʃn] (Arzt-)Rezept **II 8**, 75
present ['preznt] Geschenk **I**
° **present perfect** [ˌpreznt 'pɜ:fɪkt] *englische Vergangenheitsform* **II 6**, 56
simple **present** [ˌsɪmpl 'preznt] Präsens **II 3**, 31
⟨to pretend⟩ [prɪ'tend] so tun als ob **II 10**, 94
pretty ['prɪtɪ] hübsch **II 4**, 33
prisoner ['prɪznə] Gefangene/r **II 2**, 21
to take prisoner [ˌteɪk 'prɪznə] gefangen nehmen **II 2**, 15
prize [praɪz] Preis (*Gewinn*) **I**
probably ['prɒbəblɪ] wahrscheinlich **II 1**, 12
problem ['prɒbləm] Problem **I**
° **professional** [prə'feʃənl] professionell **II 4**, 37
° **programme** ['prəʊgræm] Programm **II 10**, 92
° **progressive** (*form*) [prəʊ'gresɪv] Verlaufsform **II 3**, 31
° past progressive [ˌpɑ:st prəʊ'gresɪv] *Verlaufsform der Vergangenheit* **II 9**, 82
° **promenade** [ˌprɒmə'nɑ:d] Promenade **I**
° **prompter** ['prɒmptə] Souffleur/Souffleuse **II 4**, 33
to be **proud of** ['praʊd‿ˌəv] stolz sein auf **II 6**, 60
to **pull** [pʊl] ziehen **II 9**, 87
pullover ['pʊlˌəʊvə] Pullover **I**
pump [pʌmp] Luftpumpe **I**
pupil ['pju:pl] Schüler/in **I**
° **puppet** ['pʌpɪt] Marionette **II 4**, 37
purse [pɜ:s] Portmonee, Geldbeutel **II 1**, 12
to **put*** [pʊt] setzen, stellen, legen **I**
to put down [ˌpʊt 'daʊn] abstellen, weglegen **II 9**, 81
to put in [ˌpʊt‿'ɪn] einsetzen, hineintun **I**
to put the telephone down [pʊt ðə 'telɪfəʊn ˌdaʊn] den Hörer auflegen **II 7**, 68
puzzle ['pʌzl] Rätsel **I**

Q

quarter ['kwɔ:tə] Viertel **I**
quarter past (eleven) ['kwɔ:tə pɑ:st] Viertel nach (elf) **I**
quarter to (twelve) ['kwɔ:tə tə] Viertel vor (zwölf) **I**
question ['kwestʃn] Frage **I**
° **questionnaire** [ˌkwestʃə'neə] Fragebogen **I**
quick [kwɪk] schnell **II 1**, 12
quiet ['kwaɪət] ruhig, still **I**
quiz [kwɪz] Ratespiel, Quiz **I**

R

rabbit ['ræbɪt] Kaninchen **II 9**, 80
race [reɪs] Wettlauf, Rennen **I**
radio ['reɪdɪəʊ] Radio **I**
rain [reɪn] Regen **II 10**, 95
to **rain** [reɪn] regnen **I**

°**RE** (= **Religious Education**) [ˌɑːr‿ˈiː = ˈrɪˌlɪdʒəs ˌedjuːˈkeɪʃn] Religionsunterricht **II 1**, 8
to **read*** [riːd] lesen **I**
ready [ˈredɪ] fertig, bereit **I**
⟨to realize⟩ [ˈrɪəlaɪz] einsehen **II 10**, 94
really [ˈrɪəlɪ] wirklich **I**
recipe [ˈresɪpɪ] (Koch)Rezept **II 6**, 52
red [red] rot **I**
°**reduced in size** [rɪˌdjuːst‿ɪn ˈsaɪz] verkleinert **I**
to **remember** [rɪˈmembə] behalten, sich merken, sich erinnern **I**
to **repair** [rɪˈpeə] reparieren **I**
report [rɪˈpɔːt] (Zeitungs-)Reportage **II 8**, 77
request [rɪˈkwest] Bitte, Wunsch **I**
to make a request [ˌmeɪk‿ə rɪˈkwest] eine Bitte äußern, einen Wunsch äußern **I**
to **rescue** [ˈreskjuː] retten, bergen **II 7**, 68
°mountain **rescue** [ˈmaʊntɪn ˈreskjuː] Bergwacht **II 7**, 67
to **rest** [rest] sich ausruhen **II 8**, 74
restaurant [ˈrestərɔːŋ] Restaurant **II 5**, 42
rhyme [raɪm] Reim **I**
°**rhythm** [ˈrɪðəm] Rhythmus **II 5**, 48
rich [rɪtʃ] reich **II 2**, 20
ride [raɪd] Fahrt **II 3**, 25
to have a ride on [ˌhæv‿əˈraɪd‿ɒn] fahren auf **II 3**, 25
°white knuckle ride [ˌwaɪt nʌkl ˈraɪd] wilde Fahrt auf Achterbahn und Ähnlichem **II 3**, 28
to **ride*** [raɪd] reiten, fahren (Fahrrad, Motorrad) **II 7**, 62
riding school [ˈraɪdɪŋ ˌskuːl] Reitschule **II 9**, 80
right [raɪt] rechts **I**
on the right [ɒn ðə ˈraɪt] rechts sein, rechts liegen **I**
right [raɪt] richtig **I**
right? [raɪt] nicht wahr?, richtig? **I**
to be right [bɪ ˈraɪt] Recht haben **II 7**, 67
right away [raɪt‿əˈweɪ] sofort **I**
ring [rɪŋ] Ring **I**
to **ring*** [rɪŋ] klingeln **II 6**, 59
river [ˈrɪvə] Fluss **II 2**, 20
road (= **Rd.**) [rəʊd] Straße **I**
°**roast beef** [ˌrəʊst ˈbiːf] Rinderbraten **II 6**, 52
°**roast potatoes** [ˌrəʊst pəˈteɪtəʊz] im Ofen gebratene Kartoffeln **II 6**, 52
rock [rɒk] Fels **I**
role play [ˈrəʊl pleɪ] Rollenspiel **I**
⟨to roll⟩ [rəʊl] rollen **II 3**, 28
⟨rolling⟩ [ˈrəʊlɪŋ] rollend **II 7**, 66
room [ruːm] Raum, Zimmer **I**
°**rope** [rəʊp] Seil, Strick **II 2**, 21
round [raʊnd] um … herum **I**
⟨you being round⟩ [juː ˌbiːɪŋ ˈraʊnd] dass du da bist **II 8**, 78
°**roundabout** [ˈraʊndəbaʊt] Karussell **II 3**, 28
row [rəʊ] Reihe **II 4**, 39
°to **row** [rəʊ] rudern **II 7**, 65
°**rubbish** [ˈrʌbɪʃ] Abfall, Müll **I**
rule [ruːl] Regel **II 7**, 68
to **run*** [rʌn] laufen, rennen **I**
to run off [ˌrʌn‿ˈɒf] weglaufen **II 3**, 30

S

saddlebag [ˈsædlbæg] Satteltasche **I**
salad [ˈsæləd] gemischter Salat **I**
°bring-and-buy **sale** [ˌbrɪŋ‿n ˈbaɪ seɪl] Flohmarkt **II 10**, 90
for **sale** [fə ˈseɪl] zu verkaufen **II 9**, 87
the **same** [ðə ˈseɪm] derselbe/dieselbe/dasselbe **I**
sand [sænd] Sand **I**
sandcastle [ˈsændkɑːsl] Sandburg **I**
sandwich [ˈsænwɪdʒ] Butterbrot **I**
Saturday [ˈsætədeɪ] Samstag, Sonnabend **I**
sauerkraut [ˈsaʊəkraʊt] Sauerkraut **II 6**, 55
sausage [ˈsɒsɪdʒ] Würstchen, Wurst **I**
to **save** [seɪv] retten; sparen **I**
to **say*** [seɪ] sagen **I**
to say hello to [ˌseɪ həˈləʊ‿tə] grüßen **I**
scared [ˈskeəd] verängstigt **I**
to be scared of [ˈskeəd‿əv] Angst haben vor **II 2**, 17
scene [siːn] Szene **II 4**, 39
behind the scenes [bɪˌhaɪnd ðə ˈsiːnz] hinter den Kulissen **II 4**, 39
school [skuːl] Schule **I**
°nursery school [ˈnɜːsrɪ ˌskuːl] Kindergarten **I**
Science [ˈsaɪəns] Naturwissenschaft(en) **II 1**, 8
⟨to scratch⟩ [skrætʃ] kratzen **II 9**, 86
sea [siː] das Meer, die See **I**
seal [siːl] Robbe **II 9**, 84
at the **seaside** [ət ðə ˈsiːsaɪd] am Meer, an der See **I**
season [ˈsiːzn] Jahreszeit **I**
seat [siːt] Sitz, Sitzplatz **I**
°front seat [ˌfrʌnt ˈsiːt] Vordersitz **II 10**, 95
to **see*** [siː] sehen **I**
to **seem** [siːm] scheinen **II 9**, 87
⟨self-assured⟩ [ˌselfəˈʃɔːd] selbstbewusst **II 8**, 78
to **sell*** [sel] verkaufen **I**
to **send*** [send] schicken **II 7**, 68
sentence [ˈsentəns] Satz **I**
September [sepˈtembə] September **I**
she [ʃiː] sie **I**
sheep [ʃiːp] Schaf, Schafe **I**
°**sheepdog** [ˈʃiːpˌdɒg] Hirtenhund **I**
shelf [ʃelf] Regalbrett **I**
°**sheriff** [ˈʃerɪf] Sheriff **II 2**, 15
shirt [ʃɜːt] Hemd **II 4**, 33
shock [ʃɒk] Schock **II 2**, 18
shoe [ʃuː] Schuh **I**
to **shoot*** [ʃuːt] schießen **II 2**, 15
shop [ʃɒp] Laden, Geschäft **I**
shop assistant [ˈʃɒp‿əˌsɪstənt] Verkäufer/in **I**
to go to the shops [ˌgəʊ tə‿ðə ˈʃɒps] einkaufen gehen **I**
shopping centre [ˈʃɒpɪŋ ˌsentə] Einkaufszentrum **II 5**, 42
shopping list [ˈʃɒpɪŋ ˌlɪst] Einkaufsliste **II 6**, 59
short [ʃɔːt] kurz **II 4**, 33
short cut [ˌʃɔːt ˈkʌt] Abkürzung **II 7**, 68
should [ʃʊd] sollte(n) **II 10**, 93
shoulder [ˈʃəʊldə] Schulter **II 8**, 71
to **shout** [ʃaʊt] rufen, schreien **I**
to **show*** [ʃəʊ] zeigen **I**
⟨showman⟩ [ˈʃəʊmən] Schausteller **II 3**, 28
side [saɪd] Seite **II 4**, 39
sign [saɪn] Schild **II 5**, 47
°**signal** [ˈsɪgnl] Signal, Hinweis **II 2**, 22
silly [ˈsɪlɪ] dumm, albern **I**
simple [ˈsɪmpl] einfach **II 2**, 22
simple past [ˌsɪmpl ˈpɑːst] Vergangenheitsform **II 2**, 22
simple present [ˌsɪmpl ˈpreznt] Präsens **II 3**, 31
to **sing*** [sɪŋ] singen **I**
singer [ˈsɪŋə] Sänger/in **II 10**, 91
sister [ˈsɪstə] Schwester **I**
to **sit*** [sɪt] sitzen **I**
to sit down [ˌsɪt ˈdaʊn] sich hinsetzen **I**
to sit up [ˌsɪt‿ˈʌp] sich aufsetzen **II 8**, 73

situation [ˌsɪtjʊ'eɪʃn] Lage, Situation **II 10**, 93
skate [skeɪt] Schlittschuh, Rollschuh **II 5**, 47
skateboard ['skeɪtbɔ:d] Skateboard **I**
skater ['skeɪtə] Skateboardfahrer/in, Rollschuhläufer/in, Schlittschuhläufer/in **II 8**, 71
°**skin** [skɪn] Haut **I**
skirt [skɜ:t] Rock **II 4**, 33
to **sleep*** [sli:p] schlafen **I**
⟨sleepy⟩ ['sli:pɪ] schläfrig **II 9**, 86
slippery ['slɪpərɪ] rutschig, glatt **II 7**, 67
slow [sləʊ] langsam **II 9**, 83
small [smɔ:l] klein **I**
smile [smaɪl] Lächeln **II 10**, 96
to **smile** [smaɪl] lächeln **II 5**, 50
°to **smoke** [sməʊk] rauchen **II 5**, 47
snack bar ['snækbɑ:] Imbissstube **I**
snake [sneɪk] Schlange **I**
⟨to sniff up⟩ [ˌsnɪf‿'ʌp] aufschnuppern **II 9**, 86
snow [snəʊ] Schnee **I**
so [səʊ] so, also, deshalb **I**
°**soap** [səʊp] Seife **I**
sock [sɒk] Socke **II 5**, 43
some [sʌm] etwas, ein bisschen, ein paar **I**
somebody ['sʌmbədɪ] jemand **II 5**, 45
someone ['sʌmwʌn] jemand **II 6**, 52
something ['sʌmθɪŋ] etwas **II 1**, 7
sometimes ['sʌmtaɪmz] manchmal **I**
somewhere ['sʌmweə] irgendwo **II 5**, 45
son [sʌn] Sohn **II 4**, 36
song [sɒŋ] Lied **I**
soon [su:n] bald **I**
sore throat [ˌsɔ: 'θrəʊt] Halsweh **II 8**, 75
Sorry. ['sɒrɪ] Entschuldigung., Tut mir Leid. **I**
sorry about ['sɒrɪ ˌəbaʊt] tut mir Leid wegen **II 3**, 31
sound [saʊnd] Klang, Geräusch **I**
°sound effects ['saʊnd‿ɪˌfekts] Toneffekte **II 4**, 39
°sound practice ['saʊnd ˌpræktɪs] Ausspracheübung **I**
to **sound** [saʊnd] klingen, sich anhören **II 10**, 93
⟨soup⟩ [su:p] Suppe **II 6**, 56
south [saʊθ] Süden, Süd-, südlich **II 7**, 62
souvenir [ˌsu:və'nɪə] Mitbringsel, Souvenir, Andenken **I**
°**spade** [speɪd] Spaten **I**
°**Spanish** ['spænɪʃ] spanisch, Spanisch **I**
to **speak*** [spi:k] sprechen **I**
to speak to ['spi:k tə] sprechen mit **I**
special ['speʃl] besondere/r/s **I**
to **spell*** [spel] buchstabieren **I**
to **spend*** [spend] ausgeben; verbringen **I**
spoon [spu:n] Löffel **I**
sport [spɔ:t] Sport **I**
sports centre ['spɔ:ts ˌsentə] Sportzentrum **II 1**, 11
spot [spɒt] Fleck **I**
spring [sprɪŋ] Frühling **I**
°to **spy** [spaɪ] sehen, erspähen **II 1**, 7
°I spy *(with my little eye ...)* [ˌaɪ 'spaɪ] Ich sehe was, was du nicht siehst *(Spiel)* **II 1**, 7
stage [steɪdʒ] Bühne **II 4**, 34
stall [stɔ:l] Stand **II 3**, 30
stamp [stæmp] Briefmarke **I**
to **stand*** [stænd] stehen **I**
I can't stand ... [aɪ 'kɑ:nt‿'stænd] ich kann ... nicht leiden/... ausstehen **II 6**, 52
°to stand up [ˌstænd‿'ʌp] aufstehen **I**
to **start** [stɑ:t] beginnen, anfangen **I**
station ['steɪʃn] Bahnhof **I**
°**statue** ['stætʃu:] Statue, Denkmal **I**
to **stay** [steɪ] bleiben, (zu Besuch) wohnen **I**
stay [steɪ] Aufenthalt **II 10**, 96
°**steep** [sti:p] steil **II 7**, 67
°**step** [step] Schritt, Stufe **I**
still [stɪl] ruhig **I**
still [stɪl] noch **I**
stomach-ache ['stʌməkeɪk] Bauchweh, Magenschmerzen **II 8**, 75
stone [stəʊn] Stein **I**
to **stop** [stɒp] aufhören **II 1**, 13; halten, anhalten **I**; verhindern, stoppen **II 2**, 16
Stop it! ['stɒp‿ɪt] Hör/Hört auf! **II 1**, 13
department **store** [dɪ'pɑ:tmənt stɔ:] Kaufhaus **II 5**, 42
story ['stɔ:rɪ] Geschichte, Erzählung **I**
straight [streɪt] direkt, gerade(wegs) **II 2**, 22
strange [streɪndʒ] seltsam, merkwürdig **II 2**, 18
street [stri:t] Straße **I**
⟨strong⟩ [strɒŋ] stark **II 10**, 94
°to get **stuck** [get 'stʌk] stecken bleiben **I**
°**student** ['stju:dnt] Student/in **II 7**, 65
subject ['sʌbdʒɪkt] Fach **II 1**, 8
suddenly ['sʌdnlɪ] plötzlich **II 1**, 12
sugar ['ʃʊgə] Zucker **I**
°**summary** ['sʌmərɪ] Zusammenfassung **II 3**, 31
summer ['sʌmə] Sommer **I**
°summer fete [ˌsʌmə 'feɪt] Sommerbazar, Sommerfest **II 9**, 87
Sunday ['sʌndeɪ] Sonntag **I**
sunny ['sʌnɪ] sonnig **I**
°**sunroof** ['sʌnru:f] Schiebedach **II 10**, 95
super ['su:pə] super, toll **I**
supermarket ['su:pəˌmɑ:kɪt] Supermarkt **I**
to be **sure** [bɪ 'ʃɔ:] sicher sein **I**
I'm not sure. [ˌaɪm nɒt 'ʃɔ:] Ich bin mir nicht sicher. **I**
surprise [sə'praɪz] Überraschung **I**
to be **surprised** [bɪ sə'praɪzd] überrascht sein **I**
sweatshirt ['swetʃɜ:t] Sweatshirt **I**
sweet [swi:t] Bonbon **I**
sweet [swi:t] süß, niedlich **II 8**, 76
to **swim*** [swɪm] schwimmen **II 9**, 80
to go **swimming** [gəʊ 'swɪmɪŋ] schwimmen gehen **I**
swimming pool ['swɪmɪŋpu:l] Schwimmbad **II 5**, 47
swimming things ['swɪmɪŋ ˌθɪŋz] Schwimmsachen, Badezeug **I**
⟨to swing⟩ [swɪŋ] *hier:* pendeln **II 9**, 86

T

T-shirt ['ti:ʃɜ:t] T-Shirt **I**
table ['teɪbl] Tisch **I**
table tennis ['teɪbl ˌtenɪs] Tischtennis **II 1**, 11
⟨tail⟩ [teɪl] Schwanz **II 9**, 86
to **take*** [teɪk] nehmen, mieten **I**
to take a photo of [ˌteɪk‿ə 'fəʊtəʊ‿əv] ein Foto machen von **I**
to take for a walk [ˌteɪk fər‿ə 'wɔ:k] (Hund) ausführen, spazieren führen **II 9**, 87
to take ... home [teɪk] jdn. nach Hause bringen **I**
to take notes [ˌteɪk 'nəʊts] Notizen machen **I**
to take off [ˌteɪk‿'ɒf] ausziehen **II 2**, 22
to take prisoner [ˌteɪk 'prɪznə] gefangen nehmen **II 2**, 15
°**takeaway** ['teɪkəˌweɪ] *Imbissstube, Schnellgaststätte mit Straßenverkauf* **II 6**, 58
°**tale** [teɪl] Geschichte, Sage **II 2**, 15
to **talk about** ['tɔ:k‿əˌbaʊt] reden über, sprechen über **I**
fish **tank** ['fɪʃ ˌtæŋk] Aquarium **II 9**, 80
to **taste** [teɪst] schmecken, probieren **II 6**, 52

tea [ti:] Tee; *Mahlzeit am frühen Abend (Abendbrot)* **I**
°tea-cosy ['ti:kəʊzɪ] Teewärmer, Kaffeemütze **II 5**, 50
°tea shop ['ti: ˌʃɒp] Café, Teestube **II 5**, 43
teacher ['ti:tʃə] Lehrer/in **I**
team [ti:m] Mannschaft **I**
Technology [tek'nɒlədʒɪ] Computerunterricht, technisches Werken **II 1**, 8
teddy ['tedɪ] Teddybär **II 3**, 25
telephone ['telɪfəʊn] Telefon **I**
on the telephone [ɒn ðə 'telɪfəʊn] am Telefon **I**
to **tell*** [tel] erzählen **I**
temperature ['temprətʃə] Fieber **II 8**, 75
tennis ['tenɪs] Tennis **I**
table tennis ['teɪbl ˌtenɪs] Tischtennis **II 1**, 11
term [tɜ:m] Trimester, Schuljahresdrittel **II 1**, 11
terrible ['terəbl] schrecklich, furchtbar **I**
test [test] Test, Probe **II 8**, 73
text [tekst] Text **I**
than [ðæn, ðən] als **II 3**, 26
Thank you ['θæŋk‿ju:] Danke schön **I**
No, thank you. [nəʊ 'θæŋk‿ju:] Nein, danke. **I**
Thank you very much. ['θæŋk‿jʊ verɪ 'mʌtʃ] Vielen Dank. **I**
Thanks. [θæŋks] Danke. **I**
that [ðæt] das (da) **I**
that [ðæt/ðət] dass **II 4**, 39
the [ðə/ði:] der/die/das **I**
theatre ['θɪetə] Theater **II 4**, 37
their [ðeə] ihr/ihre (*Pl*) **I**
theirs [ðeəz] ihr/ihre **II 8**, 74
them [ðem] sie/ihnen **I**
then [ðen] dann **I**
just then [ˌdʒʌst 'ðen] in diesem Moment **II 10**, 95
there [ðeə] da, dort **I**
over there [ˌəʊvə 'ðeə] da drüben, dort **I**
there is [ðeər‿'ɪz] es gibt, es ist **I**
these [ði:z] diese hier **I**
they [ðeɪ] sie (*Pl*) **I**
thing [θɪŋ] Ding, Sache **I**
just the thing [ˌdʒʌst ðə 'θɪŋ] genau das Richtige **II 10**, 91
to **think*** [θɪŋk] denken, glauben **I**
to think of ['θɪŋk‿əv] denken an **II 9**, 87
thirsty ['θɜ:stɪ] durstig **II 6**, 57
this [ðɪs] dies, diese/dieser/dieses **I**
this afternoon [ðɪs‿ˌɑ:ftə'nu:n] heute Nachmittag **I**
⟨this-a-way⟩ ['ðɪsəweɪ] auf diese Weise, so **II 4**, 38
those [ðəʊz] die da drüben **I**
thousand ['θaʊznd] tausend **I**
throat [θrəʊt] Hals, Rachen **II 8**, 75
sore throat [ˌsɔ: 'θrəʊt] Halsweh **II 8**, 75
through [θru:] durch **I**
throw [θrəʊ] Wurf **II 3**, 30
to **throw*** [θrəʊ] werfen **II 2**, 21
thunder ['θʌndə] Donner **II 4**, 39
thunderstorm ['θʌndəstɔ:m] Gewitter **II 7**, 65
Thursday ['θɜ:zdeɪ] Donnerstag **I**
ticket ['tɪkɪt] Fahrkarte, Eintrittskarte **I**
°Day Rider Ticket ['deɪ‿raɪdə ˌtɪkɪt] Tagesticket **I**
to **tidy up** [ˌtaɪdɪ‿'ʌp] aufräumen **I**
tidy ['taɪdɪ] ordentlich, aufgeräumt **I**
tiger ['taɪgə] Tiger **II 9**, 84
tights [taɪts] Strumpfhose, Strumpfhosen **II 4**, 33
time [taɪm] Mal **II 5**, 49; Zeit, Uhrzeit **I**
a long time ago [ə ˌlɒŋ taɪm‿ə'gəʊ] lange her **II 7**, 65
after a time [ˌɑ:ftər‿ə 'taɪm] nach einer Weile **II 7**, 67
free time [ˌfri:‿'taɪm] Freizeit **I**
in time [ˌɪn 'taɪm] rechtzeitig **II 6**, 59
It's time for... [ɪts‿'taɪm fə] Es ist Zeit für ... **I**
next time ['nekst‿ˌtaɪm] nächstes Mal **I**
timetable ['taɪmteɪbl] Fahrplan **I**; Stundenplan **II 1**,8
tired ['taɪəd] müde **I**
title ['taɪtl] Titel **II 4**, 40
to [tʊ/tə] nach; vor (*bei Uhrzeiten*) **I**
from ... to [frəm ... tə] von ... bis; von ... nach **I**
quarter to (twelve) ['kwɔ:tə tə] Viertel vor (zwölf) **I**
today [tə'deɪ] heute **I**
together [tə'geðə] zusammen **I**
toilet ['tɔɪlɪt] Toilette **I**
tomorrow [tə'mɒrəʊ] morgen **I**
the day after tomorrow [ðə 'deɪ‿ˌɑ:ftə tə'mɒrəʊ] übermorgen **II 7**, 66
too [tu:] allzu, zu; auch **I**
at the **top of ...** [ət ðə 'tɒp‿əv] ganz oben **I**
top [tɒp] oberste/oberster/oberstes **II 5**, 45
tourist ['tʊərɪst] Tourist/in **II 7**, 66
towards [tə'wɔ:dz] auf ... zu **II 1**, 12
town [taʊn] Stadt **I**
°twin town [ˌtwɪn 'taʊn] Partnerstadt **I**
toy [tɔɪ] Spielzeug **II 10**, 91
°**tractor** ['træktə] Traktor, Trecker **I**
train [treɪn] Zug **I**
°ghost train ['gəʊst ˌtreɪn] Geisterbahn **II 3**, 25
trainers (*pl*) ['treɪnəz] Turnschuhe **II 5**, 44
to **travel** ['trævl] reisen **II 7**, 62
travel agent's ['trævl‿ˌeɪdʒənts] Reisebüro **II 7**, 63
tree [tri:] Baum **I**
to **trick** [trɪk] täuschen, austricksen **I**
trick [trɪk] Streich, Trick **II 2**, 16
Robin played tricks on him. [ˌpleɪd 'trɪks] Robin spielte ihm Streiche. **II 2**, 16
to **trip** [trɪp] stolpern **I**
trousers ['traʊzəz] Hose, Hosen **I**
⟨true⟩ [tru:] wahr **II 10**, 94
trumpet ['trʌmpɪt] Trompete **II 10**, 91
⟨trunk⟩ [trʌŋk] Rüssel **II 9**, 86
⟨truth⟩ [tru:θ] Wahrheit **II 10**, 94
to **try** [traɪ] versuchen, (aus)probieren **II 1**, 11
to try hard [ˌtraɪ 'hɑ:d] (sich) anstrengen **II 9**, 83
to try on [ˌtraɪ‿'ɒn] ausprobieren, anprobieren **II 4**, 33
Tuesday ['tju:zdeɪ] Dienstag **I**
°**tummy** ['tʌmɪ] Bauch, Magen **I**
°**tunnel** ['tʌnl] Tunnel **I**
°**Turkish** ['tɜ:kɪʃ] türkisch, Türkisch **I**
to **turn** [tɜ:n] abbiegen **I**; ⟨verwandeln⟩ **II 10**, 94
to turn back [ˌtɜ:n 'bæk] zurückgehen **II 7**, 67
to turn round [ˌtɜ:n 'raʊnd] sich umdrehen **II 1**, 12
Your turn. ['jɔ: tɜ:n] Du bist an der Reihe., Ihr seid an der Reihe., Sie sind an der Reihe. **I**
tutor ['tju:tə] Klassenlehrer/in **I**
tutor group ['tju:tə ˌgru:p] Klasse (*in einer englischen Schule*) **I**
TV [ˌti:'vi:] Fernsehen **I**
twice [twaɪs] zweimal **II 7**, 64
twice a week ['twaɪs‿ə 'wi:k] zweimal die Woche **II 9**, 80
°**twin town** [ˌtwɪn 'taʊn] Partnerstadt **I**

U

uncle ['ʌŋkl] Onkel **I**
°great uncle [greɪt‿'ʌŋkl] Großonkel **II 5**, 49
under ['ʌndə] unter **I**
⟨underneath⟩ [ˌʌndə'ni:θ] unter **II 3**, 28
to **understand*** [ˌʌndə'stænd] verstehen **I**

uniform [ˈjuːnɪfɔːm] Uniform **I**
°**unit** [ˈjuːnɪt] Lektion, Kapitel, Einheit **I**
untidy [ʌnˈtaɪdɪ] unordentlich **I**
until [ənˈtɪl] bis **II 7**, 68
up [ʌp] nach oben, herauf **II 2**, 18
up to [ˈʌp tə] auf … zu **II 2**, 21
upper [ˈʌpə] obere/oberer/oberes **II 5**, 42
upstairs [ˌʌpˈsteəz] oben (in Gebäuden) **I**
us [ʌs] uns **I**
to **use** [juːz] benutzen **II 5**, 50
useful [ˈjuːsfʊl] nützlich **II 4**, 33
usually [ˈjuːʒʊəlɪ] normalerweise, gewöhnlich **I**

V

van [væn] Kleinlastwagen **II 7**, 69
vegetable [ˈvedʒtəbl] Gemüse **II 6**, 52
verb [vɜːb] Verb **I**
very [ˈverɪ] sehr **I**
very much [ˌverɪ ˈmʌtʃ] sehr **I**
vet [vet] Tierarzt/Tierärztin **I**
vet's assistant [ˈvets‿əˌsɪstənt] Tierarzthelfer/in **I**
video [ˈvɪdɪəʊ] Video **I**
visit [ˈvɪzɪt] Besuch **II 8**, 73
to **visit** [ˈvɪzɪt] besuchen **II 3**, 25
voice [vɔɪs] Stimme **II 4**, 34

W

to **wait** (*for*) [ˈweɪt fə] warten (auf) **I**
to **wake up*** [ˌweɪk‿ˈʌp] aufwachen, aufwecken **II 2**, 18
walk [wɔːk] Spaziergang **I**
to go for a walk [ˌgəʊ fər‿ə ˈwɔːk] spazieren gehen **I**
to take for a walk [ˌteɪk fər‿ə ˈwɔːk] (Hund) ausführen, spazieren führen **II 9**, 87
to **walk** [wɔːk] zu Fuß gehen **I**
to **want** [wɒnt] wollen **I**
°**ward** [wɔːd] Krankensaal **II 8**, 76
warm [wɔːm] warm **I**
to **warn** [wɔːn] warnen **II 7**, 67
wash [wɒʃ] Wäsche, Waschen **II 10**, 96
car wash [ˈkɑː wɒʃ] Autowaschanlage **II 10**, 92
to **wash** [wɒʃ] (sich) waschen **II 2**, 20
washing-up [ˌwɒʃɪŋ‿ˈʌp] Abwasch **I**
to do the washing-up [ˌduː ðə wɒʃɪŋ ˈʌp] den Abwasch machen, spülen **I**
to **watch** [wɒtʃ] gucken, zuschauen **I**
Watch out! [ˈwɒtʃ‿ˈaʊt] Vorsicht!, Achtung! **I**
water [ˈwɔːtə] Wasser **I**
way [weɪ] Weg **I**
a long way [ə ˌlɒŋ‿ˈweɪ] eine weite Entfernung **II 10**, 92
⟨in any way⟩ [ɪn‿ˈenɪ ˌweɪ] auf irgendeine Weise **II 8**, 78
in different ways [ɪn ˌdɪfrənt‿ˈweɪz] auf verschiedene Weise **II 10**, 92
out of the way [ˌaʊt‿əv ðə ˈweɪ] aus dem Weg **II 10**, 95
°she's on her way [ˌɒn hɜː ˈweɪ] sie ist unterwegs **I**
that way [ˈðæt‿weɪ] in die Richtung **II 7**, 68
we [wiː] wir **I**
to **wear*** [weə] (Kleidung) tragen **I**
weather [ˈweðə] Wetter **I**
weather forecast [ˈweðə ˌfɔːkɑːst] Wetterbericht **II 7**, 66
Wednesday [ˈwenzdeɪ] Mittwoch **I**
week [wiːk] Woche **I**
twice a week [ˈtwaɪs‿ə ˈwiːk] zweimal die Woche **II 9**, 80
weekend [ˌwiːkˈend] Wochenende **II 2**, 15
Welcome to … [ˈwelkəm tə] Willkommen in … **I**
well [wel] gut (Adverb) **II 9**, 83; nun, na ja, gut **I**
Well done. [ˌwel ˈdʌn] Gut gemacht. **I**
to feel **well** [ˌfiːl ˈwel] sich wohl fühlen **II 8**, 72
west [west] Westen, West-, westlich **II 7**, 62
wet [wet] nass **I**
what [wɒt] was **I**
What a … [ˈwɒt‿ə] Was für ein/eine … **I**
What about…? [ˈwɒt‿əˌbaʊt] Was ist mit…?, Wie wär's mit…? **I**
What colour is/are …? [ˌwɒt ˈkʌlər‿ɪz] Welche Farbe hat/haben …? **I**
What on earth …? [ˌwɒt‿ɒn ˈɜːθ] Was in aller Welt …? **II 5**, 49
What time is it? [wɒt‿ˈtaɪm‿ɪz‿ɪt] Wie spät ist es? **I**
What's … like? [ˌwɒts … ˈlaɪk] Wie ist … ? **I**
wheel [wiːl] Rad **II 3**, 28
when [wen] wenn **II 2**, 17; wann, als **I**
where [weə] wo **I**
which [wɪtʃ] welche/welcher/welches **II 1**, 8
while [waɪl] während **II 6**, 59
⟨whistle⟩ [ˈwɪsl] Pfeife **II 4**, 38
white [waɪt] weiß **I**
who [huː] wen/wem; wer **I**
⟨whoa⟩ [wəʊ] *Ausruf* **II 10**, 94
whose [huːz] wessen **I**
why [waɪ] warum **I**
⟨wide⟩ [waɪd] weit **II 7**, 66
⟨wife⟩ [waɪf] Ehefrau **II 3**, 28
°**wig** [wɪg] Perücke **II 5**, 49
will [wɪl] wird, werden **II 4**, 34
to **win*** [wɪn] gewinnen **I**
window [ˈwɪndəʊ] Fenster **I**
windy [ˈwɪndɪ] windig **I**
°**wine** [waɪn] Wein **II 2**, 21
winner [ˈwɪnə] Gewinner/in **I**
winter [ˈwɪntə] Winter **I**
with [wɪð] bei; mit **I**
And with that … [ˌænd‿wɪð ˈðæt] Und damit … **II 10**, 95
without [wɪðˈaʊt] ohne **I**
woman [ˈwʊmən] Frau **I**
⟨to womp⟩ [wɒmp] *etwa:* schnaufen **II 9**, 86
wonderful [ˈwʌndəfʊl] wunderbar **II 5**, 49
word [wɜːd] Wort **I**
°word power [ˈwɜːd ˌpaʊə] die Kraft der Wörter **I**
work [wɜːk] Arbeit **II 2**, 20
to **work** [wɜːk] arbeiten **I**
to work late [ˌwɜːk ˈleɪt] länger arbeiten **I**
world [wɜːld] Welt **II 3**, 26
worried about [ˈwʌrɪd] besorgt wegen **II 1**, 12
to **worry** [ˈwʌrɪ] sich Sorgen machen **I**
worse [wɜːs] schlechter **II 3**, 26
(the) **worst** [ðə ˈwɜːst] am schlechtesten **II 3**, 26
Would you like …? [ˌwʊd juː ˈlaɪk] Möchtest du …?, Möchten Sie …? **II 5**, 48
Wow! [waʊ] Super!, Toll! **I**
to **write*** [raɪt] schreiben **I**
to write about [ˈraɪt‿əˌbaʊt] schreiben über **I**
to write down [ˌraɪt ˈdaʊn] aufschreiben **I**
wrong [rɒŋ] falsch **I**
What's wrong? [ˌwɒts ˈrɒŋ] Was ist los? **II 8**, 75
to get out of bed on the wrong side [get‿aʊt‿əv ˌbed‿ɒn ðə ˌrɒŋ ˈsaɪd] mit dem falschen Fuß aufstehen **II 10**, 95
to go wrong [ˌgəʊ ˈrɒŋ] schiefgehen **II 3**, 30; sich verfahren **II 7**, 64

Y

year [jɪə] Jahr, Jahrgang **I**
yellow ['jeləʊ] gelb **I**
yes [jes] ja **I**
yesterday ['jestədeɪ] gestern **II 2**, 16
the day before yesterday [ðə 'deɪ bɪˌfɔː 'jestədeɪ] vorgestern **II 7**, 65
yet [jet] noch **I**; schon **II 6**, 55
not ... yet [nɒt 'jet] noch nicht **I**
you [juː] du, ihr, Sie; dir/dich/euch/Ihnen **I**
young [jʌŋ] jung **II 3**, 25
your [jɔː] dein/deine, Ihr/Ihre, euer/eure **I**
Your turn. ['jɔː tɜːn] Du bist an der Reihe., Ihr seid an der Reihe., Sie sind an der Reihe. **I**
yours [jɔːz] deine/r/s, eure/r/s, Ihre/r/s **II 8**, 74
youth group ['juːθ ˌgruːp] Jugendgruppe **II 10**, 92

Z

°**zone** [zəʊn] Zone, Bereich **I**
zoo [zuː] Zoo **II 5**, 47

Boys' names

°**Alan** ['ælən]
°**Arthur** ['ɑːθə]
Barry ['bærɪ]
°**Clive** [klaɪv]
Colin ['kɒlɪn]
David ['deɪvɪd]
°**Eddy** ['edɪ]
Harry ['hærɪ]
°**Jack** [dʒæk]
°**Jeff** [dʒef]
John [dʒɒn]
°**Ken** [ken]
°**Kevin** ['kevɪn]
°**Lee** [liː]
°**Lenny** ['lenɪ]
Mark [mɑːk]
°**Michael** ['maɪkl]
Mike [maɪk]
°**Peter** ['piːtə]
Robert ['rɒbət]
°**Sam** [sæm]
Simon ['saɪmən]
°**Tim** [tɪm]
Tom [tɒm]
°**Washington** ['wɒʃɪŋtən]

Girls' names

°**Anna** ['ænə]
°**Annabel** ['ænəbel]
Audrey ['ɔːdrɪ]
Becky ['bekɪ]
Emma ['emə]
Helen ['helɪn]
°**Janet** ['dʒænɪt]
Judy ['dʒuːdɪ]
Kim [kɪm]
°**Mary** ['meərɪ]
°**Nina** ['niːnə]
°**Pat** [pæt]
°**Sally** ['sælɪ]
Sarah ['seərə]
Shabina [ʃæ'biːnə]
°**Sue** [suː]
°**Susan** ['suːzn]
°**Suvina** [sə'viːnə]
Virginia [və'dʒɪnjə]
°**Yasmin** [jæz'miːn]

Surnames

°**Adib** [ə'dɪb]
°**Barker** ['bɑːkə]
°**Benson** ['bensn]
°**Blackwell** ['blækwel]
°**Broadwood** ['brɔːdwʊd]
°**Brown** [braʊn]
Burton ['bɜːtn]
°**Campbell** ['kæmbl]
Cooper ['kuːpə]
Croft [krɒft]
Dane [deɪn]
Davis ['deɪvɪs]
Dickens ['dɪkɪnz]
Dixon ['dɪksən]
°**Greenwood** ['griːnwʊd]
°**Hilton** ['hɪltn]
°**Hunt** [hʌnt]
°**Ismaili** [ˌɪz'meɪlɪ]
Jenkins ['dʒeŋkɪnz]
°**Jessop** ['ðʒesəp]
Lee [liː]
MacTavish [mək'tævɪʃ]
°**Martin** ['mɑːtɪn]
Mason ['meɪsn]
°**Matthew** ['mæθjuː]
°**Miller** ['mɪlə]
°**Muddle** ['mʌdl]
Otis ['əʊtɪs]
Patel [pə'tel]
°**Patterson** ['pætəsn]
Penrose ['penrəʊz]
°**Price** [praɪs]
°**Richards** ['rɪtʃədz]
°**Ripple** ['rɪpl]
°**Singh** [sɪŋ]
°**Smith** [smɪθ]
Stevenson ['stiːvnsn]
Stuart ['stjʊət]
Umney ['ʌmniː]
Underwood ['ʌndəwʊd]
°**Wall** [wɔːl]
°**White** [waɪt]
°**Wood** [wʊd]

Vocabulary

Geographical names

Africa ['æfrɪkə]
⟨Albania⟩ [æl'beɪnjə]
the **Alps** (*pl*) [ælps]
America [ə'merɪkə]
Antarctica [æn'tɑ:ktɪkə]
Arndale Road [ˌɑ:ndeɪl 'rəʊd]
Arnot Hill Park [ˌɑ:nət hɪl 'pɑ:k]
Asia ['eɪʃə]
Australia [ɒ'streɪljə]
⟨Austria⟩ ['ɒstrɪə]

⟨Belarus⟩ ['beləˌrʌs]
° **Belfast** [ˌbel'fɑ:st]
° **Belgium** ['beldʒəm]
Ben Nevis [ˌben 'nevɪs]
Berlin [bɜ:'lɪn]
⟨Bosnia Herzegovina⟩ ['bɒznɪə ˌheətsəgəʊ'vi:nə]
Britain ['brɪtn]
⟨Bulgaria⟩ [bʌl'geərɪə]

° **Castle Road** [ˌkɑ:sl 'rəʊd]
° the **Channel** ['tʃænl]
° **Chicago** [ʃɪ'kɑ:gəʊ]
⟨Cleethorpes⟩ ['kli:θɔ:ps]
⟨Clyde⟩ [klaɪd]
° **Cornwall** ['kɔ:nwəl]
⟨Croatia⟩ [krəʊ'eɪʃə]
⟨Czech Republic⟩ [ˌtʃek rɪ'pʌblɪk]

⟨Denmark⟩ ['denmɑ:k]

Edward's Lane [ˌedwədz 'leɪn]
England ['ɪŋglənd]
⟨Estonia⟩ [es'təʊnjə]
Europe ['jʊərəp]
° **Exchange Walk** [ɪksˌtʃeɪndʒ 'wɔ:k]

⟨Finland⟩ ['fɪnlənd]
° **Fort William** [ˌfɔ:t‿'wɪljəm]
° **France** [frɑ:ns]
° **Friar Lane** [ˌfraɪə 'leɪn]

Germany ['dʒɜ:mənɪ]
⟨Greece⟩ [gri:s]

° **Heathrow Airport** [ˌhi:θrəʊ 'eəpɔ:t]
° the **High Street** ['haɪ ˌstri:t]
⟨Hudson⟩ ['hʌdsən]
⟨Hungary⟩ ['hʌŋgərɪ]

⟨Iceland⟩ ['aɪslənd]
⟨Ireland⟩ ['aɪələnd]
The **Isle of Wight** [ˌaɪl‿əv'waɪt]
⟨Italy⟩ ['ɪtəlɪ]

° **King Street** ['kɪŋ ˌstri:t]

Larwood Grove [ˌlɑ:wʊd 'grəʊv]
⟨Latvia⟩ ['lætvɪə]
° **Leeds** [li:dz]
⟨Lithuania⟩ [lɪθʊ'eɪnjə]
Loch Lomond [ˌlɒk 'ləʊmənd]
Loch Ness [ˌlɒk 'nes]
London ['lʌndən]
° **Long Row** [ˌlɒŋ 'rəʊ]
⟨Luxembourg⟩ ['lʌksəmbɜ:g]

° **M6** [ˌem 'sɪks]
⟨Macedonia⟩ [ˌmæsɪ'dəʊnjə]
° **Maid Marian Way** [meɪd ˌmærɪən 'weɪ]
⟨Malta⟩ ['mɔ:ltə]
Mansfield Road [ˌmænsfi:ld 'rəʊd]
° **Market Street** ['mɑ:kɪt ˌstri:t]
⟨Moldavia⟩ [mɒl'deɪvjə]
⟨Montenegro⟩ [ˌmɒntɪ'ni:grəʊ]
° **Mount Street** ['maʊnt ˌstri:t]

° the **Netherlands** ['neðələndz]
° **Northallerton** [nɔ:'θælətən]
North America [ˌnɔ:θ‿ə'merɪkə]
° the **North Sea** [ˌnɔ:θ 'si:]
⟨Norway⟩ ['nɔ:weɪ]
Nottingham ['nɒtɪŋəm]

° **Old Market Square** [əʊld ˌmɑ:kɪt 'skweə]

° **Paris** ['pærɪs]
° **Parliament Street** ['pɑ:ləmənt ˌstri:t]
° **Poland** ['pəʊlənd]
⟨Portugal⟩ ['pɔ:tʃʊgl]

⟨Romania⟩ [ru:'meɪnjə]
⟨Russia⟩ ['rʌʃə]

° **Scotland** ['skɒtlənd]
⟨Serbia⟩ ['sɜ:bjə]
Sherwood ['ʃɜ:wʊd]
Sherwood Forest [ˌʃɜ:wʊd 'fɒrɪst]
Skegness [skeg'nes]
⟨Slovakia⟩ [sləʊ'vækjə]
⟨Slovenia⟩ [sləʊ'vi:njə]
° **Smithy Row** [ˌsmɪðɪ 'rəʊ]
South America [ˌsaʊθ‿ə'merɪkə]
° **South Parade** [ˌsaʊθ pə'reɪd]
⟨Spain⟩ [speɪn]
° **St Peter's Gate** [snt ˌpi:təz 'geɪt]
⟨Sweden⟩ ['swi:dn]
⟨Switzerland⟩ ['swɪtsələnd]

° **Truro** ['trʊərəʊ]
⟨Turkey⟩ ['tɜ:kɪ]
⟨Tweed⟩ [twi:d]
Twycross Zoo [ˌtwaɪkrɒs 'zu:]

the **UK** (= **the United Kingdom**) [ˌju: 'keɪ]
⟨the Ukraine⟩ [ju:'kreɪn]
⟨the United Kingdom (= the UK)⟩ [ju:ˌnaɪtɪd 'kɪŋdəm]

Wales [weɪlz]
° **Wheeler Gate** [ˌwi:lə 'geɪt]
° **Yorkshire** ['jɔ:kʃə]

Other names

Belle [bel]
Bloggs ['blɒgz]
Canterville Chase [ˌkæntəvɪl 'tʃeɪs]
City Information Centre [ˌsɪtɪ‿ɪnfə'meɪʃn ˌsentə]
Dr ['dɒktə]
° **Goose Fair** [ˌgu:s 'feə]
° **Friar Tuck** [ˌfraɪə 'tʌk]
° **Greenwood School** [ˌgri:nwʊd 'sku:l]
Haywood School [ˌheɪwʊd 'sku:l]
Jackie ['dʒækɪ]
Just Jeans [ˌdʒʌst 'dʒi:nz]
Lace Museum [ˌleɪs mju:'zɪəm]
° **Taj Mahal** [ˌtɑ:dʒmə'hɑ:l]
Maxi ['mæksɪ]
Mini ['mɪnɪ]
Monny ['mɒnɪ]
the **Major Oak** [ðə ˌmeɪdʒər‿'əʊk]
° **Robin Hood Statue** [ˌrɒbɪn hʊd 'stætʃu:]
° **Sneaky Snake** [ˌsni:kɪ 'sneɪk]
° **Sniffy** ['snɪfɪ]
° **Snowy** ['snəʊɪ]
° **Spot** [spɒt]
° **Springfield Farm** [ˌsprɪŋfi:ld 'fɑ:m]
° **St Peter's Church** [snt ˌpi:təz 'tʃɜ:tʃ]
Tabby ['tæbɪ]
Teens [ti:nz]
° **Twinning Office** ['twɪnɪŋ‿ˌɒfɪs]
Two'n'Two [ˌtu:n'tu:]
° **Victoria Shopping Centre** [vɪkˌtɔ:rɪə 'ʃɒpɪŋ ˌsentə]
Will Scarlet [ˌwɪl 'skɑ:lət]

Bildquellen:

Barnaby's, London: S. 47 (li. o.)
J. Allan Cash Ltd., London: S. 28 (mi. & mi. u.); S. 47 (re. u.); S. 58 (li. u.); S. 62 (re. o. & re. u.); S. 66 (re. o.); S. 76 (re. o.)
Wolfgang Kunz/Bilderberg, Hamburg: Umschlagfoto
Adam Butler/dpa/PA, Frankfurt: S. 92 (re. u.)
Katharine Eastham, Stuttgart: S. 28 (re. u.)
Jörn Sackermann/Das Fotoarchiv, Essen: S. 28 (li. o.)
Dieter Gebhardt, Graphic- und Foto-Design BFF, Asperg: S. 63 (re. u.); S. 84 (re. o.)
Geophotos/Tony Waltham, Nottingham: S. 19 (re. u.)
Greenhill, London: S. 37 (li. o.); S. 92 (li. o.); S. 104 (re. u.)
Harding, London: S. 62 (li. o. & li. u.); S. 76 (li. u.)
Joachim Krüger, Korntal (Karte): Innenumschlag hinten
The Lace Hall, Nottingham: S. 47 (li. u.)
Mauritius, Stuttgart: S. 80 (li. o.); S. 84 (li. o. & li. mi. & re. mi. & li. u. & re. u.)
Rudi Meisel/Visum, Hamburg: S. 37 (re. u.)
Wolfgang Metzger, Mühlacker (Karte): Innenumschlag vorne
Nottingham Evening Post, Nottingham: S. 92 (mi.)
Reinhard Tierfoto, Heiligkreuzsteinach: S. 80 (re. o. & mi. o. & li. u. & mi. u. & re. u.)
Roland Schmidt, Arolsen: S. 19 (li. mi.)
Sea Fish Industry Authority, Edinburgh: S 58 (re. o.)
Melanie Smith, Peabody's Communication Group, Nottingham: S. 19 (re. o.); S. 28 (re. o. & li. u.);
Topham Picturepoint, Edenbridge: S. 37 (re. o. & li. u.); S. 47 (re. o.); S. 58 (li. o. & re. u.); S. 64 (re. o.); S. 92 (re. o.)
The World of Robin Hood; Retford, Notts: S. 15 (re. o.)

Textquellen:

I've got a lovely bunch of coconuts: S. 29, von Fred Heatherton © Irwin Dash Music Co. Ltd., London
Five hundred miles: S. 38, von Hedy West, © Ebony Musikverlag OHG, München
The rolling hills of the border: S. 66, von Matt McGinn, © Kerrs Music Corporation, Glasgow
Help: S. 78, von John Lennon/Paul McCartney, © Northern Songs Ltd., London
Going to the zoo: S. 86, von Tom Paxton, © Originalverlag: Cherry Lane Music Ltd., Subverlag: Richt & Slezak OHG, Hamburg
We are the world: S. 94, von Michael Jackson/Lionel Richie © Mijac Music/Brockman Music, für Deutschland: Neue Welt Musikverlag GmbH, München

List of irregular verbs

infinitive	simple past	past participle	German
be [bi:]	was, were [wɒz, wɜ:]	been [bi:n]	sein
begin [bɪ'gɪn]	began [bɪ'gæn]	begun [bɪ'gʌn]	beginnen
bend [bend]	bent [bent]	bent [bent]	(sich) bücken, biegen
break [breɪk]	broke [brəʊk]	broken ['brəʊkn]	brechen
bring [brɪŋ]	brought [brɔ:t]	brought [brɔ:t]	bringen
buy [baɪ]	bought [bɔ:t]	bought [bɔ:t]	kaufen
catch [kætʃ]	caught [kɔ:t]	caught [kɔ:t]	fangen
choose [tʃu:z]	chose [tʃəʊz]	chosen ['tʃəʊzn]	auswählen
come [kʌm]	came [keɪm]	come [kʌm]	kommen
cost [kɒst]	cost [kɒst]	cost [kɒst]	kosten
cut [kʌt]	cut [kʌt]	cut [kʌt]	schneiden
do [du:]	did [dɪd]	done [dʌn]	machen, tun
draw [drɔ:]	drew [dru:]	drawn [drɔ:n]	zeichnen
drink [drɪŋk]	drank [dræŋk]	drunk [drʌŋk]	trinken
drive [draɪv]	drove [drəʊv]	driven ['drɪvn]	fahren
eat [i:t]	ate [eɪt]	eaten ['i:tn]	essen
fall [fɔ:l]	fell [fel]	fallen ['fɔ:ln]	fallen
feed [fi:d]	fed [fed]	fed [fed]	füttern
feel [fi:l]	felt [felt]	felt [felt]	fühlen
find [faɪnd]	found [faʊnd]	found [faʊnd]	finden
fly [flaɪ]	flew [flu:]	flown [fləʊn]	fliegen
forget [fə'get]	forgot [fə'gɒt]	forgotten [fə'gɒtn]	vergessen
get [get]	got [gɒt]	got [gɒt]	holen, bekommen
give [gɪv]	gave [geɪv]	given ['gɪvn]	geben
go [gəʊ]	went [went]	gone [gɒn]	gehen
grow [grəʊ]	grew [gru:]	grown [grəʊn]	wachsen, (an)bauen
have [hæv]	had [hæd]	had [hæd]	haben
hear [hɪə]	heard [hɜ:d]	heard [hɜ:d]	hören
hide [haɪd]	hid [hɪd]	hidden ['hɪdn]	(sich) verstecken
hit [hɪt]	hit [hɪt]	hit [hɪt]	schlagen
hold [həʊld]	held [held]	held [held]	halten
hurt [hɜ:t]	hurt [hɜ:t]	hurt [hɜ:t]	verletzen, weh tun
keep [ki:p]	kept [kept]	kept [kept]	(be)halten
know [nəʊ]	knew [nju:]	known [nəʊn]	wissen, kennen
lay [leɪ]	laid [leɪd]	laid [leɪd]	legen
learn [lɜ:n]	learned [lɜ:nt], learnt [lɜ:nt]	learned [lɜ:nt], learnt [lɜ:nt]	lernen
leave [li:v]	left [left]	left [left]	(ver)lassen

infinitive	simple past	past participle	German
lend [lend]	lent [lent]	lent [lent]	(ver)leihen
let [let]	let [let]	let [let]	lassen
lie [laɪ]	lay [leɪ]	lain [leɪn]	liegen
make [meɪk]	made [meɪd]	made [meɪd]	machen
mean [mi:n]	meant [ment]	meant [ment]	bedeuten
meet [mi:t]	met [met]	met [met]	treffen, begegnen
pay [peɪ]	paid [peɪd]	paid [peɪd]	zahlen, bezahlen
put [pʊt]	put [pʊt]	put [pʊt]	setzen, stellen, legen
read [ri:d]	read [red]	read [red]	lesen
ride [raɪd]	rode [rəʊd]	ridden ['rɪdn]	reiten, fahren
ring [rɪŋ]	rang [ræŋ]	rung [rʌŋ]	klingeln, anrufen
run [rʌn]	ran [ræn]	run [rʌn]	laufen, rennen
say [seɪ]	said [sed]	said [sed]	sagen
see [si:]	saw [sɔ:]	seen [si:n]	sehen
sell [sel]	sold [səʊld]	sold [səʊld]	verkaufen
send [send]	sent [sent]	sent [sent]	schicken, senden
shoot [ʃu:t]	shot [ʃɒt]	shot [ʃɒt]	schießen
show [ʃəʊ]	showed [ʃəʊd]	shown [ʃəʊn]	zeigen
sing [sɪŋ]	sang [sæŋ]	sung [sʌŋ]	singen
sit [sɪt]	sat [sæt]	sat [sæt]	sitzen
sleep [sli:p]	slept [slept]	slept [slept]	schlafen
speak [spi:k]	spoke [spəʊk]	spoken ['spəʊkn]	sprechen
spell [spel]	spelled [spelt], spelt [spelt]	spelled [spelt], spelt [spelt]	buchstabieren
spend [spend]	spent [spent]	spent [spent]	ausgeben, verbringen
stand [stænd]	stood [stʊd]	stood [stʊd]	stehen
swim [swɪm]	swam [swæm]	swum [swʌm]	schwimmen
take [teɪk]	took [tʊk]	taken ['teɪkn]	nehmen, bringen
tell [tel]	told [təʊld]	told [təʊld]	erzählen, sagen
think [θɪŋk]	thought [θɔ:t]	thought [θɔ:t]	denken
throw [θrəʊ]	threw [θru:]	thrown [θrəʊn]	werfen
understand [ˌʌndə'stænd]	understood [ˌʌndə'stʊd]	understood [ˌʌndə'stʊd]	verstehen
wake [weɪk]	woke [wəʊk]	woken ['wəʊkn]	wecken, aufwachen
wear [weə]	wore [wɔ:]	worn [wɔ:n]	tragen (Kleidung)
win [wɪn]	won [wʌn]	won [wʌn]	gewinnen
write [raɪt]	wrote [rəʊt]	written ['rɪtn]	schreiben

⟨In the classroom⟩

What you can say to your friends or to the teacher

When you arrive and leave

What are we going to do today?	Was machen wir heute?
I'm sorry I'm late.	Tut mir Leid, dass ich mich verspätet habe.
I'm sorry, I've forgotten my exercise book.	Tut mir Leid, ich habe mein Heft vergessen.
What's for homework?	Was haben wir als Hausaufgabe auf?
See you next time.	Bis zum nächsten Mal.
Have a nice weekend.	Schönes Wochenende!

If there is a problem …

How are you?	Wie geht es dir?
Are you feeling ill?	Fühlst du dich krank?
What's the matter with you?	Was fehlt dir denn?
I'm fine, thank you.	Gut, danke.
I'm not feeling well.	Ich fühle mich nicht gut.
I've got a headache.	Ich habe Kopfweh.
Can I open the window, please?	Darf ich bitte das Fenster öffnen?
Can I go to the toilet, please?	Darf ich bitte auf die Toilette gehen?

If you want to ask for help …

Can you help me, please?	Können Sie mir bitte helfen?
I don't understand this.	Ich verstehe das nicht.
What do we have to do?	Was müssen wir denn machen?
What's that in English/German?	Was heißt das auf Englisch/Deutsch?
Can I say: …?/What does … mean?	Kann ich sagen: …?/Was bedeutet …?
How do you do this exercise?	Wie macht man diese Übung?
Is this right? I'm not sure.	Ist das richtig? Ich bin nicht sicher.
Sorry, I don't know.	Tut mir Leid, das weiß ich nicht.
Can you write it on the board, please?	Können Sie das bitte an die Tafel schreiben?
Can I ask a question, please?	Kann ich bitte eine Frage stellen?
Pardon? Can you repeat the question/sentence, please?	Wie bitte? Können Sie die Frage/den Satz bitte wiederholen?
Can you play the cassette again, please?	Können Sie die Kassette bitte noch mal abspielen?
Can you play the cassette with pauses, please?	Können Sie die Kassette bitte mit Pausen abspielen?
Can we do another example, please?	Können wir noch ein Beispiel machen?
Thanks./Thank you very much.	Danke./Vielen Dank.

If you work together …

Can I work with …?	Kann ich mit … zusammenarbeiten?
Can I have your crayon/ruler …?	Kann ich mal deinen Buntstift/dein Lineal haben?
Whose turn is it?	Wer ist dran?

What are we going to do first?	Was machen wir als Erstes?
Let's write ... on our poster.	Schreiben wir ... auf unser Poster.
Let's put this picture here.	Setzen/Kleben wir das Bild hier hin.
You can be ... and I'll be ...	Du kannst ... spielen, und ich werde ... spielen.
Has anybody seen my pencil?	Hat jemand meinen Bleistift gesehen?

If you want to talk about stories, poems, songs, ...

I like/don't like this story.	Diese Geschichte gefällt mir/gefällt mir nicht.
I think it's good, interesting, brilliant, funny, really exciting.	Ich finde sie gut, interessant, toll, witzig, wirklich spannend.
I think it's sad, terrible, boring.	Ich finde sie traurig, schrecklich, langweilig.
It was OK, but I've read better ones.	Sie ist ganz nett, aber ich habe schon bessere gelesen.

If you have a discussion ...

What do you think?	Was meinst du?
In my opinion ...	Meiner Meinung nach ...
I think you are right/wrong.	Ich denke, du hast Recht/Unrecht.
On the one hand ..., on the other hand ...	Einerseits ..., andererseits ...

... and what the teacher says to you

Open your books at page	Schlagt Seite ... auf.
Turn to page	Blättert auf Seite ... um.
Read the text on page	Lest den Text auf Seite ... .
Who would like to write on the transparency?	Wer möchte auf die Folie schreiben?
Come to the board, please.	Komm bitte an die Tafel.
Who would like to play the cassette?	Wer möchte die Kassette abspielen?
You're going to hear the cassette twice.	Ihr werdet die Kassette zweimal hören.
Rewind the cassette to zero, please.	Spul die Kassette bitte auf null zurück.
Who would like to play the part of ...?	Wer möchte die Rolle von ... spielen?
Write the answers in your exercise book.	Schreibt die Antworten in eure Übungshefte.
Would you collect the exercise books/ worksheets, please?	Würdest du bitte die Übungshefte/Arbeitsblätter einsammeln?
Do this exercise for homework.	Macht diese Übung als Hausaufgabe.
Be quiet. Sit down, please.	Seid ruhig. Setz dich/Setzt euch, bitte.
Please speak up.	Sprich/Sprecht bitte lauter.
No prompting, please.	Nicht vorsagen, bitte.
Excellent!	Prima!
You can do better. Try again.	Das kannst du besser. Versuch es noch einmal.
That's it. Well done.	So ist es richtig. Gut gemacht.

ICELAND
NORWAY
SWEDEN
FINLAND
RUSSIA
ESTONIA
LATVIA
LITHUANIA
RUSSIA
DENMARK
IRELAND
THE UNITED KINGDOM
Nottingham
London
THE NETHERLANDS
BELARUS
E U R O P E
POLAND
BELGIUM
GERMANY
THE UKRAINE
CZECH REPUBLIC
LUXEMBOURG
SLOVAKIA
MOLDAVIA
FRANCE
SWITZERLAND
AUSTRIA
HUNGARY
ROMANIA
SLOVENIA
CROATIA
BOSNIA–HERZEGOVINA
SERBIA
PORTUGAL
ITALY
BULGARIA
MONTENEGRO
SPAIN
MACEDONIA
ALBANIA
GREECE
TURKEY
MALTA
0
500
1 000 km
A F R I C A